The
Best
of
Electric
Crockery
Cooking

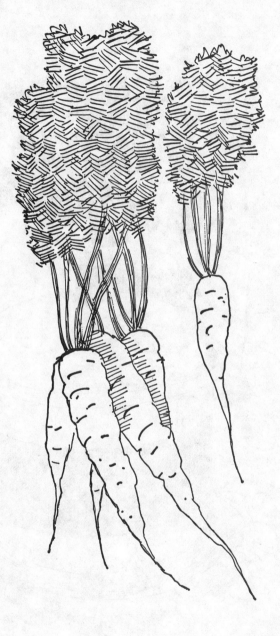

The Best of
Electric Crockery Cooking
Jacqueline Hériteau

Grosset & Dunlap · Publishers · New York
A FILMWAYS COMPANY

*To Earl Hubbard,
American artist, philosopher,
and poet of the space age,
who discovered that man
does not live by thought alone.*

ACKNOWLEDGMENTS

This volume owes many of its recipes to my French relatives, the Hériteau clan, and to my American friends, fellow housewives, and associates, in particular to Anne Le Moine, who contributed many recipes based on slow-cook economy dishes she developed during World War II in France. My gratitude to the Dry Bean Advisory Board, which was kind enough to give me advance information on its in-depth testing of dried beans in slow-cookers. A very special thank you to Lee Schryver, the editor of this volume, for guidance, counsel—and patience, and to Hawthorn Books, Inc., publishers of The How to Grow and Cook It Book of Vegetables, Herbs, Fruits and Nuts, *and of* Oriental Cooking the Fast Wok Way *for permission to reprint recipes that appear in those books.*

CONTENTS

INTRODUCTION

BEFORE YOU BEGIN . . . *in an age when we increasingly demand wholesome foods and at the same time need more freedom from routine cooking chores, the electric crock cooker is a blessing. It produces those savory braised meats, casseroles, stews, soups, compotes, and wonderful old-fashioned puddings that haven't been seen since the wood-burning stove went out of business. It's a money-saver, because the slow-cooking thrives on scraps, lesser cuts, and leftovers. It's happy-making, because this is one pot the cook really does not have to watch. It's a boon not only for making family meals but for party cooking, and it has revolutionized my approach to summer eating, the evening meal, and breakfast.*

The recipes here are those I've found the slow-cooker does best. Some I like to do in the cooker because of the free time that it gives me; others are just fun to try—baked goods, jams, fondues have a special flavor when slow-cooked. Getting to know your crock cooker and what it can do will open a whole new world of cooking for you —the world of cooking our grandmothers knew.

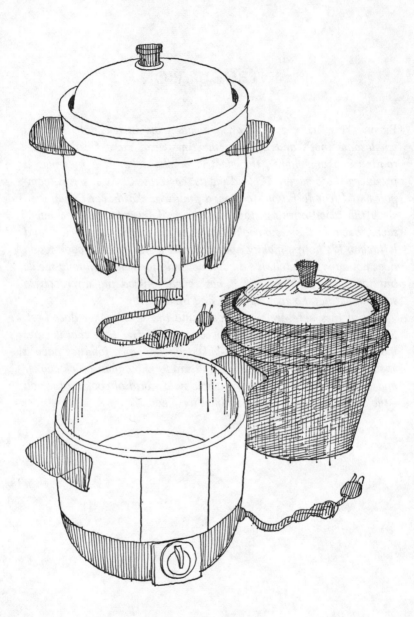

PART ONE

HOW TO USE YOUR SLOW-COOK ELECTRIC CROCK POT

Chapter 1

Meal Planning with a Slow-Cook Crock Pot

THE SLOW-COOKING ELECTRIC crock pot has brought back to American cooking many foods that vanished with the wood-burning stove—casseroles, soups, stews, dishes made from variety meats, grains, cereals, and dried vegetables.

The slow-pot doesn't replace the oven, the broiler, or the stove top. It's not the best way to cook fresh fish or corn on the cob. But it can bring new variety to your meals and improve their quality while giving you more time for other things. And it certainly makes possible better meals at a significantly lower cost.

What the slow-cook pot can do for meal planning and budget scheduling is easy to understand if you think of how our grandmothers cooked.

At the turn of the century, fresh vegetables and luxury meats, such as steaks, chops, and roasts, were only occasionally available. Basic meal planning, particularly in the months when gardens were dormant, revolved around dried grains and vegetables and basic meat cuts that required a lot of cooking. Variety meats—hearts, for instance—were available and economical. Ours was still an agrarian society, although the Industrial Revolution was in full force; workers, generally involved with physical labor, burned a lot of calories and needed substantial food. Breakfast was a real meal, lunch a full-scale dinner, and dinner almost as hearty as lunch. The cook had a great deal of cooking to do.

The kitchen stove was relied on for much of the home's heat in winter. These two needs—that for indoor heat and that for plenty of food—combined with the foods available, resulted in cooking based on day-long simmering in a big Dutch oven. The food was delicious—savory stews and bean dishes, thick mouth-watering soups to eat with crusty bread, biscuits, and buns. The cooking heat was free, since the stove was used to warm the house, and the most economical, most available ingredients tasted best when slow-cooked.

When the wood-burning stove was superseded and long-distance transportation of fresh produce became practical, the meal picture changed. At the same time, the need for three large meals a day began to wane. Little by little, we've learned to quick-cook on stove tops and under broilers and to use ingredients that can be cooked and eaten in less than an hour. Today, any "real" cooking—that is, slow-preparation cooking—tends to be done primarily for entertaining. We don't want to spend money keeping the stove going for 8 and 10 hours. We don't want to spend hours watching slow-cooking dishes to see they don't burn. We've forgotten how to use lesser meat cuts, variety meats, dried grains and vegetables. Just once in a while, after a superb dish of from-scratch baked beans, or Indian pudding, or whisky-rice pudding, we are reminded that meals can be more than grilled hamburgers and frozen vegetables.

The great popularity of the slow-cook electric crock pot is due to the fact that it restores to us the dishes our grandmothers made and at the same time saves us money and time.

USING THE SLOW-COOK POT
TO SAVE TIME

HOW THE SLOW-POT COOKS: To understand how the slow-cook pot can save you kitchen time, you have to know how it works. Think of the slow-cooker as a large kettle, or pot, that cooks so slowly that no steam escapes from under its close-fitting lid. The utensil closest to it is probably the Dutch oven, which is made of heavy cast iron (sometimes enameled) and has a heavy lid that keeps in most of the steam. It is used over a very slow fire, and it makes such heavenly stews and casseroles that most people really interested in cooking have one. I've never been in a European household that didn't rely on a Dutch oven for some part of every big meal.

There are important differences between the Dutch oven and the slow-cook crock pot. The Dutch oven caramelizes the sugars in the ingredients, giving dishes a rich, brown-gravy flavor. However, unwatched, a Dutch oven tends to go dry. You can't leave it to its own devices; you must check it every hour or so, to make sure there's enough liquid to keep ingredients from burning or drying out.

The slow-cook pot, on the other hand, cooks so slowly that no steam escapes. You can leave it unwatched for hours—perhaps days —without fear of burning the food. The slowness of the cooking process breaks down the fibers in tough ingredients without destroying flavor or texture. The pot can take all day to cook almost anything. That's the key factor in understanding how to use it to free yourself from the kitchen without sacrificing those savory meals most families love.

HIGH AND LOW SETTINGS: Timing and heat levels, and how to handle slow-cookers that register heat in Fahrenheit or Centigrade degrees instead of on High and Low, are explained in Chapter 2. But before you use a slow-cooker, you should understand the two settings High and Low.

Generally, Low means that food will cook at 200° to 240° Fahrenheit (about 100° to 115° Centigrade). At this setting, most casseroles, meats, stews, soups, and other foods require a minimum of 6 hours before they will be ready to eat. At the High setting, food cooks at 300° to 340° F. (about 149° to 170° C.) and will be ready in about half the time.

This means you can use your electric crock pot like a Dutch oven and have dinner ready in 2 to 4 hours. Or you can use it to free yourself for twice that many hours—or more—by cooking at Low.

Most recipes here and in other slow-pot cookbooks give cooking times at the Low setting. By making the most of the slow-pot's ability to cook food for a very long time, unsupervised, without ruining it, we can be away much of the day and still produce a very good meal.

PLANNING FAMILY MEALS: The major item in most family meals—specifically the main meal of the day—is the meat course. The slow-cooker adds variety here by preparing to perfection all sorts of casseroles and even some of the variety meats and lesser cuts that are hard to make palatable by conventional cooking. Turning lesser meat cuts into delicious stews and casseroles is a special talent of the slow-cooker. By bubbling ingredients for hours and hours, it produces a flavor you can't get any other way.

There are two ways to slow-cook meats and casseroles.

Some recipes let you combine everything, with little or no preparation, and the dishes are ready to serve the minute they are cooked. Boiled dinners, poached ham and tongue are typical. This is the fastest and easiest way to use the cooker for meat.

Other recipes require more time and effort. Many of the best stews and casseroles are in this group. You may have to brown the meats and/or other ingredients in a skillet before you put them, and the scrapings and pan juices, into the slow-pot, with or without other ingredients. You can omit the browning, but you will sacrifice flavor. The slow-pot can't do it all alone.

Many recipes, for meats and other foods, require more work after slow-cooking and before serving. Sauces may be thin—remember, the slow-cooker lets no liquid escape. Some sauces are exquisite thin, but others are a little flavorless. These should be boiled down to about half their quantity, to heighten flavor. I use relatively little flour in cooking—my family tends to be on the round side, so I eliminate anything fattening if I can—but I sometimes thicken a thin slow-pot sauce with flour, as described on page 28.

In selecting a recipe for a family meal, study the one that suits your mood to see how long it will free you from the kitchen, how much must be done before you can cover the pot, how much time will be needed after the dish has finished cooking.

Meats aren't the only hearty courses the slow-pot can produce for family meals. The slow-pot's stews and casseroles, even the braised meats, have a similarity of texture. You wouldn't enjoy week after week of slow-cooked meat dishes. You can change the pace by slow-cooking a vegetable casserole and serving with it a grilled or broiled meat, ready in minutes. Or serve grilled, broiled, or cold sliced meat with a hearty slow-cooked bean or dried-vegetable or grain dish. Or serve quick-cooked vegetables and meat with a slow-pot soup or rich slow-pot dessert.

PLANNING PARTIES WITH A SLOW-COOKER: The slow-cooker is a terrific help at party time. Some of the best party dishes were meant to be cooked in a slow-cook pot—Boeuf Bourguignon and Cassoulet (pages 144, 155) for instance, which are among the many dishes from other countries much appreciated here when they are well prepared. The electric crock cooker does them beautifully.

The slow-cooker also makes easier another group of party dishes. Blanquette de Veau (page 152)—an exquisite, creamy veal casserole —is typical. It takes me 2 hours to make it stove-top fashion. By using the slow-pot on Low to cook the meat during the day, I can finish the dish in a little over 30 minutes—while my guests are having their second drink. I start it in the morning, do my shopping for the party, and am free until shortly before serving the meal. When I am working away from home, the slow-pot is a big help with entertaining.

MAKING BREAKFAST EASY—AND GOOD: I have three children, and I am not one of those lucky people who wake up bright-eyed and bushy-tailed. I wake up mostly asleep. Using a timer with a slow-cook pot lets me work miracles for the morning meal. Delicious, nutritious, old-fashioned grains and cereals—Irish oats, for instance, and cornmeal grits—are now regular events. The children love these old-fashioned foods—served with brown sugar and light cream, or with melted butter and a drizzle of honey or maple syrup—and go off to school well fueled for the day. The fact that they nibble a sandwich for lunch doesn't trouble me, because I know breakfast was sound.

On weekends, when there's more time to spend around the breakfast table, I slow-cook overnight delicious fruit breads (Chapter 11). They are a little more like pudding than bread. It's wonderful to wake up to the smell of the breads cooking. Prepared the night before, they are placed in the crock pot with a few ice cubes to keep them cool, and the timer is set to start them baking so they'll be ready for breakfast.

Among other foods to cook overnight are dried fruits. My family is accustomed to having fruit at breakfast. One night when I discovered I had no fresh fruit, I set raisins and dried apples to cooking in the slow-pot. In the morning, the fragrance of the cinnamon was delightful, and the still-warm compote, served with a dollop of cream and hot buttered toast, became a big favorite.

I can rhapsodize about overnight cooking of breakfast foods. For so many years, this meal was restricted to orange juice, eggs, bacon, and toast, or juice and cereal. The slow-pot has made innovations possible, and they are all much appreciated. In the case of breakfast, the slow-cook pot contributes variety, rather than a saving in time.

CREATE YOUR OWN RECIPES

You can add almost anything to a good piece of beef, set all to cooking in the crockery pot, and create a wonderful dish that is particularly your own.

Madame Bertrand, chief cook and first lady of a family of peasants with whom I lived for a few years in Southern France, never owned a recipe book, as far as I could tell. About 8 or 9 o'clock in the morning, you'd find her standing by her big wood-burning stove looking thoughtfully at the dinner meat. Usually, she browned it in a skillet, turned it into a big kettle, simmered the pan juices with boiling water, and added that to the kettle. Then she'd survey the garden, to see what vegetables were available—a tomato or two, a sweet pepper, young turnips, baby carrots—and add whatever pleased her fancy, along with onions and garlic (garlic always in Southern France), usually thyme, a bit of rosemary, a stray mushroom picked in the fields by her son, salt, and pepper. Covered, the dish cooked all day and was ready to serve whenever her son and husband returned from the fields or the market in Cannes.

If she didn't make stew, she made soup the same way. Odds and ends that simmered all day with herbs and onions were the base; at night, she'd add rice or noodles, or tomatoes, or grated cheese, and serve the soup with chunks of crusty bread, butter, and a salad.

The slow-cooker makes Madame Bertrand's inventiveness accessible to us all. If we don't have a vegetable garden, we do have the crisper, where ends of vegetables always languish, and we have spices and condiments. The rest is a matter of imagination and knowing which flavor combinations we like best. I've included some of my favorite last-minute flavorings in each meat chapter.

USING THE SLOW-COOK POT
TO SAVE MONEY

ECONOMY MEAT CUTS: Most of these have two things in common —good flavor and toughness of fiber. The slow-cook pot makes them into really delicious stews and casseroles with very little effort on your part. Beef shank cross cut, top round, flank steak, short ribs, veal shank, lamb neck, and lamb breast are a few of the cuts to consider. Cooked in conventional fashion, these usually can instantly be labeled "economy." Done in the slow-cooker, with herbs and vegetables, they can become family favorites.

VARIETY MEATS: These low-cost meats aren't often seen in big-city supermarkets because most of us have forgotten how to cook them. However, country markets often carry them, and city butchers usually are willing to procure them on request. They are strongly flavored, and some need special handling.

One reason, besides the savings, for using them is that they are very sound nutritionally. Another reason is that they bring variety to meals. Hearts, beef and baby beef liver, pig's feet (trotters), lamb and other kidneys are some of the variety meats for which I have collected slow-cook recipes for dishes my family and friends enjoy very much. You won't want to make them all. The pâtés, for instance, you might not like as a staple, and headcheese isn't everyone's cup of tea; but gourmets consider them treats, and you should at least investigate what your slow-cook pot can do for them.

SOUP, STOCK, AND THE HOSPITALITY POT: I am not only French, as you could guess from my name, but also Scottish. That combination may or may not be responsible for my joy in the crockery cooker's ability to use discards and scraps to make meals better and more varied.

In Canada, in my Canadian grandmother's kitchen, there was always a big pot on the back of the coal-burning stove, and into it she tossed all sorts of scraps, such as stubs of peeled carrots, chicken necks, bits of rice, which in a modern home might have been aimed at the garbage can. In France, when my French grandmother was cooking, similar scraps went into a large ceramic pot set on the back of a wood-burning stove. These big kettles simmered all day, and at dinner time, with the addition of a little rice or some special flavoring—home-canned tomatoes, perhaps—the delicious, hearty soup became the first course. Years ago in Sweden, where it's cold and distances are great, it was a duty to feed anyone who came to the door. Guests scraped leftovers from their plates into a big kettle on the stove, so the meal helped keep the "hospitality pot" going—and tasting a little different every day.

The crockery cooker comes close to being for us what those hospitality kettles were for our grandmothers. Because it cooks for only a few cents a day, making your own stocks and your own soups, soups so good they're a meal, is once again a good investment.

Making stock in a crockery cooker will improve all aspects of your cooking. Stock is a thin-flavored, thin soup made from meat bones or fish, and it is called for in many gourmet recipes. Used instead of water in the cooking of casseroles, the braising of vegetables, the making of soups and sauces and gravies, stock adds a depth of flavor you cannot otherwise attain.

Recipes for stock usually call for pounds of meat and bones. Have you priced soupbones recently? They are out of sight. I use bones removed from roasts before or after cooking. Or I use saved-up chicken backs and necks. It takes a while to gather enough, but since we all have freezers, we can easily save bones and other discards. And the stock made from them is economical, nutritious, and good.

I also make and save gravies for use in my slow-cooker stews, stocks, and casseroles. You get lots of delicious gravy by adding a little stock or bouillon, even water, to the skillet meat was sautéed in or to the roaster a bird or roast was baked in, and scraping up the pan juices as it simmers. You can store small quantities of leftover gravies and pan drippings in the freezer. You can, of course, add Gravy Master or a similar gravy base to soups and stocks, but it won't give the fine, clear, sharp flavor you get from gravy and pan drippings.

In order to have plenty of gravy for use in slow-cooked dishes, I roast a special way. I sear most roasts, then reduce the heat and add ½ to 1 cup of stock (or bouillon or water) to the roaster. I sear beef at 450° to 475° F. (232° to 246° C.) for 20 minutes, then turn the heat down to 375° F. (190° C.) and add stock. I sear chicken at 425° to 450° F. (218° to 232° C.) for 15 to 20 minutes, then turn the heat down to 325° F. (163° C.) and add ½ cup of chicken stock or bouillon made with a chicken-bouillon cube or granules (Steero is my favorite brand). Pork, lamb, and veal are seared at about 450° F. (232° C.); then the heat is turned down to between 350° and 375° F. (177° to 190° C.), and ½ or 1 cup of chicken or veal stock is added. I baste meat and chicken several times, and if the stock dries up, I add another ¼ or ½ cup about 20 minutes before cooking is finished.

Other discards the crockery cooker thrives on are parsley stems, celery leaves, odds and ends of root vegetables such as carrots, parsnips, and turnips.

The stocks you can make in your slow-cooker become real soups when you add not only discards but meat or vegetables. Canned soup may be all right with luncheon sandwiches if there's nothing else available, but a slow-cooked soup that includes a chicken or a piece of beef or a delicious combination of vegetables or beans makes a splendid meal. Who said we have to have meat and potatoes every night? Try some of the soups in Chapter 8, "Soups That Make One-Dish Dinners." They can bubble all day while you are away. In less than half an hour, when you return home, you can whip up hot biscuits (use a mix—the mixes are good) to go with the soup. Serve a salad and a nice dessert, and even the most meat-and-potatoes household will tell you it's a treat to have something different.

Furthermore, a soup dinner feeds multitudes for very little. And it's romantic, because our grandmothers often served soup for family suppers.

THE RICH, OLD-FASHIONED DESSERTS: In some households, dessert is equated with sin—the sin of calories. And that's a mistake. You can include dessert if you reduce calories by serving smaller portions of meat—and also economize without leaving diners feeling empty. The slow-pot makes to perfection wonderful old desserts—Indian and rice puddings, custards, and dozens of other favorites. Made in the slow-cooker, they cost less and taste infinitely better than the ersatz, quick-cook versions that come in costly packages. Furthermore, though they are rich in calories, many are also rich in nutritional value.

A meal of soup and salad, topped by an old-fashioned pudding, is a happy event and saves many meat dollars. Remember, as you contemplate high-protein meals to save on calories, that large servings of meat actually are high in calories as well as expensive.

JAMS, RELISHES, AND PRESERVES: Making your own preserves the slow-cook way is economical, too.

In experimenting with jams, relishes, and preserves in the crockery pot, I've found that the color is a little off—a little dark. The flavor, however, is fabulous. The slowness of the cooking makes marmalade, for instance, an experience in orangeness no quick-cooked marmalade can match.

Making these old-fashioned goodies in a crockery cooker seems easier, probably because you do them in two stages. The old way, you stand around cutting up the ingredients, stand around while they go through the preliminary cooking, then stand around stirring while they simmer down to the final, thickened state. The crock-pot way, you get the ingredients ready, go off and do a day's worth of something else while they slow-cook, and return to stir during the boiling-down process.

I often make crockery-pot preserves overnight. I start them after dinner, let them cook overnight, and finish them after breakfast. This may not save kitchen time, but it is easy—and, as I said, the flavor is fabulous.

And that, finally, is one of the nicest things about having a slow-cook pot. Even when it doesn't save much time or money, the taste of the foods is so wonderful that this method becomes a real pleasure for the family and the cook.

USING THE SLOW-COOKER TO COOK FOR ONE

Cooking the slow-pot way for a single person makes economic sense when you freeze extras. Slow-cooking one-meal portions isn't economical. Almost all casserole recipes here are for 4 to 6 or 8 persons. Cut the recipes in half when you are cooking for only yourself, and freeze extras in heavy-duty, plastic wrappers. Label them so you'll know what they are. Or refrigerate half the leftover and freeze half. This makes sense especially with soups and stews.

Another way is to cook basic meat cuts—half a chicken, pork chops, beef, lamb—in a little stock (recipes here tell how much liquid to include) and, after cooking, flavor the stock with ingredients from other recipes. Flavor the first meal as in the recipe chosen. For example, you might cook chicken as directed for the veal in Blanquette de Veau (page 152), finish the first night's sauce as in that recipe, and freeze the remaining chicken and stock in one-meal portions. The next time, you might thaw one portion overnight in the refrigerator, and the following evening dress the sauce with vegetables or flavorings from almost any veal or pork recipe. Simmer a little of the flavoring ingredients in the stock, thickened with butter or margarine and flour (see page 28).

USING THE SLOW-COOKER IN HOT WEATHER

One of the great bonuses in having a slow-cooker is that it lets you prepare hot-weather menus without warming the kitchen. Most cookers give off almost no heat—certainly much less than an oven— so in summer I turn often to my slow-cook recipes for hot dishes. A chicken casserole is pleasant with a crisp summer salad. Vegetable combinations done in the slow-cooker are particularly appealing with meats grilled outdoors, and they're wonderful take-along dishes for summer parties when no one wants to do any real cooking, but everyone still enjoys real eating.

Chilled aspics are excellent for summer buffets and parties. Since these usually begin by poaching meats, they are well suited to slow-pot cooking (see page 137). Some of the soups the slow-cooker makes well are fine summer luncheon dishes if they are chilled—for instance, Vichyssoise. In the winter, I make slow-pot soups during the day, but in the summer, I make them overnight, chill them, and serve with crusty bread and butter, cheese, and fresh fruit. It takes all the misery out of being the cook when the thermometer soars.

USING THE SLOW-COOKER TO PROVIDE MORE FUN ON WEEKENDS

A slow-cooker can smooth complicated weekends and holiday periods. For instance, on Friday you can put a slow-cook dish in the cooker, store it in the refrigerator, and go away for the weekend knowing Monday's dinner is ready to start cooking Monday morning. Or you can put the dish in the cooker Friday, take the pot to the country, refrigerate it overnight, and plug it in Saturday morning, freeing yourself for a day of activities without having to think about food. It's a wonderful cook's helper on weekends.

It's also a wonderful helper if you work all day and won't be home for dinner. When I don't expect to go home after work, I start a dish cooking in the morning, one that needs no further attention, and know the children can help themselves to a nourishing, tasty meal.

USING THE SLOW-POT FOR OVERNIGHT COOKING

In some areas, electrical rates are lower at night. In every chapter in this collection there are loads of dishes that are practical to cook overnight, so you might as well cash in on those rates.

Overnight cooking has other advantages. When you cook breakfast overnight, it's warm in the morning, and the kitchen smells as though someone had been up all night preparing nice things for you. Desserts to be served cold in the evening can be cooked overnight; they have the day to chill. As I have said, many jams and preserves can be cooked during the night and finished in the morning.

Aspics and tureens, soups and stews that cook for hours can be cooked overnight and be set aside until you are ready to deal with them. Then the slow-pot is available for cooking during the day. For two-step party dishes, do the long part of the cooking overnight; in the morning, refrigerate the dish and finish it just before dinner.

It takes a little planning and reorganizing to get used to the slow-cooker's working for you while you sleep, but it's worth the effort, particularly when you are dealing with special or party dishes, jams, or breakfast foods. It's pleasant to be free, as many of us are only in the evening, to work on fancy dishes and family treats. And it's marvelous to wake up in the morning knowing that much of the day's cooking is done.

NUTRITION AND FLAVOR

Anyone interested in good nutrition—as we all should be—can feel happy about food that comes from a slow-cooker, because slow-cooking tends to preserve nutrients. During the cooking of stews, casseroles, soups, and compotes—dishes the slow-pot does superbly—nutrients leached from the ingredients go into the cooking liquid, which becomes the sauce. The nutrients don't dissolve in steam. Of course, some nutrient loss can occur with any cooking method, and garden fresh corn-on-the-cob simmered for hours tastes so second-rate that I can't believe it hasn't lost nutrients (and don't really care, to tell the truth, since the flavor and texture are dreadful). Though I believe that slow-cooking preserves nutritional values, I doubt manufacturers' claims (meant to promote slow-cook pots) that fast-cooking is very destructive. The flavor of slow-cooked foods is enough to sell a cook on that method; there's no need to downgrade traditional methods.

The possibility of bacteria growth during slow-cooking doesn't seem to be a hazard. In an unofficial report on slow-cookers, the USDA states that foods cooked at temperatures below 200° to 240° F. (Low on most slow-cookers) may encourage the growth of potentially harmful bacteria. Since most cookers don't cook below 200°, except during the warm-up period, we needn't be concerned. If bacteria did develop in susceptible foods during a long, slow warm-up period, they probably would be killed when the 200° to 240° temperature was reached. That is the generally held view. Our grandparents were sound and sturdy, and most of their foods were slow-cooked—so we have history to reassure us.

Chapter 2

How to Use and Care for Your Slow-Cooker

To GET THE MOST from your electric crock pot, you must learn how to use it. That's no harder than learning to use a blender.

Compare the way a typical dish is done on top of the stove or in the oven and the way it is done in a slow-cook pot.

Beef stew is a staple in most cooks' repertoire. The basic procedure is to heat a large skillet or a Dutch oven and brown in it onions and the meat pieces, floured or unfloured. Then you flavor with salt and pepper, herbs and spices, add water, cover, and cook. As the water boils down, you add more. You may add vegetables at the beginning (some of them will be slightly overdone) or you may hang around the kitchen waiting to add them at intervals, as gourmet cooks do. The carrots go in first, since they are slow to cook, and the potatoes 30 minutes later, since they cook more quickly. The total cooking period will be 1 or 2 hours.

You can cook a beef stew in a slow-pot exactly the same way. Brown the meat; put it into the pot; turn the setting to High; add water; add the vegetables all at once or at intervals; check now and then to make sure the water level is all right. The cooking period will be 2 to 4 hours or so. If you use the Low setting, the stew will take at least twice as long.

ADAPTING YOUR FAVORITE RECIPES
TO SLOW-COOK PROCEDURES

ADD LESS LIQUID: There are two basic things to remember when you adapt your recipes. The first is that, whether set on High or on Low, the slow-cooker lets no, or almost no, steam escape. This means that all the liquid you put into the pot, plus the liquid from the solid ingredients, is likely to be there when the cooking is over.

SOUPS: In a regular pot, I need 8 to 10 cups of water to make soup with 2 cups of dried split green peas; in the slow-cooker, 6 to 8 cups (depending on whether I want thick or thin soup) are plenty. In other words, in adapting soup recipes, I use ⅔ to ¾ the amount of liquid the original recipes call for.

If that reduction isn't enough, it won't cause a disaster. When the soup has finished, just turn the heat to High and simmer until it has the consistency that pleases you.

CASSEROLES AND STEWS: When adapting your recipes for these, halve the liquid called for. If, besides water or stock, the original recipe calls for vegetables with a high liquid content—tomatoes, for instance—cut down even further on the liquid.

If a recipe calls for dried vegetables or grains, you'll have to think carefully, because these absorb water—just how much is difficult to say. Raw rice absorbs twice its measure of water, sometimes a fraction more. Young, dried navy beans seem to absorb more water than do old ones. Read directions on the package; add the amount of water you think the dried foods will take up plus a little more so there will be as much sauce as you need.

Or find a recipe in this book whose ingredients are somewhat similar and add the amount of liquid called for.

BRAISING: When you braise in the slow-cooker, add very, very little liquid or the ingredients will be boiled, not braised.

PLACE THE VEGETABLES UNDER THE MEAT: The second basic thing to remember has to do with vegetables. For reasons I've never yet seen explained, vegetables cook more slowly in slow-cook pots than do meats. Since the highest heat in the pot is usually at the bottom, when you are making meat-and-vegetable stews always place the vegetables on the bottom, with the slowest-to-cook ones at the very bottom.

I should warn you that potatoes, turnips, and other pale vegetables don't come from the slow-cooker a pearly white; they are a little tan, though rich with stew flavor. If you want showy-colored vegetables for party occasions, cook them separately and add them to the slow-pot for the last ½ hour of cooking.

THICKENING THIN SAUCES: In judging the amount of liquid needed for slow-cook recipes, there's always an element of guesswork. You have no control over and no way of gauging the moisture in any piece of meat because it varies with the animal, the cut, and the quality. Likewise, moisture in carrots varies depending on how long ago they were picked and how much rain fell while they were growing.

If the sauce after cooking is too thin, boil it down to half or until it looks right. Or make a roux, a flour thickener, like this:

ROUX, OR THICKENER FOR THIN SAUCES

2 Tbs. butter, margarine, or fat skimmed from cooking liquid	3 Tbs. all-purpose flour Hot cooking liquid

In a medium-large skillet over medium-low heat, heat the butter 1 or 2 minutes. Add the flour all at once, and stir quickly to make a smooth paste. Still stirring, pour in the hot cooking liquid all at once (all the liquid from the slow-cooked dish); stir quickly until the sauce thickens—2 or 3 minutes. Turn it back into the pot; set the heat on High, and let the ingredients simmer a few minutes before serving.

BAKING IN AN ELECTRIC CROCK POT: This is quite different, not only in timing but in procedure. Why bake in a slow-pot? Just for the fun of seeing the difference, for one thing. I bake this way when I want fruit breads and such for breakfast without getting up early and when I want to go to a football game and return home to find corn muffins waiting. I also use my slow-pot for steamed puddings, which are much harder to bake in any other utensil.

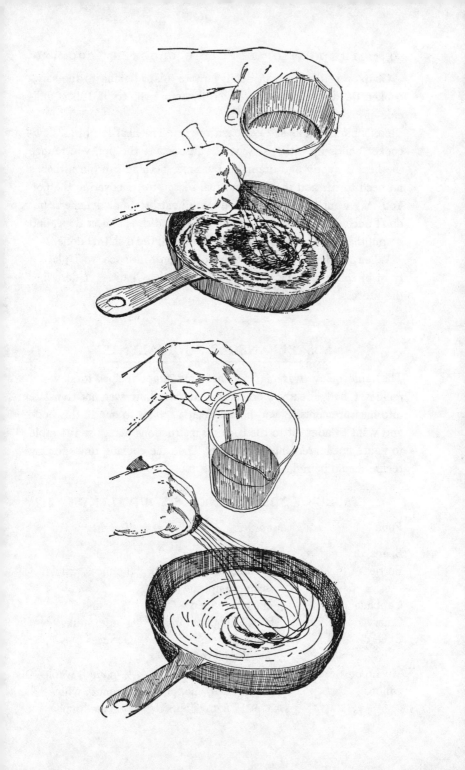

Chapter 11 discusses in detail how to adapt baking to the slow-cooker. Read the instructions carefully before you try it. It isn't difficult—just different.

DON'T UNCOVER THE SLOW-COOKER TO STIR: The heat level in a slow-cooker builds up rather slowly. If you uncover the pot, you reduce the heat instantly and dramatically. Since nothing can burn, there's no need to stir and therefore no real reason for uncovering the pot. You may want to investigate the ingredients' state of doneness, but don't uncover the pot until you believe the dish is almost done, and do put the cover back as quickly as possible if the dish isn't done.

When I bake, I want a tiny bit of steam to escape, so I place a twist of foil under the cover to tilt it a little. Chapter 11 describes the process.

MISCELLANEOUS EQUIVALENTS

The table below was made to help me adapt recipes to slow-pot recipes I had already worked out. It tells how weights translate into measurements. If you have a recipe similar to one in this book and want to adapt it to the cooking instructions here, use the table to figure out ingredient equivalents. Then the cooking times for my recipe should be right for your recipe, too.

TABLE OF MISCELLANEOUS EQUIVALENTS

Food	Measure	Weight
Beans, dry	2 to 2½ cups, raw	1 pound
Berries	1⅓ cups, whole; scant 1 cup, sieved	8 ounces, whole
Cabbage	3 cups, shredded	½ pound
Celery	About ½ cup, cut up	2 large stalks
Cheese	½ cup, grated, lightly packed	2 ounces
Mushrooms, fresh	About 2½ cups, sliced	½ pound, whole
Onions	About 4 cups, chopped	1 pound, whole
	About ⅓ cup, chopped	One medium

Food	Measure	Weight
Peas, green		
Fresh, small	1 cup, shelled	1 pound, unshelled
Fresh, large	1½ cups, shelled	1 pound, unshelled
Frozen	1½ cups, cooked	10-ounce package, raw
Raisins, small seedless, and currants	¾ cup	4 ounces
Rice	1 cup, raw or 3 cups, cooked	8 ounces, raw
Sugar, granulated and superfine	1 Tbs.	⅓ ounce
	⅓ cup	2 ounces
	1 cup	6½ ounces
	5¼ cups	2.2 pounds
Tomatoes		
Fresh	1½ cups, peeled, seeded, juiced	1 pound, whole
Canned	1¾ cups strained pulp	35-ounce can
Vegetables, leaf		
Fresh	½ cup plus, cooked, squeezed, chopped	10-ounce package, raw
Frozen	½ cup, squeezed, chopped	10-ounce package, raw
Vegetables, raw	3½ cups, diced or sliced	1 pound, whole

WORKING WITH THE RECIPES IN THIS BOOK

Recipes aren't blueprints of the road to culinary bliss; they are merely indications of how to go. Only you know your own and your family's favorite flavors and how to produce them. In any recipe, the condiments, spices, herbs can be changed to suit your taste, or omitted if you don't like strong flavors.

In working with slow-cook pots, I've learned to use about twice as much flavoring as for quick-cook recipes. Experiment, using more or less than I have suggested here. Always check sauces and add salt or pepper if needed. For that matter, if they taste bland, you can add more of the herbs called for and simmer another few minutes before serving.

DON'T PANIC—SUBSTITUTE: When you are preparing a dish and discover that a necessary ingredient is missing, don't panic—substitute. The following table lists some of the things I run out of occasionally and the substitutes I use.

TABLE OF SUBSTITUTES

Bouillon or stock	1 bouillon cube dissolved in 8 ounces hot water
Bread crumbs	Rolled-out saltines
Butter	Margarine, rendered chicken fat, vegetable oil, shortening, or rendered pork fat
Carrots	Parsnips or baby white turnips
Cream, light	Whole milk or heavy cream thinned with milk
Croutons	Cubes of crustless white bread, sautéed in butter
Curry powder	Turmeric plus cardamom, ginger powder, and cumin
Flour, all-purpose, as a thickener	Cornstarch
Garlic	Garlic salt or garlic powder
Ginger, fresh	Powdered ginger. One slice ginger equals about ¼ teaspoon powdered
Lemon juice	White vinegar, lime juice, or white wine
Lettuce	Spinach or any leafy green
Mayonnaise, fresh	For ½ cup mayonnaise: commercial mayonnaise plus ½ teaspoon lemon juice and ½ teaspoon prepared mustard
Milk	Powdered milk and water, blended
Mustard, prepared	Powdered mustard
Olive oil	Vegetable oil
Parsley	Chervil
Pepper, black	White pepper or paprika

Scallions	Green, plain, or frozen onions, or onion powder to taste
Shallots	⅔ onion plus a garlic clove
Vinegar, tarragon	Pinch of dried tarragon heated in wine vinegar for 3 minutes, then strained
Vinegar, wine	Cider, or red or white vinegar with a little wine

WHICH SLOW-COOKER DOES WHAT?

There are more than two dozen brands of slow-cooker on the market, and more turn up all the time. As the slow-pot's popularity grows, industry copies the most successful models and produces yet other versions.

Slow-cook recipes give a much wider leeway in cooking times than do conventional recipes. Timing depends on which cooker you buy. A 2-hour span is usual: "Turn to Low, and cook, covered, 6 to 8 hours" is a common recipe instruction. When you cook on High, time is halved: "3 to 4 hours," giving you a 1-hour leeway. This means that on Low, the dish may be expected to be done at the earliest in 6 hours in some cookers and at the latest in 8 hours in others; on High, it may be done at the earliest in 3 hours and at the latest in 4 hours.

If you've just acquired a slow-cooker, how can you tell whether dinner will be ready at 6 o'clock or at 8? You will have to adjust recipe timing to your cooker.

Learning the cooker's timing pattern is the first—almost the only—thing needed for success with slow-cook recipes. Timing in this book is a little shorter than suitable for the slowest pots.

The Timing Table on page 35 suggests cooking patterns for slow-pots I've studied, but they are only indications. Some cookers said to cook at exactly the same heating curve don't. I cut a pork rib roast in half and put the halves in different brands of slow-pot. Timing instructions for both were similar, but one roast was cooked long before the other. Two models made by the same manufacturer cooked at slightly different speeds. Slow-cooker literature warns that line surges and other peculiarities of electrical current affect cooking times.

What all these variables mean is that your slow-cooker has its own heating pattern. For the first week or two, expect things to be done a little earlier or later than recipes indicate. Check the cooker contents 1 hour earlier—2 hours earlier for long-cooking dishes— until you get the hang of your model's pattern.

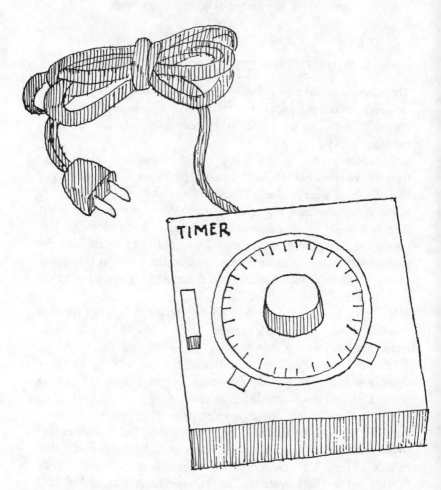

Even if the foods are ready early and continue to cook, they won't be harmed. They may be a little overdone, but they won't dry out or burn. True, dense cuts of beef (pot roast in the round, for instance) are stringy and dry when overdone, but the slow-cooker makes a delicious sauce which you can ladle over the meat slices.

Once you understand your cooker's timing, you can adjust recipe instructions and turn out perfect dishes at about the time you expect.

Many, perhaps most, slow-cook dishes are almost impossible to overcook. Casseroles and stews and vegetable mélanges are delicious only when cooked slowly for hours. You really do have all that free time the majority of recipes provide.

If your slow-cooker cooks more slowly than a recipe indicates, and you are eager to have the dish done, turn to High the last hour or two.

FIGURING COOKING TIME: Recipes in this book have been timed to slow-pots that cook at between 200° and 240° F. on Low (about 100° to 115° C.) and 300° to 340° F. on High (about 149° to 170° C.). Study the cooking heats described for your model. Check the table where cooking speeds of several brands of cooker are listed. Then try a recipe, using your adjusted timing. The result will tell you whether to shorten or lengthen cooking time. Timings for most slow-pot recipes are pretty standard; they reflect the cooking curves of slower units but not the slowest.

TIMING TABLE AND CHART OF HEAT LEVELS

Brand name of electric slow-cooker Note: These are not pressure cookers	For Low Cook at	For High Cook at
CORNING ELECTROMATIC TABLE RANGE, 2½ quarts Note: Halve recipes in this book for this unit, and add ½ cup liquid, as it dries foods more than do the other types of cooker. When baking, add ½ cup water to the unit, and use a trivet. It really isn't designed for slow-baking.	240° F.	350° F.
CORNWALL CROCKERY COOKER, 4 quarts	Medium	Hi
CORNWALL TRAY MODEL CROCKERY COOKER, 2½ quarts Note: Halve recipes. Add at least ½ cup water to recipes that do not call for a liquid. Use ½ cup more liquid in	No. 3 Heat	Do Not Use

recipes that do call for liquid. The first few times you use the unit for slow-cooking, make notes on how much difference there was between actual cooking times and cooking times in the recipes and how much extra liquid was needed. When baking, add ½ cup water to the pot, and use a trivet.

| CORNWALL TRAY MODEL CROCKERY COOKER, 4½ quarts | No. 2 Heat | No. 3 Heat |

Note: Add 1 cup water when recipes do not call for water; use ½ cup more liquid to recipes including liquid. When baking, add ½ cup water to the pot, and use a trivet. Watch the pot the first few times you use it for slow-cooking or slow-baking, to see if timing for recipes here fits and to test how much more liquid is needed.

| CORNWALL TRAY MODEL CROCKERY COOKER, 8 quarts | No. 2 Heat | No. 3 Heat |

Note: See notes for 4½-quart Cornwall on adding water. If you double recipes to fill the 8-quart container, use regular cooking times; if you use recipes as written, reduce cooking times by 1 or 2 hours. This cooker tends to cook fast.

| DOMINION CROCK-A-DIAL, 3 quarts | Low | High |

Note: This model seems to cook a little more slowly than most.

| EMPIRE EASY MEAL SLOW COOKER, 2½ quarts | Medium | Between Medium and High |

Note: Halve recipes, and add a little liquid, about ½ cup. Watch the pot the first few times you use it with the recipes here, to gauge how closely its

cooking times fit the recipes and how
much more liquid may be needed.

FARBERWARE POT-POURRI,	200° F.	300° F.
3 and 4½ quarts		

Note: These units cook more quickly
than the recipes here indicate. Reduce
cooking times by about ⅓, and watch
the pot the first few times, to gauge
timing.

GRANDINETTI CROCKERY	Low	High
COOK POT, 3½ and 5 quarts		

Note: For 3½-quart unit, keep recipe
ingredients on the skimpy side. A few
recipes may not quite fit the pot. Uses
less energy than most.

HAMILTON BEACH	Low	High
CONTINENTAL COOKER,		
3 quarts		
CROCK-WATCHER	Low	High
SIMMER-ON	Low	High

Note: The Continental Cooker and the
Crock-Watcher have autoshift controls
that start foods on a hotter setting than
the real Low. In combination with the
autoshift hot-cook period, the Low
setting cooks at about the same pace as
the recipes here indicate. Without the
autoshift, on Low these cookers cook
more slowly than recipes indicate.
Study your model the first few times
you use it, and adjust recipes according
to its performance.

NESCO POT LUCK COOKER,	200° F.	250° F.
4½ quarts		

Note: Steam escapes through holes in
the lid, and this means you lose some
of the liquid. Add another ¼ or ½ cup
liquid to recipes, or block the holes

with crumpled foil. This model cooks a
little faster than recipes here indicate.
Watch your pot the first few times you
use recipes from this book, and adjust
cooking periods to the pattern of your
pot, if necessary. *Consumer Reports*
tests show this model uses more
energy than most.

PENNEY'S SLOW COOKER/ FRYER, 4 quarts	Just left of the crockery- cooking band	Between 325° and 350° F.

PRESTO SLOW COOKERS,   High   Between
   2¾ and 5 quarts   High and
Note: Halve ingredients in recipes   Brown
in this book for the 2¾-quart model.
Reduce cooking times by about 2
hours on Slow-cook recipes, and
reduce times for High-cook recipes
by about half. Study the time your unit
takes to cook; compare with timing
given for the recipes here, particularly
for baking. The smaller unit really
isn't suited to baking.

REGAL MARDI GRAS POT   No. 2 Heat   No. 3 Heat
   O' PLENTY, 4 quarts
Note: This cooks a little faster than
recipes here, and the food may need
stirring. Study the way your model
handles meats, and adjust your
cooking plans accordingly. It pays to
add a little water to the recipes until
you have a notion of how your model
performs. Drains 1600 watts energy—
a lot for a crockery pot—according to
Consumer Reports.

RIVAL CROCK-POT CASSEROLE   Low   High
   3500, 2 quarts
Note: Cooks a little slower on Low
than mine.

	Low	High
RIVAL CROCK-POT, 3, 4½, and 5 quarts	Low	High
SEARS CROCKERY COOKER, 4½ quarts	Medium	Hi
SEARS CROCKERY COOKER 65292, 4 quarts	Medium	High

Note: Cooks a little slower on Low than mine.

SEARS TRAY MODEL, 2½ quarts	No. 3 Heat	Do not use High recipes

Note: Halve recipes in this book. This unit doesn't seem to cook fast enough to use High given for recipes. Add 1 cup water when recipes do not call for liquid, and add ½ cup liquid to recipes that include liquid. When baking, add ½ cup water to the pot, and use a trivet. Not really suited to slow-baking.

SEARS TRAY MODEL, 5 quarts	No. 2 Heat	No. 3 Heat

Note: Add 1 cup water when recipes do not call for liquid, and add ½ cup liquid to recipes including liquid. When baking, add ½ cup water to the pot, and use a trivet.

SUNBEAM CROCKER COOKER/ FRYER, 4½ quarts	Just left of crockery- cooker band	Between 325° and 350° F.

Note: Recipes here come out just right if you set the dial just left of the crockery-cooker band.

SUNBEAM CROCKER FRYPAN, 2 quarts	200° F.	300° F.

Note: Halve the recipes in this book, and add ½ to 1 cup liquid per recipe, including those where no liquid is called for. Watch the pot the first few times you use it for recipes here, to gauge the differences between its way of cooking and those indicated in the recipes.

WARDS AND VAN WYCK SIM-R-WARE, 4 quarts	Low	Do not use High recipes

Note: The High setting may cook a
little faster than the recipes given
here. Set on Low, these cook a little
slower than mine, according to
Consumer Reports.

WEAR-EVER H38032 and C38033, 3½ quarts	Low	High
WEST BEND LAZY DAY SLO-COOKER, 5 quarts	No. 2 Heat	No. 4 Heat

Don't let all this information make you feel it is a problem to get
the timing just right. Remember that to cook properly with a stove,
you must know the stove. This is also true with the slow-cooker.

Keep records on the recipe pages of time changes that seem de-
sirable and of variations in ingredients. If a dish needs a teaspoonful
more salt, or if you prefer it without the bay leaf, make a note. It
won't damage the book to write on its pages; on the contrary, that
will make it specially yours. Someday you may pass it along to a
younger sister, a daughter, or a friend. If you record how you like a
dish, your daughter can make it "just the way Mother did." Or
sister, or friend. That's how cooking traditions are established—not
in the cold print of someone else's favorite flavors.

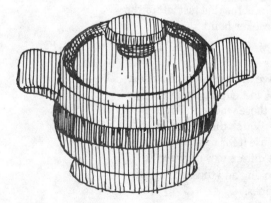

CONTINUOUS-HEAT VS. THERMOSTATIC-CONTROL COOKERS

In the evaluation of cooking times, a *Consumer Reports* article makes some differentiation between slow-cookers whose heat is continuous and those whose heat is thermostatically regulated. Of twenty-four models tested, six continuous-heat pots cooked the average stew made with tough beef on Low in 10 to 12 hours and on High in 5 to 7 hours.

The six were Wear-Ever H38032 and C38033, Penney's Cooker Catalog #0350, Rival Crock Pot 3100 and 3300, and Grandinetti 532. These supply two cooking heats and include models I've based my cooking times on. With the other continuous-heat cookers tested, 15 hours or more were required for a stew. I've found that more tender and delicate cuts of meat, such as chicken and veal, cook in 5 to 7 hours on Low and tougher meats in 8 to 10 or 10 to 12 hours, as noted in my recipes.

However, I haven't tested every recipe in this book in every slow-cooker manufactured. To find out how your cooker works—let me say it again—make a stew with tough beef and one with chicken or veal. Then you will have precise readings to help you adjust slow-cooker recipes to your pot.

Consumer Reports found cooking times unreliable in thermostatically controlled slow-pots—as much as 4 to 6 hours off the timings given in the manufacturers' recipe booklets. Even so, these models present no problems. Just adjust the control to the heating ranges represented by High and Low in this book—between 200° and 240° F. for Low and between 300° and 340° F. for High—and your cooker will finish the dishes in approximately the times given.

ADDITIONAL TIPS FOR USING SLOW-COOKERS

USING A TIMER WITH YOUR SLOW-COOKER: A timer—an electrical fixture that plugs into a wall socket and turns the slow-cooker on and off at specific times—costs from under $10 to about $25. I've recommended its use especially for baking and for overnight cooking of breakfast foods. By using a timer, you can, for example, wake up to the aroma of fresh-baked orange-nut bread. Slow-cookers generally bake on High and for fewer hours than most of us spend in bed; however, you can set the timer to turn on the cooker during the night. Or you can set it to start the cooking right away and turn off the pot during the night.

The timer can prolong your absentee hours; while you are away, it can turn on the cooker whenever you wish. If a dish requires 5 to 7 cooking hours and you will be away 10, the timer makes that possible. In my opinion, it is a good investment.

There is the question of whether foods may spoil while waiting for the pot to be turned on. I wouldn't choose a boiling-hot day and an easily spoiled meat like chicken for timed cooking. If you are concerned about a casserole with ingredients susceptible to spoilage, keep them in the refrigerator until you are ready to combine them, and use ice cubes, added just before you leave the house, for the liquid content. The cubes will melt slowly, keeping everything cool until the cooking starts.

ADJUST RECIPES TO THE SIZE OF YOUR SLOW-COOKER: The recipes in this book were worked out with about 4½-quart units. Three-, 3½-, 4-, and 5-quart slow-cookers will handle most of them. For smaller units, cut the ingredients in half. For a slow-pot to cook at approximately the recommended times, it should be about half full.

CARE AND CLEANING OF THE SLOW-POTS: There are three major types of pot: a tray-model container set on a heating unit like a small single burner; a pot that is part of the heating unit; a pot that goes into, or is part of, a larger container with heating wires around its walls. I think you will find that the last two are the easiest to work with. However, the unit on a heating element works perfectly well if the temperature settings correspond to those for the recipes you use.

Tray models made of crockery (some are enamel-coated metal) may crack if there is no liquid in the recipe. If the pot is drying out, add ¼ cup or more of bouillon, wine, or water. Liquid is added because steam is escaping and the crock's interior is becoming dry. You needn't worry that the liquid will alter the dish; it should evaporate.

One-piece crockery cookers—those that contain the heating wires —usually should not be immersed in water for washing. Keeping them clean is a little more awkward than washing a pot that can be removed from a larger container or a heating unit. Still, it's not much more trouble than electric coffeepots, and we're all accustomed to washing those without soaking the electrical contact.

If baked-on food in a wired pot is especially greasy, try letting water with a few tablespoons of ammonia soak in the pot. Wash it thoroughly after the ammonia has been poured out. If there is a lot of baked-on food, fill the pot with hot, soapy water and a few tablespoons of baking soda, and let it stand a few hours. If the food doesn't rinse off easily, scrub it with a plastic scouring pad. Enamel or metal interiors stay new longer if steel wool and cleaning compounds are avoided. It is important not to scrape or scratch crockery pots. The glaze could be damaged, and foods would stick to the scratched places. For stains, simmer 3 or 4 tablespoons of Teflon cleaner and water in the pot for an hour; that should cleanse it.

Units coated with Teflon, as are some tray models, should be washed thoroughly before the first use, then coated lightly with vegetable oil to season them. Don't use sharp knives and utensils that could scratch or damage the Teflon coating. Scour only with plastic pads. Some shades of Teflon discolor after a time, but this doesn't affect the nonstick quality. Products for cleaning stained Teflon are available. After a stain-removal session, scrub away the cleaning product; wash the pot's interior thoroughly, and coat it with vegetable oil.

HANDLE SLOW-COOKERS WITH CARE: Each cooker comes with instructions for its care and handling. Follow them.

Be wary of extreme or sudden changes of temperature. If your cooker is a removable unit, don't keep it in the refrigerator with leftovers and then place it directly into or onto the heating unit; the sudden application of heat could break it. I never heat my crockery pot on the stove. Crockery was once used for stove-top cooking, but eventually it would break. That's one reason it was replaced by metal. Think of crockery as you think of glass. Handled gently, it will last virtually forever. (Glass pots such as those made by Corning can stand quick temperature changes; if you have one of these, you may use it for freezer or refrigerator storage if you wish.)

THE METRIC SYSTEM AND YOU

The metric system, now used everywhere except in the United States, is fairly simple, but until we get accustomed to it and our cooking equipment is converted to it, we'll have to fiddle with equivalents. Here are two simplified tables I've worked out that may be of help to you. I assume that we will be using the metric system soon. Meanwhile, with these tables you can convert any treasured metric-measured recipes to the recipes in this book.

WEIGHT MEASUREMENTS AND NEAR METRIC EQUIVALENTS

Approximate Ounces and Pounds	Metric
⅛ ounce	5 grams
⅓ ounce	10 grams
½ ounce	15 grams
1 scant ounce	25 grams
1 ounce	30 grams
1¾ ounces	50 grams
2⅔ ounces	75 grams
3½ ounces	100 grams
¼ pound (4 ounces)	114 grams
4⅜ ounces	125 grams
½ pound (8 ounces)	227 grams
9 ounces	250 grams
1 pound (16 ounces)	464 grams
1.1 pounds	500 grams
2.2 pounds	1,000 grams

LIQUID MEASUREMENTS AND NEAREST CONVENIENT METRIC EQUIVALENTS

Ounces and Quarts	Spoons and Cups	Metric
¹⁄₁₆ ounce	1 tsp.	5 grams
⅓ ounce	2 tsp.	10 grams
½ ounce	1 Tbs.	15 grams
1¾ ounces	3⅓ Tbs.	½ deciliter

Ounces and Quarts	*Spoons and Cups*	*Metric*
2⅔ ounces	⅓ cup	1 deciliter minus 1⅓ Tbs.
3½ ounces	⅓ cup plus 1 Tbs.	1 deciliter
8 ounces	1 cup	¼ liter
1 pint (16 ounces)	2 cups	½ liter minus 1½ Tbs.
17 ounces	2 cups plus 2½ Tbs.	½ liter
1 quart (32 ounces)	4 cups	1 liter minus 1 deciliter
1 quart 2 ounces	4⅓ cups	1 liter

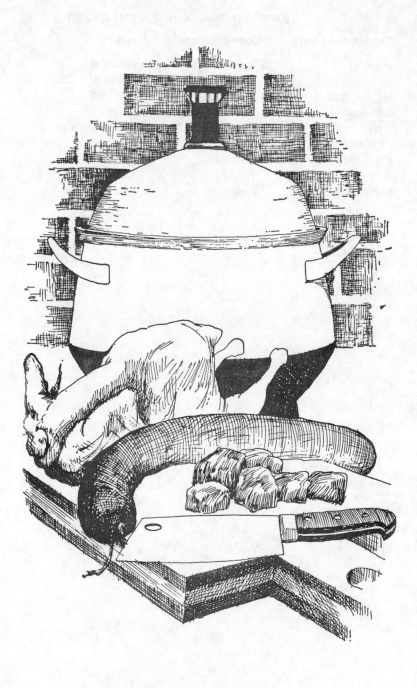

PART TWO
MEAT DISHES FOR FAMILY MEALS

Chapter 3

Beef and Veal

BRAISED MEATS, CASSEROLES, and stews are the dishes the slow-cooker does extraordinarily well. Making lesser cuts of meat into really good food is its special talent. It bubbles ingredients very slowly for hours, and the finished dishes have a flavor you just can't get any other way.

Almost all recipes in this section call for some liquid. A few add only vegetables to the meat and flavorings— The meat and vegetables contribute enough moisture to make some sauce by the time cooking is finished. However, a few recipes have neither liquid nor particularly moist vegetables. Some slow-cookers on the market— usually pots that heat on tray units—require some liquid. If you have one of these models and are using a no-liquid recipe, add the minimum amount of liquid your cooker's instructions call for. Rather than water, use meat stock or bouillon made with granules or cubes. Leftover soup or tomato juice might be good in some recipes.

BEEF FOR THE SLOW-COOKER

There are at least six cuts of beef you might use in the slow-cook recipes that follow. These cuts, described briefly, are listed on pages 51 and 52. Some of the more expensive cuts noted as suitable for braising, stews, and casseroles might also be good for roasting—that depends on the quality of the beef.

The basic cuts fall into two categories: beef with lots of gristle and fat running through the meat fibers and beef that is a solid chunk of rather dense meat. The tender meat we use for steaks—sirloin, for instance—and prime rib roasts are marbled with thin veins of fat. These are the expensive cuts and are at their best broiled, roasted, sautéed, or grilled. When they are cooked at high temperatures, the fat melts away while the tissues tenderize rapidly, and the result is one of America's favorite foods.

The less tender, dense cuts of beef (except filet mignon) cook to shoe-leather texture at high heats. Cooked quickly, cuts threaded with gristle are just about inedible. Cooked very slowly, both types become tender.

Many cuts are interchangeable. Top and bottom round make excellent pot roasts; if they are first quality, they also make good oven roasts. Poke a good-quality sirloin roast and compare its tenderness with that of a good-quality top- or bottom-round roast; then, the next time you buy a round roast, you'll have some guide for deciding whether to oven-roast or pot-roast it. Firmness doesn't necessarily mean a hard-to-eat cut, but it usually does mean the cut should be slow-cooked.

The best stews, in my opinion, are those made with meat that has some fat clinging to it. Short ribs—the ends cut from a rib roast —are superb in stews. Any of the lesser cuts with some fat will make a good stew in the slow-cooker. Chuck roasts are sometimes perfect for oven-roasting; sometimes, however, they are tough and make a much better stew (in fact, a delicious stew) than a roast.

Although many cuts that include a bone are good for oven-roasting, a few—some of the chuck cuts, for instance—are better slow-cooked. I think bone-in meat has more flavor than boneless meat, but the bone can prevent the cut's fitting into the slow-cooker. So when you buy beef for slow-cooking, keep in mind the shape and size of your cooker. If you've bought a bone-in piece that doesn't fit the cooker and doesn't seem suitable for preparing some other way, just cut the meat into stew-size chunks. Or bone and roll the piece, securing it with stout, clean cord or thread. Freeze the bone for soup making, and nothing will be lost.

For most family meals, I start my planning by investigating buys at the meat counter. Since I know that the slow-cooker can make almost any beef cut good, I tend to buy the current bargain, then check my recipes to see which suits the meat. If I have bought more than the recipe calls for, I freeze the extra or increase the other recipe ingredients, and use all the meat.

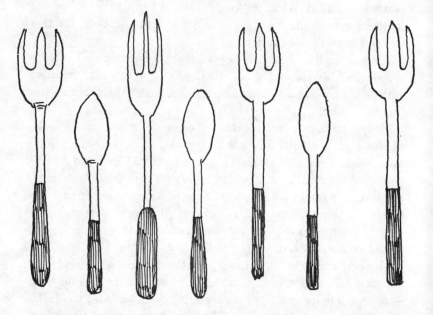

GROUND BEEF OR HAMBURGER IN THE SLOW-COOKER: Customarily, meat loaf is baked in the oven, and meat sauce for spaghetti and lasagna is cooked on the stove top. Both are excellent slow-cooked, however, so I've included recipes for them. Sometimes it's helpful to prepare them in the morning and have them ready to serve the instant the dinner bell rings. Many ground-beef and hamburger dishes can be made in a slow-cooker, and I've suggested a few because it is so practical to cook them this way and they are popular.

TIMING BEEF DISHES: Most slow-cook beef recipes allow you 8 to 10 hours or more away from the kitchen. The size of the meat pieces affects cooking time. When you are braising beef, be aware that a cut smaller or larger than the one called for in the recipe requires shorter or longer cooking time.

Another thing that affects timing is the coldness of a large cut when it is put into the pot. Crockery pots warm up very, very slowly. If the cut is large, dense, and almost freezing cold, the pot will take much longer to warm up and thus much longer to cook. So to have the dish ready in the shortest time given by the recipe, make sure the meat has been out of the refrigerator at least an hour before you put it into the pot.

BEEF CUTS ESPECIALLY SUITED TO SLOW-COOKING

Shoulder Roast: This cut, from the bottom of the animal's chuck section, is sold in two parts. The front has a round bone and is carried in my markets as "arm roast." The back is without bone. The meat is lean and rather dry and benefits from the slow, moist cooking of an electric crock pot.

Rump Roast: This may be bone-in, as a triangular piece of meat, or boneless and rolled. It has some fat and can be roasted if the quality is very good; it also makes a super pot roast when done in the slow-cooker.

Chuck Roast: A very good flavor is one of the pluses of chuck. It can be boiled and often is roasted when the quality is very good, since there is a fair amount of fat. Leaner chucks make wonderful slow-cooked meats.

Brisket: Often sold for corned beef, brisket comes in two cuts. The first is lean and dry, and slow-cooking is the best method. The second is fatter and can be cooked in the oven or slow-cooked.

Plate: A stringy cut, sold flat or rolled. The best way to prepare it is in the slow-cooker.

Short Ribs: These are ends cut from a rib roast. They are very fatty but very flavorful and make wonderful pot roasts or boiled beef.

INVENT YOUR OWN SLOW-COOK BEEF DISHES

You can adapt any of your favorite beef dishes to slow-cooking by finding a similar recipe here and following the cooking procedures. If your recipe adds more than a pound of ingredients, increase cooking time by half an hour or an hour.

Inventing beef dishes is easy and satisfying. You can make a stew or casserole from almost any beef cut by browning the meat in a skillet, with onion and a bit of garlic, and simmering with about 1 cup of beef or veal stock and a bay leaf, 3 sprigs of parsley, a pinch of ground dried thyme, and a pinch of ground clove or 4 or 5 whole cloves. Vegetables that go well with beef include carrots (on the sweet side), parsnips, celery, potatoes. A good combination with beef is mushrooms, tomatoes, sweet peppers, and onions. Give a lift to thin beef sauces by adding a tablespoon of a good prepared mustard about 15 minutes before serving, or a minced clove of fresh garlic, or a few spoonfuls of wine vinegar, red wine, or tomato paste.

BEEF RECIPES

POT ROAST WITH SOUR-CREAM SAUCE, GERMAN STYLE
10 to 12 hours

A good recipe for lean beef in the round. If a lot of fat is floating on the sauce when cooking is over, skim it off before adding the sour cream. This pot roast is especially nice with noodles or cooked green cabbage.

1 *tsp. salt*	1 *cup dry red wine*
3 *to 4 lb. top or bottom round of beef*	½ *tsp. salt*
	¼ *tsp. black pepper*
1 *medium onion, peeled, sliced*	2 *Tbs. all-purpose flour*
	½ *cup sour cream*

To Cook: Sprinkle 1 teaspoon salt in a large skillet, set over medium-high heat, and brown the roast well on all sides. Remove roast to the slow-cooker. Add the onion to the skillet, and brown lightly, stirring often. Pour in the wine; scrape up pan juices, and turn into the slow-cooker with ½ teaspoon salt and the pepper. Cover, turn to Low, and cook 10 to 12 hours.

Before Serving: Skim 2 tablespoons fat from the liquid in the cooker and heat in a medium skillet, over low heat. Stir in the flour to make a smooth paste. Then add the cooking liquid all at once; stir continuously until the sauce is smooth and has thickened—about 5 to 7 minutes. Remove skillet from heat; stir in the sour cream. Serve sauce over the pot roast.

Makes 6 to 8 servings.

POT-AU-FEU
12 to 18 hours

This is boiled beef, one of the favorites of all French family dishes. It is perfect only when it is slow-cooked. At home, we serve it in soup bowls with big chunks of crusty French bread. You may select a rump pot roast for this; other choices are bottom round, sirloin tip, or chuck pot roast. Leftover veal scraps and a marrow-bone or two can be added.

3 *lb. rump pot roast*
4 *chicken wings, or*
    equivalent in chicken
    necks, backs, and
    gizzards
3 *large carrots, scraped and*
    quartered
3 *parsnips, or 3 medium*
    young white turnips,
    scraped
3 *large stalks celery, cut*
    into 4-inch pieces
1 *small onion, peeled and*
    stuck with 4 whole cloves

1 *can (10 oz.) beef bouillon,*
    or 10 oz. water and
    2 beef bouillon cubes
1 *large bay leaf*
6 *sprigs fresh parsley,*
    or 1 tsp. dried parsley
½ *tsp. ground thyme*
4 *cloves garlic, peeled*
    (optional)
8 *peppercorns*
2 to 3 *tsp. salt*
Sea salt or coarse
    kosher salt, if available

To Cook: Place all the ingredients, except the sea salt, in the slow-cooker, with the vegetables and herbs on the bottom. Cover and cook on Low for 12 to 18 hours. Discard chicken pieces. Serve from a tureen into soup dishes. Offer the sea salt on the side. It is to be sprinkled over the meat by each diner.

Makes 5 or 6 servings.

SWISS STEAK
6 to 8 hours

1½ lb. boneless round or rump
    steak, 1½ inches thick
2 Tbs. all-purpose flour
1 tsp. salt
¼ tsp. black pepper
2 Tbs. vegetable oil
1½ cups peeled fresh
    tomatoes or canned
    whole tomatoes, sliced

3 large onions, peeled
    and thinly sliced
1 large stalk celery, diced
1 large clove garlic, peeled
    and minced
1 Tbs. Gravy Master or
    Kitchen Bouquet

To Cook: Remove any excess fat from the meat, and lay meat on a cutting board. Sprinkle with half the flour, salt, and pepper. With the back of a heavy kitchen knife or the edge of a saucer, pound flour and seasonings into the meat. Repeat on the other side, using the remaining flour, salt, and pepper. In a large skillet, over medium-high heat, brown each side of the meat in the oil for 2 or 3 minutes. Lift the meat into the slow-cooker. Add remaining ingredients to the skillet; stir and scrape to get up all the pan juices. Pour this mixture over the meat. Cover and cook on Low for 6 to 8 hours.

Makes 4 to 6 servings.

SWISS STEAK JARDINIÈRE
6 to 8 hours

This is a variation to play on Swiss steak. It uses mushrooms, fresh or canned.

1½ lb. round or rump steak, cut in slices ½ inch thick

¼ cup all-purpose flour

1 tsp. salt

¼ tsp. black pepper

2 Tbs. vegetable oil

½ cup chopped onion

1 medium clove garlic, peeled and minced

1½ cups fresh or canned whole tomatoes, quartered

6 medium carrots, peeled and halved

2 medium green peppers, seeded and cut into 1-inch pieces

1 lb. fresh mushrooms, rinsed, patted dry, and cut in half; or 2 cans (6- to 8-oz. size) whole mushrooms, drained

To Cook: Remove any excess fat from the meat slices, and lay them on a cutting board. Sprinkle with half the flour, ½ teaspoon salt, and half the pepper. With the back of a heavy kitchen knife or the edge of a saucer, pound the flour into the meat. Repeat on the other side, using ½ teaspoon salt and remaining flour and pepper. In a large skillet over medium-high heat, brown the meat slices on each side in the oil 2 or 3 minutes. Lift the meat into a bowl. Add the onion, garlic, and tomatoes to the still-hot skillet and sauté, scraping up the pan juices, for 2 or 3 minutes. Turn into the slow-cooker. Add the carrots and green peppers, then the meat. Cover and cook on Low for 6 to 8 hours.

Before Serving: Lift the meat and vegetables onto a heated serving platter. Skim the cooking liquid to gather 1 or 2 tablespoons fat, and put fat in a large skillet. Over medium-high heat, sauté the mushrooms, tossing constantly, until moisture has dried and pieces are tender—about 5 minutes. Add salt. Pour cooking liquid from the slow-cooker over the mushrooms; simmer briefly, scraping up pan juices. Sauce should be the consistency of heavy cream. Pour over meat and vegetables.

Makes 4 to 6 servings.

GOULASH, SOUTHERN STYLE
8 to 10 hours

Nice with mashed potatoes and a green salad.

1 *lb. round steak, cut into*	2 *tsp. salt*
¼-inch cubes	1¼ *cups cold water*
3 *Tbs. vegetable oil*	1 *Tbs. brown sugar*
¼ *tsp. paprika*	3 *small bay leaves*
¾ *cup thinly sliced onion*	3 *Tbs. all-purpose flour*

To Cook: In a large skillet, over medium-high heat, brown the meat in the oil with the paprika, stirring constantly. Add the onion, and stir until browned. Add the salt, water, brown sugar, and bay leaves. Scrape and stir to get up the pan juices. Turn into the slow-cooker. Cover and cook on Low for 8 to 10 hours.

Before Serving: Remove the bay leaves. Skim 3 tablespoons fat from the sauce in the cooker, and turn into a skillet set over medium-low heat. Stir in the flour. As soon as the mixture is smooth, pour in the juices from the cooker, and stir quickly to smooth the sauce. Let simmer a few minutes, or until it is as thick as heavy cream. Turn the meat into the sauce; heat through, and serve.

Makes 4 servings.

SIMPLE BEEF CURRY
6 to 8 hours

This is an easy curry, made with bottom round and meant to be served with plain boiled rice, though it's nice with noodles, too.

1 *large onion, peeled,*	1 *Tbs. curry powder*
chopped	2 *cups beef bouillon, or 2*
1 *large clove garlic, peeled,*	*cups water with Steero*
minced	*beef-bouillon granules*
3 *Tbs. butter or vegetable oil*	
1 *lb. bottom round of beef,*	
cut in 1-inch cubes	

To Cook: In a large skillet, over medium-high heat, sauté the onion and the garlic in the butter until the onion is beginning to turn dark gold. Add the meat cubes and curry powder, and sauté until meat is browned on all sides. Turn the meat into the slow-cooker. Add the beef bouillon to the skillet, and scrape up the pan juices. Turn into the slow-cooker. Cover and cook on Low for 6 to 8 hours, or until the meat is tender.

Before Serving: If the sauce seems a little thin, turn the curry into a skillet, and simmer until sauce is reduced and thick. Taste, and add salt if needed.

Makes 4 to 6 servings.

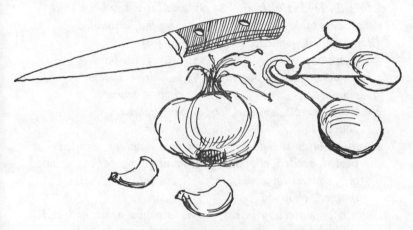

WALTER FISCHMAN'S RED-BEEF APPETIZER
8 to 10 hours

This is a Chinese way with beef, well suited to dense, rather tough cuts such as top round. Cooled and sliced thinly, Red Beef makes a great appetizer, especially for an Oriental meal.

½ cup soy sauce
¼ cup dry sherry
2 cups water
2 heaping tsp. light-brown sugar

3 scallions, minced
2 or 3 slices fresh or frozen ginger, minced
1½ lb. top round of beef

To Cook: Place all the ingredients in the slow-cooker. Cover and cook on Low for 8 to 10 hours, or until tender.

Before Serving: Let the beef cool in the cooking liquid. Then drain; slice thinly across the grain, and serve.

Makes 10 to 12 servings.

BEEF BRISKET, CREOLE STYLE
8 to 10 hours

A hot version, distinctly Southern, to make in early summer when fresh vegetables are available. If you like the recipe but don't care for red-hot foods, omit the dried chili. If you include the chili, wear rubber gloves while you prepare it and don't touch your face with your hands.

3 to 4 lb. brisket of beef
2 Tbs. vegetable oil
3 large onions, peeled, chopped
4 large cloves garlic, peeled, chopped
2 medium carrots, scraped, chopped
2 medium-large tomatoes, peeled, seeded, chopped; or 3 canned tomatoes, drained, chopped
1 cup chopped celery leaves, packed
1 medium white turnip, scraped, chopped
1 large parsnip, scraped, chopped

1 small dried red-hot chili, seeded, crumbled
1 bay leaf
4 sprigs fresh parsley
½ tsp. dried thyme
6 whole allspice
6 peppercorns
2 tsp. salt
16 new potatoes, scraped
6 small young carrots, scraped, cut into lengthwise quarters
Green cabbage, washed and cut in thin wedges
Salt

To Cook: Trim excess fat from the brisket. Roll it up and tie securely with string. Wipe the bottom of a large skillet with the oil and, over medium-high heat, brown the meat all over. Lift the roll into the slow-cook pot; it should curve to fit the bottom without too much trouble. Add the onion, garlic, and chopped carrots to the skillet and cook, stirring constantly, until slightly browned. Transfer to the slow-pot. Add all remaining ingredients except the last four; add water just to cover the brisket. Pour enough water into the skillet to scrape up the pan juices, and turn these into the pot. Cover, turn heat to Low, and cook 8 to 10 hours.

About an hour before the dish is to be served, place potatoes in a large kettle with cold water; cover, and cook over high heat. When they begin to soften, about 10 to 15 minutes after boiling begins, add the young carrots, with a little more water to cover them if needed. When carrots are half-done, place the cabbage on them; cover, and continue to cook until cabbage is done. All three vegetables should be ready by then. Drain well, and salt very lightly.

Before Serving: Drain the brisket; remove the string, and carve meat into thin slices. Place on a deep serving platter or in a large, shallow soup tureen; arrange the vegetables around it, and pour stock over all. Serve in soup plates.

Makes 8 to 10 servings.

MARINATED CHUCK ROAST OR BRISKET OF BEEF
8 to 10 hours

If your household likes hearty, plain food, try beef brisket this way. It's one of my favorite recipes and ever so easy. The only caution is that the beef must marinate overnight. Serve with parsley potatoes.

3 *lb. chuck roast or brisket of beef*	1 *tsp. Tabasco sauce*
2 *Tbs. Kitchen Bouquet*	⅛ *cup lukewarm water*

To Cook: Place the roast in a shallow bowl, and spread Kitchen Bouquet and Tabasco sauce over all the surface. Marinate overnight, covered, in the refrigerator. Remove from refrigerator as soon as you get up in the morning, and allow meat 15 or 20 minutes to warm up to room temperature. Add water to the slow-cooker, just enough to be about ¼ inch deep. Add the beef; cover and cook on Low for 8 to 10 hours.

Before Serving: If the juices in the cooker are thin, simmer in a small saucepan over high heat for a few minutes to thicken. Place the meat on a serving platter; pour thickened pan juices over it, and serve at once.

Makes 5 or 6 servings.

BRISKET OF BEEF, ITALIAN STYLE
8 to 10 hours

In this recipe, the brisket cooks all day; then the juices are thickened by simmering just before serving. Buttered spaghetti or rice is a good companion for this dish.

3 *lb. brisket of beef*	1 *tsp. salt*
1 *clove garlic, peeled and minced*	½ *tsp. dried thyme*
3 *Tbs. tomato paste*	1 *tsp. dried oregano*
1 *large onion, peeled and minced*	½ *tsp. black pepper*

To Cook: Bring the meat to room temperature while you combine remaining ingredients in a small bowl. Smear all surfaces of the meat with this mixture; then place in the slow-cooker. Cover and cook on Low for 8 to 10 hours.

Before Serving: If the cooking juices seem a little thin, simmer until thickened in a small skillet, over high heat. I usually add a little salt to the sauce.

Makes 6 to 8 servings.

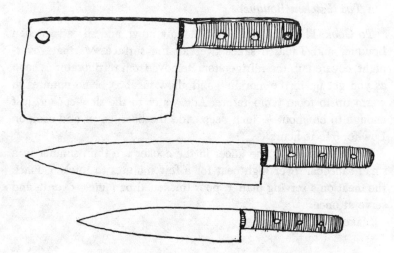

WALTER FISCHMAN'S THINNING POT ROAST
8 to 10 hours

This is a pot roast Walter makes from the cut sold in New York as a California pot roast: it's chuck beef. Thickened with dried mixed vegetables, which you'll find in foreign food markets at reasonable prices, the sauce tastes like the richest, most delicious of gravies, but is relatively calorie-free.

3 *lb. chuck pot roast*	2 *large cloves garlic, peeled*
1½ *cups beef bouillon*	*and minced*
(College Inn), or 1½	½ *tsp. dried thyme*
cups water with Steero	1 *Tbs. chili powder*
beef granules	2 *tsp. dried lemon peel*
½ *cup dry red wine*	2 *Tbs. soy sauce*
2 *tsp. salt*	1 *cup dried mixed vegetables*
	½ *tsp. pepper*

To Cook: Place all the ingredients in the slow-cooker. Cover and cook on Low for 8 to 10 hours.

Before Serving: Remove the beef to a serving dish, and keep warm. Put the rest of the pot contents in a blender, and blend until liquefied. (If there's too much for the blender, turn the stock into a saucepan; simmer to reduce; then blend.) Remove and discard fat as it rises to the top of the blender. Pour the thick, rich sauce over the meat, and serve.

Makes 8 to 10 servings.

BRAISED SHORT RIBS OF BEEF
7 to 10 hours

Short ribs are really delicious if they are cooked slowly and at length—and they're among the most inexpensive of beef cuts. This dish may be served on a bed of boiled noodles. A dash of Tabasco sauce peps it up.

2 Tbs. all-purpose flour
2 tsp. salt
½ tsp. black pepper
2 lb. short ribs of beef, cut into 3- to 4-inch pieces
2 Tbs. vegetable oil
4 medium potatoes, pared and halved

5 small white onions, peeled
4 large carrots, scraped and quartered
8 stalks celery, cut into 2-inch pieces
¾ cup boiling water

To Cook: In a large bowl, combine the flour, salt, and pepper, and toss the meat in mixture until well coated on all sides. In a large skillet, over medium-high heat, brown the meat in the oil. Remove each piece as soon as it is browned, and set in a bowl. Turn the vegetables into the hot skillet; sauté them quickly (2 or 3 minutes), and turn into a bowl. Remove the skillet from the heat, and stir in the remaining flour mixture, working quickly to make a smooth paste. Add the boiling water, stirring constantly to smooth the sauce, and scrape the bottom of the skillet to get up all the juices. Turn the sauce into the slow-cooker, and add the vegetables, then the meat. Cover and cook on Low for 7 to 10 hours.

Makes 4 servings.

SWEET-AND-SOUR POT ROAST
10 to 12 hours

When you're tired of the same old flavors in pot roast, try this.

3 to 4 lb. boneless beef shoulder or chuck pot roast
1 Tbs. vegetable oil
12 small potatoes, peeled
6 medium carrots, peeled and quartered

1 cup chopped onion
1 can (15 oz.) tomato sauce
¼ cup firmly packed light-brown sugar
¼ cup Worcestershire sauce
2 Tbs. white vinegar
1 tsp. salt

To Cook: Trim any excess fat from the meat. In a large skillet, over medium-high heat, brown the meat on all sides in the oil—takes 4 to 5 minutes. Place the potatoes and carrots in the slow-cooker, and add the meat. Pour off and discard all but a tablespoon or so of the fatty oil in the skillet. Over medium-high heat, sauté the onion in the skillet for 1 minute. Then add the tomato sauce, sugar, Worcestershire, vinegar, and salt; stir, scraping up the pan juices, until the sugar dissolves. Pour the sauce over the meat. Cover and cook on Low for 10 to 12 hours, or until the meat is very tender.

Before Serving: If the sauce seems thin, turn it into a skillet, and simmer it, over medium-high heat, until the consistency of heavy cream. Turn into a gravy boat, and serve on the side.

Makes 8 to 10 servings.

BEEF STEW
8 to 10 hours

⅓ cup all-purpose flour
¼ tsp. black pepper
½ tsp. celery salt
1¾ lb. boneless chuck or
    round beef, cut into
    1½-inch cubes
¼ cup vegetable oil
1 cup minced onion
3 medium cloves garlic,
    peeled and minced

1½ cups boiling water
3 heaping Tbs. tomato paste
½ tsp. salt
1 tsp. Worcestershire sauce
12 small carrots, peeled;
    or 3 large carrots,
    peeled and quartered
4 or 5 medium potatoes,
    peeled and quartered
¼ cup finely minced parsley

To Cook: In a large bowl, combine the flour, pepper, and celery salt. Toss meat in this mixture. In a large skillet, over medium-high heat, heat the oil and brown the meat, stirring often, until darkened on all sides. As soon as each piece finishes browning, lift it into a small bowl. When all the meat is done, toss the onion and garlic together in the fat remaining in the skillet. Remove the skillet from the heat. Stir in the leftover flour mixture; then stir in the boiling water, working quickly to keep the sauce smooth. Add the tomato paste, salt, and Worcestershire. Scrape the bottom of the skillet to get up all the pan juices, and turn into the slow-cooker. Place the carrots and potatoes in the cooker, and scrape the meat over them. Cover and cook on Low for 8 to 10 hours.

Before Serving: Garnish the finished stew with the parsley.

Makes 4 servings.

BEEF STEW À LA ROMANA
8 to 10 hours

A tomato-rich beef stew with Italian flavorings. The sauce will be a little thin; thicken it with a roux, as described on page 28, if you wish.

⅛ cup diced salt pork; or
    6 *slices fatty bacon, diced*
3 *lb. stew beef*
1 *medium onion, peeled,*
    sliced
1 *clove garlic, peeled, minced*
½ *cup dry red wine*
1 *can (29 oz.) whole*
    tomatoes
1 *tsp. salt*
¼ *tsp. oregano*

¼ *tsp. pepper*
6 *large carrots, peeled,*
    cut in 2-inch chunks
1 *lb. small white onions, peeled*
4 *medium potatoes, peeled,*
    quartered
2 *sweet green peppers,*
    seeded, cut in wedges
2 *Tbs. flour (optional)*
2 *Tbs. grated Parmesan cheese*
    (optional)

To Cook: In large skillet, over medium-high heat, cook the salt pork until all fat has been rendered. Remove with a slotted spoon to the slow-pot. Brown the stew beef, onion, and garlic in the pan drippings, turning often. Add to the skillet the wine, tomatoes, can juices, salt, oregano, and pepper, scraping up the pan juices as mixture simmers. Place in the slow-pot, in layers, the carrots, onions, potatoes, and peppers. Turn the skillet contents into the pot. Cover, turn to Low, and cook for 8 to 10 hours.

Before Serving: When cooking is over, if you would like the sauce to be thicker, place 2 tablespoons of fat skimmed from the stew liquid in a small skillet, over medium heat. Stir in the flour and 1 cup of the cooking liquid, stirring constantly until the sauce is thick. Turn into the slow-pot; set on High, and simmer a few minutes. Just before serving, add the Parmesan cheese, if you wish, to the sauce, and mix well.

Makes 8 servings.

GOULASH, HUNGARIAN STYLE
8 to 10 hours

This is also nice cooked without potatoes and served with boiled, buttered noodles.

3 Tbs. butter or margarine	1½ lb. chuck, rump, or round
3 cups thinly sliced onion	beef, cut into 1-inch cubes
4 medium potatoes, peeled	2¼ tsp. salt
and quartered	4½ tsp. paprika
	1 cup water

To Cook: In a large skillet, over medium-high heat, melt the butter, and cook the onion until golden—5 or 6 minutes. With a slotted spoon, remove the onion to the slow-cooker. Place the potatoes on the onion. Add the meat to the skillet, and sauté until well browned on all sides. Sprinkle the meat with salt and paprika, and lift into the slow-cooker. Add the water to the skillet; scrape up the pan juices; turn into the cooker. Cover and cook on Low for 8 to 10 hours, or until tender.

Makes 4 or 5 servings.

BEEF STEW WITH ZUCCHINI
8 to 10 hours

In midseason when zucchini comes in, try this recipe for beef stew. Select small, fresh zucchini whose skin is fresh enough to be broken easily with a thumbnail, and don't pare them. You can use marrow or summer squash instead of zucchini.

2 lb. boneless chuck or stew	1 medium green pepper,
beef, cut into 1½-inch	seeded and chopped
cubes	1 bay leaf
1 Tbs. vegetable oil	2 large stalks celery, cut into
2 tsp. salt	2-inch pieces
¼ tsp. pepper	6 medium potatoes, pared and
1 medium onion, peeled and	quartered
sliced	2 zucchini, stemmed and cut
½ cup water	into 1-inch slices
¼ tsp. marjoram	2 Tbs. all-purpose flour

To Cook: In a large skillet, over medium-high heat, thoroughly brown the meat pieces in the oil. Sprinkle half the salt and pepper over the meat. Lift the meat into a bowl. Sauté the onion in the skillet until translucent; then lift it into the slow-cooker. In the still-hot skillet, swirl the water, scraping up the pan juices; then turn the liquid into the slow-cooker. Add the marjoram, green pepper, bay leaf, celery, potatoes, and zucchini, and sprinkle with the remaining salt and pepper. Place the meat on top. Cover and cook on Low for 8 to 10 hours.

Before Serving: Remove the meat and vegetables to a serving plate, and keep warm. Skim 1 or 2 tablespoons of fat from the cooking liquid, and heat in a medium skillet, over medium-low heat. Stir the flour into the fat. Pour the hot cooking liquid over the flour mixture, and beat rapidly to make a smooth sauce. Simmer until the sauce is as thick as whipped cream; then pour over the meat and vegetables.

Makes 6 to 8 servings.

BEAN-POT STEW
6 to 8 hours

An authentic, old Maine recipe that makes a nice, slow-cooked, one-dish dinner. A bit bland, perhaps.

2 Tbs. vegetable oil	4 Tbs. rolled oats
1 lb. top round, cubed	3 medium potatoes, peeled,
1 medium onion, peeled,	quartered
diced	1 cup water
2 small carrots, peeled, diced	1 tsp. salt
1 small turnip, peeled, diced	⅛ tsp. pepper
1 cup dried baby limas	

To Cook: In a large saucepan, over medium-high heat, warm the oil, and sauté the meat, onion, carrots, and turnip until the meat is browned all over. Place the limas in the slow-cooker and scrape the skillet contents over them. Sprinkle on rolled oats and push the potato pieces down into the meat-and-vegetable mixture. Add the water and seasonings. Cover and cook on Low for 6 to 8 hours.

Makes 4 to 6 servings.

SLOW-COOKED BARBECUE
3 to 5 hours

This is good for a pick-up meal after a party. Serve on toasted hamburger rolls and with a mixed garden salad.

1½ lb. boneless chuck steak,
   1½ inches thick
1 clove garlic, peeled
   and minced
¼ cup wine vinegar
1 Tbs. brown sugar
1 tsp. paprika

2 Tbs. Worcestershire
   sauce
½ cup catsup
1 tsp. salt
1 tsp. dry or prepared
   mustard
¼ tsp. black pepper

To Cook: Cut the beef on a diagonal, across the grain, into slices 1-inch wide. Place these in the slow-cooker. In a small bowl, combine the remaining ingredients. Pour over the meat, and mix. Cover and cook on Low for 3 to 5 hours.

Makes 4 or 5 servings.

FLANK-STEAK POT ROAST
8 to 10 hours

The preparations for this are a little like making a jelly roll and take me about 35 minutes. You'll need skewers or wooden toothpicks to hold the meat in a roll.

1 flank steak (about 2 lb.)
1 cup unflavored bread
   crumbs
¼ cup minced onion
1 Tbs. minced parsley
½ tsp. salt
¼ tsp. black pepper
½ tsp. ground sage
1 Tbs. butter or margarine

1 Tbs. vegetable oil
1 tsp. wine vinegar
½ cup hot water
½ tsp. whole peppercorns
2 Tbs. butter or margarine
¼ cup all-purpose flour
1 Tbs. soy sauce or
   Worcestershire sauce
½ cup beef bouillon

To Cook: On a slant, against the grain of the meat, slash one side of the steak. Turn the steak slashed side down. In a medium bowl, combine crumbs, onion, parsley, salt, pepper, and sage. Cover the steak with this stuffing, leaving half an inch free all around the edges. Smooth the stuffing firmly into place, and dot with 1 tablespoon butter. Roll up the steak, like a jelly roll, starting at the side opposite the widest edge. If a little stuffing spills, tuck it back into the ends after the steak has been rolled up. Secure with skewers or wooden toothpicks. In a medium skillet, over medium-high heat, brown the meat on all sides in the oil; then lift it into the slow-cooker, and dribble the vinegar over the top. To the hot oil in the skillet, add the water; scrape up the pan juices, and pour them over the meat. Sprinkle with peppercorns. Cover and cook on Low for 8 to 10 hours.

Before Serving: In a medium skillet, over medium-low heat, melt 2 tablespoons butter, and stir in the flour. Pour the juices from the cooker and soy sauce into the mixture, and stir quickly to a smooth sauce. If the sauce seems too thick, add a little hot bouillon or water; usually there's juice left in the cooker when you remove the meat, so add that to thin the sauce. If the sauce seems too thin, simmer a few minutes to reduce and thicken it. Serve with the meat.

Makes 4 or 5 servings.

FLANK STEAK, SOUTHERN STYLE
8 to 10 hours

Flank steak is a wedge of rather thin beef that comes from the animal's flank. It is boneless and can be prepared lots of ways. This way is a favorite, nice with boiled rice.

1 *flank steak (about 2 lb.)*	¾ *cup catsup*
2 *Tbs. vegetable oil*	1 *tsp. salt*
3 *cups sliced onion*	⅛ *tsp. black pepper*
1 *large clove garlic, peeled and minced*	⅛ *tsp. ground thyme*

To Cook: With a sharp knife, lightly slash the surface of the steak. In a large skillet, over high heat, heat the oil and brown the steak quickly on both sides. Remove from the heat, and lift the meat into the slow-cooker. At once turn the remaining ingredients into the hot oil, and scrape the pan to gather all the juices. Turn the sauce into the cooker. Cover and cook on Low for 8 to 10 hours.

Makes 5 or 6 servings.

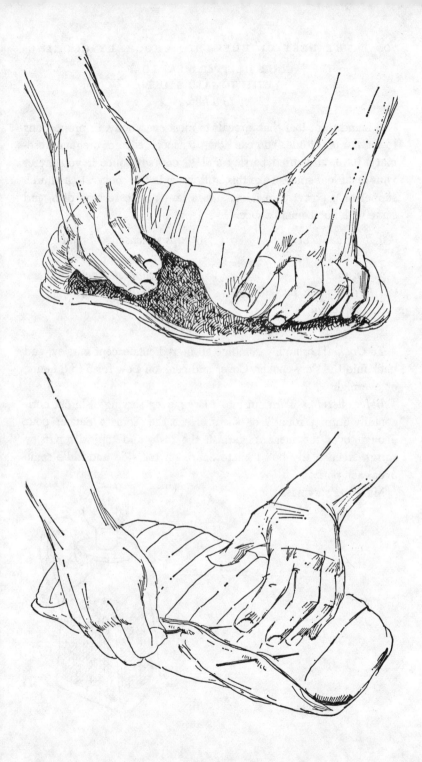

CHURCH-SUPPER MEAT LOAF
WITH TOMATO SAUCE
6 to 8 hours

A bland meat loaf that appeals to most everybody, in proportions to serve a multitude. You can add 1 teaspoon each of oregano, rosemary, basil, and dried parsley and ¼ cup soy sauce if you prefer your meat loaf spicy. Take this, still warm in the cooker, to a church supper or a party; turn it out into a large, deep serving dish, and serve with hot Tomato Sauce.

6 *lb. ground beef*
2 *lb. ground pork*
3 *tsp. salt*
4 *large onions, peeled,*
    shredded

6 *cups unseasoned bread*
    crumbs
2 *cups evaporated milk*
2 *recipes Tomato Sauce*
    (*page 230*)
Parsley sprigs

To Cook: Thoroughly combine all ingredients except parsley, and pack into the slow-cooker. Cover and cook on Low for 6 to 8 hours, or overnight.

Before Serving: Turn out into a large, deep serving dish; cut horizontally into 3 rounds or slices. Heat the Tomato Sauce; pour enough over the meat to garnish the dish, and top with parsley sprigs. Keep really hot Tomato Sauce on the side and ladle some over each portion.

Makes 24 servings.

MEAT LOAF
5 to 7 hours

This is my family's favorite meat-loaf recipe. Use it as a guide to adapt your family's meat-loaf recipe to slow-cooking.

½ cup whole or
    condensed milk
2 slices white bread
1½ lb. ground beef or
    hamburger
2 eggs

1 small onion, peeled
1½ tsp. salt
½ tsp. pepper
1 tsp. dry mustard
1 can (12 oz.) whole
    tomatoes

To Cook: Place the milk and bread in a large mixing bowl, and let stand until the bread has absorbed all the milk. With two forks, break the bread into crumbs. Beat the ground beef into the crumbs until well mixed. Make a hollow in the center of the meat and break the eggs into it. Beat the eggs a little; then grate the onion into the eggs. Add salt, pepper, and mustard. Beat the eggs into the beef. Shape the mixture into a round cake and place in the slow-cooker. Drain the tomatoes, and place them on the meat. Cover and cook on Low for 5 to 7 hours.

Before Serving: Uncover the pot; turn the heat to High, and bubble away some of the sauce. It should be thick, not thin.

Makes 6 servings.

MEATBALLS IN MUSHROOM SAUCE
4 to 6 hours

1 lb. ground chuck beef
¼ lb. ground pork shoulder
1 medium onion, peeled
    and minced
½ cup raw converted rice
1 egg, slightly beaten
1½ tsp. salt
¼ tsp. black pepper
⅛ tsp. ground allspice

1 cup unflavored bread
    crumbs
½ cup milk
1 can condensed cream-of-
    mushroom soup
¼ tsp. salt
⅛ tsp. black pepper
2 tsp. soy sauce or
    Worcestershire sauce

To Cook: In a large bowl, combine the beef, pork, onion, rice, egg, 1½ teaspoons salt, ¼ teaspoon pepper, the allspice, bread crumbs, and milk. Shape the mixture into balls about the size of a golf ball. In the slow-cooker, combine the soup, ¼ teaspoon salt, ⅛ teaspoon pepper, and the soy sauce. Add the meatballs, and mix quickly. Cover and cook on Low for 4 to 6 hours.

Makes 6 servings.

MEAT SAUCE
8 to 10 hours

Meat sauce that has cooked ever so slowly all day is really better than meat sauce made in a hurry. This is very good on any of the pastas or baked beans or rice. Offer grated Parmesan cheese with the sauce.

3 Tbs. olive oil or vegetable oil	1 tsp. sugar
1 large onion, peeled and chopped	1 tsp. dried basil
	1 tsp. dried oregano
2 large cloves garlic, peeled and minced	2 large green peppers, seeded and chopped
1½ lb. ground beef or hamburger	2 large stalks celery, diced
1 can (16 oz.) whole Italian tomatoes	½ lb. mushrooms, stemmed; or 1 can (10 oz.) mushrooms
1 can (6 oz.) tomato paste	2 tsp. salt
⅔ cup water	½ tsp. pepper

To Cook: In a large skillet, over medium-high heat, heat the oil and sauté the onion and garlic until the onion is well browned but not burned. With a slotted spoon, remove to the slow-cooker. Turn the meat into the skillet; break it up, and sauté it on high heat, stirring often, until it is in little lumps and well browned. Turn meat into the slow-pot. Add the tomatoes, tomato paste, and water to the still-hot skillet, and scrape up the pan juices. Turn off the heat, and add the remaining ingredients to the sauce. Combine well; then stir into the contents of the slow-pot. Cover and cook on Low for 8 to 10 hours. The sauce is relatively well cooked after about 4 hours, but it will taste best after a long cooking period.

Before Serving: If the sauce seems a little thin (which it

shouldn't), simmer it in a skillet for 4 or 5 minutes before serving.
Makes 3 to 6 servings.

CHILI CON CARNE
5 to 7 hours

This is a meaty variation on Mexican chili sauce. It's hot, and I
combine it with rice. It can be made from very lean chuck or from
hamburger. If you make it with hamburger, skim away any fat from
the sauce before serving.

1 *lb. lean ground chuck beef or hamburger*	1½ *Tbs. chili powder*
1 *cup chopped onion*	½ *tsp. salt*
1 *large clove garlic, peeled and minced*	1 *can (7½ oz.) whole tomatoes*
1 *tsp. oregano*	⅔ *cup canned tomato purée*
¼ *tsp. pepper*	1 *cup drained canned red kidney beans*
1 *tsp. ground cumin*	4 *cups hot cooked rice*

To Cook: Place all the ingredients except the rice in the slow-
cooker. Cover and cook on Low for 5 to 7 hours.

Before Serving: If the sauce seems thin after the cooking is finished, pour it into a small skillet and simmer over medium heat until thick. Pour over the chili and serve with hot cooked rice on the
side.

Makes 6 servings.

MOTHER'S RICE DISH
6 to 8 hours

This is a rice, hamburger, onion, and tomato combination that is
super-simple and tastes terrific.

1½ *cups converted rice*	1½ *cups water*
½ *cup vegetable oil*	1 *large onion, chopped*
1 *lb. hamburger or ground beef*	1 *large green pepper, seeded and chopped*
1 *16 oz. can whole tomatoes*	1½ *tsp. salt*
1 *can (6 oz.) tomato paste*	

To Cook: In a medium skillet, over medium heat, sauté the rice in the oil until the rice becomes opaque. Remove the rice to the slow-cooker. In the same skillet, sauté the hamburger over high heat. Crumble it as you sauté it and let the underside heat enough to stick and turn brown. Turn the hamburger into the slow-pot. Add the tomatoes, tomato paste, and water to the skillet; scrape up the pan juices. Add the onion, green pepper, and salt; then turn the skillet contents into the cooker. Cover and cook on Low for 6 to 8 hours. Makes 4 to 6 servings.

BEEF SHANK CROSS CUT WITH VEGETABLES
7 to 9 hours

Beef shank cross cut is an excellent piece of stewing meat. There's lots of cartilage in it, and the slow-cooking method is exactly what it needs. Cooked here with vegetables, it makes a fine one-dish dinner.

3 lb. beef shank cross cut, 1 inch thick
2 Tbs. all-purpose flour
2 tsp. salt
¼ tsp. pepper
1 Tbs. vegetable oil
¼ cup water
1 large sprig parsley
½ tsp. thyme
1 bay leaf
1 small onion, peeled and stuck with 4 whole cloves

3 medium carrots, peeled and cut into pieces 1 inch long
4 large stalks celery, cut in pieces 3 inches long
12 to 15 Brussels sprouts, or 1 package (10 oz.) frozen sprouts (optional)

To Cook: In a large bowl or a plastic bag, toss the meat with the flour combined with the salt and pepper. In a medium skillet, over medium-high heat, heat the oil and brown the meat well on all sides. Remove the meat to a bowl. Pour the water into the still-hot skillet, and scrape up the pan juices. Turn the liquid into the slow-cooker. Add the herbs, onion, carrots, and celery. Place the meat on top. Cover and cook on Low for 7 to 9 hours, or until meat is completely tender.

Before Serving: Cook the fresh Brussels sprouts in lots of boiling salted water for 10 to 15 minutes, or until they are pierced easily with a fork. Or cook frozen sprouts as instructed on package. Lift meat and vegetables to warm serving platter and add sprouts. In a medium skillet, simmer cooking juices until the consistency of heavy cream. Pour over the meat and vegetables.

Makes 4 to 6 servings.

VEAL FOR THE SLOW-COOKER

Only a few veal cuts are best done in a slow-cooker. Veal is young beef; the meat is fine grained and, when of good quality, almost white. It is tender, wonderful quick-cooked in thin slices, breaded or lightly pan-fried. The few veal cuts that are good for stews aren't often available in my area, but when they are I snatch them because they make a delicious change.

Sometimes I do veal sold for roasts in a slow-cooker. Roast veal can be good, but the cuts most often seen for roasting are likely to be fatless, rather dense, and somewhat dry. Slow-cooked with a sauce, they are very good, though not particularly economical.

Veal cuts suggested in recipes here can be replaced by cuts available in your markets. Many veal dishes are equally good with pork or chicken.

TIMING OF VEAL DISHES: Veal tenderizes a little more quickly than beef. Most recipes here call for 5 to 7 hours of cooking. If you want more free time than that, use a timer (see page 41) to switch on the cooker. If your kitchen is warm, include a couple of ice cubes with the liquid ingredients; they'll keep the meat cool until the cooker turns on.

VEAL CUTS ESPECIALLY SUITED
TO SLOW-COOKING

Neck: An inexpensive and tough cut, it makes good stews and soups, stock, and jellies for aspic.

Foreshank of Veal: This is the cut used for Osso Bucco (page 153) and other boiled beef dishes, and the slow-cooker does it best.

Breast of Veal: This is usually inexpensive, and you can do a lot with it in the slow-cooker. Breast veal requires a good deal of cooking. Boned, it can be stuffed any number of ways.

INVENT YOUR OWN
SLOW-COOK VEAL RECIPES

You can adapt any of your favorite veal dishes to slow-cooking simply by finding a similar recipe here and following my procedures.

You can easily make a veal casserole of your own invention. Place the cut-up veal in the slow-pot, along with light beef or chicken stock (about 1 cup) and the French herbs—for instance, a bay leaf, 3 parsley sprigs, a pinch of thyme—a medium onion, peeled and stuck with 4 or 5 whole cloves. Or cook the veal with herbs that flavor Italian dishes—rosemary, thyme, bay, basil and oregano.

Vegetables especially good with veal are sweet peppers, tomatoes, onions, mushrooms, and combinations of these. Potatoes, carrots, and peas are nice with veal, too.

A veal casserole whose sauce seems thin and tasteless is sometimes improved by adding a sprinkling of grated Parmesan cheese. Or if you want a richer sauce for veal that has little or no fat, stir 1 or 2 tablespoons of butter into the sauce at the very last. If a sauce is lifeless, add 1 or 2 teaspoons of strained lemon juice before serving; or add 1 or 2 teaspoons of white wine or vinegar, and simmer on the stove top for a few minutes before serving.

VEAL RECIPES

BREAST OF VEAL, STUFFED
4 to 6 hours

Often sold at a reasonable price, breast of veal can be stuffed and slow-cooked in many ways.

2½ lb. boned veal breast
¼ cup butter or margarine
6 Tbs. minced onion
2 cups fresh bread crumbs
1 tsp. salt
⅛ tsp. pepper
1½ tsp. ground sage
¾ cup minced parsley
3 Tbs. vegetable oil
¼ cup hot water
1 bay leaf
1 small onion, stuck
    with 3 cloves
¼ tsp. dried thyme

To Cook: If the veal has cartilage, trim it off. Lay the meat on a cutting board. In a large skillet, over medium heat, melt the butter and sauté the onion until translucent. Add the bread crumbs, salt, pepper, sage, and parsley; toss until well combined. Spread over the veal, leaving ¼ inch free at the edges. Roll up and secure the meat as described in Flank-Steak Pot Roast (page 67). Add the oil to the skillet, and brown the roll on all sides. Place in the slow-cooker. Add the water to the skillet; scrape up the pan juices, and add to the cooker with the bay leaf, onion, and thyme. Cover and cook on Low 4 to 6 hours. Remove onion and bay leaf before serving.

Makes 4 to 6 servings.

BREAST OF VEAL WITH SABLAISE STUFFING
4 to 6 hours

This is a delicately flavored dish, nice with cold, dry white wine, small boiled potatoes or rice, and a green salad.

2½ lb. boned breast of veal	½ cup water
½ recipe for stuffing	1 tsp. salt
in Flank Steak	2 medium cloves garlic,
with Sablaise Stuffing	peeled, crushed
(page 145)	1 Tbs. white Dijon or
1 Tbs. all-purpose flour	Maille mustard
2 Tbs. vegetable oil	2 tsp. minced parsley

To Cook: Lay the veal flat on a cutting board and stuff with Sablaise Stuffing. Roll up and secure the meat, as described for Flank-Steak Pot Roast (page 67). Roll in the flour. Add the oil to the skillet the stuffing cooked in and brown the veal roll on all sides thoroughly. Place it in the slow-cooker. Add the water and salt to the skillet and scrape up the pan juices. Turn into the slow-cooker. Cover and cook on Low for 4 to 6 hours, or until tender.

Before Serving: About 30 minutes before the meat is done, mix the garlic and mustard into the cooking liquid around the meat; turn the heat to High and simmer 30 minutes. If the sauce seems thin, leave the cover off during this cooking period. Add a little more mustard and salt to the sauce if you like strong flavors. Garnish with minced parsley.

Makes 6 to 8 servings.

BREAST OF VEAL, STUFFED,
GERMAN STYLE
4 to 6 hours

2½ to 3 lb. breast of veal	⅛ tsp. pepper
½ tsp. salt	½ tsp. paprika
⅛ tsp. pepper	3 Tbs. butter or margarine
2 Tbs. butter or margarine	1 cup chicken stock, or
¾ cup minced onion	1 chicken bouillon cube
2 Tbs. minced celery	and 1 cup water
3 slices day-old bread,	1 Tbs. cornstarch
crusts removed, cubed	2 Tbs. cold chicken stock
2 Tbs. half-and-half	or water
2 whole eggs, slightly beaten	¼ cup currant jelly
½ tsp. salt	1 tsp. lemon juice

To Cook: Lay the veal on a cutting board, and season with ½ teaspoon salt and ⅛ teaspoon pepper. In a large skillet, over medium heat, heat 2 tablespoons butter and sauté the onion and celery until the onion is translucent—4 or 5 minutes. Add the bread and toss well. Remove from the heat, and beat the half-and-half and the eggs into bread mixture, along with ½ teaspoon salt, ⅛ teaspoon pepper, and the paprika. Stuff the breast, as described for Flank-Steak Pot Roast (page 67). Heat 3 tablespoons butter in the skillet and brown the stuffed breast, over medium-high heat. Place the meat in the slow-cooker. Add ¼ cup chicken stock to the skillet; scrape up the pan juices, and turn into the cooker. Cover and cook on Low for 4 to 6 hours.

Before Serving: Remove the meat to a heated serving dish. Measure the cooking liquid, and add enough chicken stock to make 1 cup; place in a medium skillet, over medium-low heat. Combine cornstarch and 2 tablespoons cold chicken stock. Stir into the simmering sauce and heat, stirring, until thickened. Add the jelly and lemon juice and simmer, stirring, another 3 to 5 minutes. Pour over the meat.

Makes 4 to 6 servings.

POT ROAST OF VEAL
5 to 7 hours

Make this with boned rump or shoulder veal, roast, or any of the lesser veal cuts listed on page 75.

3 *Tbs. vegetable oil*
3 *to 4 lb. rump or shoulder*
   veal
1 *tsp. salt*
⅛ *tsp. pepper*
2 *carrots, peeled, cut in*
   ¼-inch rounds

6 *large stalks celery, cut*
   in 2-inch chunks
2 *Tbs. water*
2 *Tbs. butter or*
   margarine
2 *Tbs. all-purpose flour*
¼ *cup dry white wine*

To Cook: In a medium skillet, over high heat, heat the oil and brown the meat on all sides. Season with salt and pepper. Place the vegetables in the cooker and set the meat on top. Remove skillet from heat, add water, scrape up the pan juices, and turn into the cooker. Cover and cook on Low for 5 to 7 hours, or until meat is completely tender.

Before Serving: Remove the meat and vegetables to a serving dish, and keep warm. In a medium skillet, over medium-low heat, melt the butter and stir in the flour. Add the hot cooking liquid and stir quickly to make a smooth sauce. Add the wine and simmer 5 minutes, or until nicely thickened. Taste and add salt and pepper if needed. Pour over the meat.

Makes 8 to 10 servings.

VEAL POT-AU-FEU (BOILED DINNER)
WITH MUSTARD SAUCE
6 to 8 hours

Before I make this, I save a couple of well-browned, pan-sautéed steak bones or bones from a rib roast, along with drippings from the steak skillet or the roasting pan. I add them to the slow-pot. Serve pot-au-feu in soup bowls with a little cooking liquid added to each portion of meat and vegetables.

1 Tbs. fat from beef drippings, or vegetable oil
2 chicken backs and necks
3 to 4 lb. rolled shoulder
  of veal
2 tsp. salt
¼ tsp. pepper
2 small white turnips,
  peeled, cut in 2-inch
  pieces
3 parsnips, peeled, cut
  in 2-inch pieces
2 carrots, peeled, cut in
  2-inch pieces

8 small white onions, peeled
3 medium potatoes, peeled,
  quartered
Leaves from a head of celery
4 sprigs parsley, or 1 tsp.
  dried parsley, or 8 to 10
  parsley stems
1 large bay leaf
1 tsp. dried thyme
4 whole cloves
3 large cloves garlic,
  peeled, chopped
10 oz. hot water
Mustard Sauce (below)

To Cook: Heat the fat in a large skillet, over high heat; brown the chicken pieces. Push to one side and brown the veal. Place remaining ingredients, except water and Mustard Sauce, in the cooker; set the chicken and veal on top. Scrape out the skillet with a little hot water and turn into the cooker. Add the rest of the water. Cover and cook on Low for 6 to 8 hours, or until the veal is very tender.

Before Serving: Place the meat and vegetables in a serving dish. Strain the cooking liquid; save 1½ cups for Mustard Sauce, and pour the rest over the meat. Serve with Mustard Sauce on the side.

Makes 6 to 8 servings.

MUSTARD SAUCE

1½ cups cooking liquid
  from Veal Pot-au-Feu
1½ Tbs. white Dijon or
  Maille mustard
1 cup heavy cream

1 Tbs. cornstarch
¼ cup dry white wine
Salt
2 Tbs. finely minced
  parsley

To Cook: In a small saucepan, over high heat, boil down the cooking liquid to half—about 20 minutes. Mix a few tablespoons of the liquid with the mustard and stir back into the sauce. Stir in the cream and reduce the heat. Simmer until reduced to about 1½ cups. Combine the cornstarch and wine and add to the sauce. Simmer, stirring constantly, 3 or 4 minutes. Taste and add a little salt if needed. Stir in the parsley; mix well. Serve hot.

VEAL PAPRIKA
4 to 6 hours

Nice with noodles and buttered broccoli.

2 *lb. boned veal shoulder or round, in 1-inch cubes*	1 *Tbs. paprika*
2 *slices bacon, minced*	2 *Tbs. all-purpose flour*
½ *cup minced onion*	1 *cup chicken stock,*
1 *medium clove garlic, peeled, minced*	*or 1 chicken bouillon cube with 1 cup water*
1 *tsp. salt*	¾ *cup sour cream*
⅛ *tsp. pepper*	*Paprika*

To Cook: In a medium skillet, over medium-high heat, sauté the veal cubes and the bacon until meat is brown on all sides. Add the onion and garlic and sauté, stirring, 2 or 3 minutes. Remove from heat; add the salt, pepper, 1 tablespoon paprika, and the flour, and toss thoroughly. Pour in the stock; stir until the sauce is smooth. Then scrape into the slow-cooker. Cover and cook on Low for 4 to 6 hours, or until the meat is tender.

Before Serving: Lift the meat into a warm serving bowl. If the sauce seems thin, simmer in a small skillet until thickened. Then remove from the heat and stir in the sour cream. Reheat just enough to warm the cream; don't boil. Pour over the meat and garnish with a dash of paprika.

Makes 4 to 6 servings.

VEAL STEW
6 to 8 hours

This is nice with plain, boiled new potatoes, or mashed potatoes, or noodles.

2 lb. boned shoulder of veal, in 2-inch cubes
¼ cup all-purpose flour
1½ tsp. salt
⅛ tsp. pepper
2 Tbs. butter or margarine
¼ cup minced onion
2 medium cloves garlic, peeled, minced

8 medium carrots, peeled
12 small white onions, peeled
1½ cups boiling water
2 tsp. celery seed
1 tsp. salt
2 tsp. strained lemon juice
2 Tbs. minced parsley

To Cook: Place the veal in a large bowl and toss with the flour, 1½ teaspoons salt, and the pepper. In a large skillet, over medium heat, melt the butter and sauté the minced onion and garlic 2 or 3 minutes. Remove to the slow-cooker. Add the vegetables and meat to the skillet and sauté until meat is brown all over—5 to 10 minutes. Scrape mixture into the cooker. Pour the water into the skillet and scrape up the pan juices. Turn into the cooker with the celery seed and 1 teaspoon salt. Cover and cook on Low for 6 to 8 hours.

Before Serving: Remove the meat and vegetables to a serving platter and keep warm. Turn the cooker to High; add the lemon juice and simmer 5 to 10 minutes. Pour over the meat, garnish with parsley, and serve.

Makes 4 to 6 servings.

VEAL STEW, MADAME BERTRAND STYLE
3 to 5 hours

A French Riviera way with veal. Serve with buttered thin spaghetti.

1 tsp. salt
⅛ tsp. pepper
2½ lb. boned veal shoulder,
    in 1½-inch cubes
1 Tbs. white-wine vinegar
2 Tbs. olive oil or vegetable
    oil
¾ cup sliced fresh mushrooms
    or canned mushroom
    slices
½ cup minced onion

1 10-oz. can whole tomatoes, or
    1¾ cups canned tomatoes
    and juice
1 large sweet green pepper,
    seeded, cut in 1-inch
    strips
1 tsp. sugar
1½ tsp. salt
2 tsp. dried oregano
½ cup converted rice

To Cook: Salt (1 teaspoon) and pepper the veal cubes and sprinkle with vinegar. In a medium skillet, over medium heat, heat the oil and sauté the mushrooms and onion 4 or 5 minutes. Add the meat and sauté until lightly browned. Turn into the slow-cooker. To the skillet, add the tomatoes, pepper, sugar, 1½ teaspoons salt, the oregano, and rice; sauté, stirring, 3 or 4 minutes. Scrape all into the slow-cooker. Cover and cook on Low for 3 to 5 hours.

Makes 5 or 6 servings.

VEAL CURRY

Follow the recipe for Simple Beef Curry (page 56), but use 1 pound of cubed veal from the shoulder instead of beef.

Chapter 4

Pork, Ham and Chicken

ADVENTURES IN PORK COOKERY

ONCE UPON A TIME, it was said of the pig that the cook used everything but the squeal. The head, feet, knuckles, intestine, blood, even the skin had a use and were an important part of a farm's economy. Today, pork remains one of the more economical meats, and particularly during winter months, we turn to it when the budget is running low. However, we have become accustomed to pork chops and loin roasts, and, of course, ham in various forms, because we haven't had any reasonable way of dealing with the other pig parts.

The slow-cooker makes available the kind of cooking that used to turn pork variety meats into delicacies. Headcheese, Creole Style (page 91) is typical of old recipes that required hours and hours of cooking. It does take a lot of preparation, but a slow-cooker frees you from the tedious business of watching a boiling pot before you roll up your sleeves and start turning pig's heart, tongue, and feet into good food. A similar but simpler version is my father's recipe for Galantine de Porc Marcel. Hog's Headcheese (page 92), also called Souse Meat and Pigtail Stew, is another way to use pork oddments. This type of recipe won't shorten time in the kitchen, but it will make eating more interesting—in other words, try these recipes when you feel like cooking, rather than when you want to avoid it. They will make trips to the meat market an adventure. What fun is it to see pig's feet if you don't know what to do with them? For that matter, what fun is meat shopping when you do the same old things with the same old cuts day in and day out? It's a bore. The fact that these meats cost relatively little makes them even more fun.

CONVENTIONAL PORK CUTS—AND HAM

Recipes here for conventional pork cuts and ham allow you 8 to 12 hours of free time. The slow-cooker is, I think, ideal for some pork products and not for others. It's fine for ham small enough to fit in your cooker. Ham is superb when cooked very slowly; as far as I am concerned, the slow-cooker can do no wrong with ham. I haven't had the same luck with all pork cuts. Pork should be cooked slowly, of course, but I have found that loin and end-of-loin roasts (the rib section) really are better slowly roasted. The slow-pot just doesn't do much for them; the meat seems to become tough and stringy.

The slow-pot does do pork chops superbly. As you know, pork chops—unlike most other chops—are difficult to cook through without drying out. The slow-cooker eliminates that problem—it cooks the chops all day and turns them out falling-off-the-bone tender and sweet. I've slow-cooked pork chops with nothing added but a little beef bouillon, and they were delicious. However, it's worth the trouble to add a few other ingredients and make the chops into a casserole with gravy.

Though pork doesn't resemble beef, several of the beef-casserole recipes in Chapter 3 can be used for pork chops. Buy small, thick chops; remove the excess fat, and cook them whole or halved, rather than cut into 2- or 2½-inch pieces.

Pork hocks appear occasionally in my supermarket, and they're among the specialty meats a slow-cooker does wonders with. Adapt your own favorite pork-hock recipes and follow the timing in the recipe for Bavarian Pork (page 93).

Sausages and very fatty pork products should be sautéed to remove most of the fat if they are to be slow-cooked alone. Meat with a large fat content isn't ideal for slow-cooking—with some exceptions. For some bean and other casseroles, sausages make the dish. I've included a few of these. Stuffed Cabbage Catalan (page 157) calls for ground pork (like spicy sausage meat); the New England Boiled Dinner (page 98) includes a Polish sausage (any large, flavorful German sausage will do—except knockwurst, which would duplicate the corned-beef flavor); and Cassoulet (page 155), which is made with beans, calls for a garlic sausage.

PORK CUTS THAT ARE ESPECIALLY GOOD SLOW-COOKED

Pork Hocks: From the lower part of the picnic ham, these are sold fresh and, sometimes, smoked. They make very good soups and stews. There's a lot of bone, but lots of chunks of flavorful meat, too.

Pig's Feet: The pig's front feet are said to be better. They are sold pickled in vinegar, though country markets sometimes offer them fresh. They are very good slow-cooked for aspic jellies and other special dishes.

Boneless Smoked Shoulder Butt: This also is called a cottage roll or daisy ham roll. Usually it will fit into a slow-cooker. It is very nice slow-cooked.

Blade Pork Chops: Though not quite as fancy as chops from the rib section, these are very good done in various ways in the slow-cooker.

Salt Pork: A very fatty (almost meatless) cut used primarily for flavoring dishes such as Boston baked beans. It is salted rather than smoked or brine-pickled. In Europe, it is used for sautéing casserole meats. Joe Booker Stew (page 98), which includes beef, is based on the flavor of salt pork and is typical of ways salt pork once was used in New England cooking.

CREATE YOUR OWN PORK RECIPES

Using the basic information given here for cooking pork chops and other cuts, you can invent your own recipes and adapt your favorites. You can thicken the cooking liquids with flour and flavor the gravy with sage, Worcestershire or soy sauce, onions, garlic, minced parsley, sherry, curry. You can add sauerkraut, beets, cabbage—all go well with pork, and so do sweet things, like apples and dried fruits, yams and sweet potatoes.

Leftover slow-cooked pork can be used in salads or served cold with a sharp sauce, such as Mustard Sauce (page 80) and Vinaigrette Dressing (page 123). Frozen in one-cup lots, the pork can be used in many Chinese dishes.

PORK RECIPES

PORK CHOPS
8 to 10 hours

This is a mother's-day-at-the-office recipe. You do all the work at the beginning and can let the dish cook almost indefinitely. I serve fresh sour cream with it. To dress up the dish, boiled potatoes and braised celery may be added before serving.

12 *to* 16 *small pork chops*
6 *large Bermuda or sweet*
   onions, peeled and
   thickly sliced
2 *tsp. salt*
½ *tsp. pepper*

¾ *cup chicken broth, or* 1
   cup water with Steero
   chicken granules
1 *tsp. chopped chives*
   (*optional*)

To Cook: Trim any extra fat from the chops. In a large skillet, over high heat, melt down the fat; discard the bits of pork. Turn the heat to medium and sauté the onion slices in the fat until translucent. Keep the rounds intact if you can. Remove to a bowl. Turn the heat to medium high and brown each chop well on both sides; keep them in the skillet only long enough to brown—3 or 4 minutes. Remove the chops to a bowl as they are done. Salt and pepper the chops as they finish browning. Turn off the heat; add the broth to the skillet, and scrape up the pan juices. In the slow-cooker, layer the chops and the onions, beginning and ending with onions. Pour the broth over all. Cover and cook on Low for 8 to 10 hours. Sprinkle with chives before serving.

Makes 8 to 12 servings.

PORK CHOPS WITH BEANS
8 to 10 hours

The large end of a loin roast makes chops with a bone straight down the center and some gristle. When these turn up at a good price, I buy them for slow-cooker recipes. Sometimes, when a whole loin of pork is selling economically, I have the large end cut into chops for the slow-cooker and oven-roast the rib portion.

4 *pork chops less than 1 inch*	¼ *cup chili sauce*
thick	1 *tsp. brown sugar*
1 *tsp. salt*	½ *tsp. prepared mustard*
⅛ *tsp. pepper*	1 *cup drained cooked or*
1 *medium clove garlic,*	*canned kidney beans*
peeled, minced	1 *cup drained cooked or*
1 *large onion, peeled,*	*canned lima beans*
chopped	

To Cook: Rub a large skillet, over medium-high heat, with a bit of fat cut from a chop. Lay the chops in the hot skillet and brown well on both sides. Season with salt and pepper and place in the slow-cooker. Sauté the garlic and onion in the skillet 2 or 3 minutes, and turn into the cooker. Remove skillet from the heat; pour the chili sauce into it and scrape up the pan juices. Stir in the sugar and mustard and turn into the cooker. Cover and cook on Low 6 to 8 hours. Add kidney beans and limas to the cooker, placing them under the meat. Cover and cook on Low another 1 or 2 hours.

Makes 4 to 6 servings.

PORK CHOPS WITH MUSHROOM SAUCE
8 to 10 hours

This is an easy way with pork chops and very popular in my family.

8 to 10 *small, thick pork chops*	⅛ *tsp. sage*
2 *tsp. salt*	1 *can (12 oz.) cream-of-mushroom soup*
¼ *tsp. pepper*	1 *Tbs. dried onion flakes*

To Cook: Trim excess fat from the chops and use it to grease a large skillet. Over high heat, brown each chop lightly on both sides. Salt and pepper each as it finishes and place it in the slow-cooker. Add the sage. Turn the soup (undiluted) and the onion flakes into the still-hot skillet. Scrape up the pan juices and turn into the cooker. Cover and cook on Low for 8 to 10 hours.

Makes 6 to 8 servings.

PORK CURRY

Follow the recipe for Simple Beef Curry (page 56), but use 1 pound of cubed pork instead of beef.

PORK SHOULDER, BAVARIAN STYLE
6 to 8 hours

3 *lb. pork shoulder*	1 *large onion, peeled, sliced thin*
1 *tsp. salt*	
½ *cup beef stock, or 1 beef bouillon cube and ½ cup water*	2 *carrots, peeled, grated*
	3 *black peppercorns, crushed*
	½ *tsp. caraway seed*

To Cook: Place the meat in the slow-cooker, along with the other ingredients. Cover and cook on Low for 6 to 8 hours.

Before Serving: Simmer the cooking liquid in a small skillet to reduce it.

Makes 6 to 8 servings.

PORK AND PEARS
8 to 10 hours

This is a version of a German recipe called Shoemaker's Pot. Use Seckel pears, still firm.

2 lb. boneless pork loin roast, blade end	6 Seckel pears, peeled, halved, and cored
½ tsp. salt	1 Tbs. caraway seed
⅛ tsp. pepper	1 beef bouillon cube
¼ tsp. dried marjoram	1 Tbs. Worcestershire sauce
¼ tsp. dried dill	½ cup water
3 large potatoes, peeled, diced	2 Tbs. cornstarch
	2 Tbs. cold water

To Cook: Season the pork with salt, pepper, marjoram, and dill. Arrange the potatoes in the slow-cooker; set the pork on top. Place the pears on the pork, and add the caraway seed, bouillon cube, Worcestershire, and ½ cup water. Cover and cook on Low for 8 to 10 hours, or until the pork is tender.

Before Serving: Remove the meat to a serving platter and arrange the pears around it. Combine the cornstarch and cold water and pour into the slow-cooker. Turn the heat to High and stir until the sauce has thickened. Pour over the meat.

Makes 4 to 6 servings.

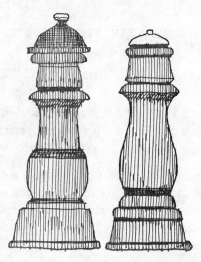

HEADCHEESE, CREOLE STYLE
8 to 10 hours

This is a dish from the South, where it is made with the head of a pig. It is a special treat, a recipe to select when you are planning a buffet and want to show off a little. Do the preliminary cooking overnight and finish the headcheese the next day.

4¼ lb. pig's feet
2 lb. pig heart
1 lb. pig tongue
Hot water to cover (about
    2 quarts)
¼ cup salt
1 Tbs. white vinegar
¼ cup strained lemon juice
2 Tbs. butter or margarine

1 cup chopped onion
1 bay leaf
1 tsp. ground sage
1 tsp. ground mace
½ tsp. hot red pepper
1 tsp. pepper
1 cup minced parsley
1 cup minced scallions or
    onions

To Cook: Wash the meats and trim any fat from the heart and tongue. Place in the slow-cooker with the water, salt, vinegar, and 1 tablespoon lemon juice. Cover and cook on High until the liquid froths. Skim off the foam two or three times. Reduce the heat and cook on Low overnight (8 to 10 hours), or until all the meats are tender. It's hard to overcook. Remove the meats from the pot. Skin the tongue and discard the little bones and gristle. Cut the heart into quarters and remove the veins and arteries. Put the meat (it will pull away easily from the bones) through the food grinder, using the coarsest blade, or chop coarsely. For about 5 cups of meat, measure 3½ cups of stock from the cooker. In a large skillet, over medium heat, melt the butter and sauté the chopped onion until translucent. Add ½ cup of stock and simmer until liquid is reduced by half—about 15 to 20 minutes. Stir in the ground meat, remaining 3 cups stock, remaining lemon juice, the bay leaf, sage, mace, and peppers. Raise the heat and bring to a boil. Reduce the heat; cover and simmer 10 minutes. Turn off the heat and stir in the parsley and scallions. Add salt if needed. Then scrape mixture into a square cake tin (9-by-9-by-2-inches deep); cover lightly, and refrigerate overnight, or at least 6 hours, before serving. Or divide into small ceramic tureens.

Before Serving: Heat the bottom of the cake tin or tureens a minute or two. Then turn upside down and unmold on a serving platter. Makes 1 (9-by-9-by-2-inch) loaf.

HOG'S HEADCHEESE
8 to 10 hours

Called Souse Meat or Pigtail Stew, depending on what part of the country you come from. This is another of those recipes devised to use everything but the pig's squeal. In the South, this was served with collard greens garnished with fried salt-pork bits and baked sweet potatoes.

1 *lb. fresh pork oddments—*	1 *tsp. salt*
ears, nose, feet, head or	1¼ *tsp. poultry seasoning*
parts of it	¼ *tsp. pepper*
1 *lb. neck of beef*	1 *red-pepper pod (optional)*
Water to cover (about 1½	
quarts)	

To Cook: Place all ingredients in the slow-cooker; cover and cook on Low for 8 to 10 hours. Remove the pepper pod, if you have used one, and lift out the meat. When it has cooled a little, remove the skin and pick the meat from the bones. Chop the meat coarsely in a large bowl. Check seasonings and add more if needed. Add enough broth to make a soupy but very thick mixture. You can serve this hot or pack it into tureens and refrigerate or store in the freezer. Makes 4 to 6 servings.

GALANTINE DE PORC MARCEL
8 to 10 hours

My father's recipe for a wonderful pork spread, excellent for sandwiches, great with salad for lunch, and wonderful served on plain saltines as a cocktail appetizer. It keeps well for about 2 weeks in the refrigerator and about 6 months in the freezer. Wrap well before storing. For a big party, pack into a fancy fluted mold; for storing, pack into small ceramic tureens or bread-loaf tins.

2½ lb. boneless pork shoulder	¼ tsp. pepper
1½ lb. (3 to 4) pork hocks (shanks)	¼ tsp. savory
	¼ tsp. dried thyme
2 cups water	¼ tsp. nutmeg
1 large onion, stuck with 8 whole cloves	3 small cloves garlic, peeled, minced
2½ tsp. salt	1 Tbs. minced parsley

To Cook: Place everything but the garlic and parsley in the slow-cooker; cover, cook on Low for 8 to 10 hours. Remove the meat and reserve the cooking stock. Peel rinds from the hocks and purée rinds in the blender with the garlic, parsley, and 1 cup very hot stock. Remove meat from the hocks and chop this and pork-shoulder meat coarsely in a large bowl. Stir in the puréed mixture. Check the seasonings and add salt if needed. Pack into a 3-quart mold; cover and refrigerate overnight before serving. Or pack into 6 small ceramic tureens or 2 small bread-loaf tins and store.

Makes 12 to 18 servings.

BAVARIAN PORK
10 to 12 hours

The slow-pot is a great asset in preparing this Pennsylvania dish, since the hocks must cook for hours before being finished in an oven.

2 to 3 lb. fresh pork hocks (6 to 8)	¼ tsp. pepper
	About 4 cups water
2 large onions, peeled	2 green apples, cored
1 bay leaf	3 lb. undrained sauerkraut
2 stalks celery, diced	½ cup light-brown sugar, firmly packed
2½ tsp. salt	

To Cook: Place the hocks, onions, bay leaf, celery, salt, pepper, and water to cover in the slow-cooker. Cover and cook on Low for 10 to 12 hours, or until hocks are thoroughly cooked.

Before Serving: Preheat the oven to 325° F. Remove the hocks from the cooker and place in a small casserole, closely packed. Cut the apples into wedges and place them over the hocks. Cover both with sauerkraut, not drained, and sprinkle with the sugar. Bake for 45 minutes.

Makes 6 to 8 servings.

ODDS-AND-ENDS STEW
6 to 8 hours

This is a fine way to use odds and ends of pork and meat trimmed from roasts or leftover chops, saved in the freezer. If you have some gravy drippings, add those after first removing the fat congealed on the surface.

4 *slices bacon, minced*	½ *cup beef stock, or 1 beef*
½ *lb. pork, in 1-inch cubes*	*bouillon cube and* ½
½ *lb. beef in 1-inch cubes*	*cup water*
½ *lb. lamb, in 1-inch cubes*	½ *tsp. salt*
4 *carrots, peeled, sliced*	⅛ *tsp. pepper*
2 *large onions, peeled, sliced*	½ *tsp. dried marjoram*
3 *large potatoes, peeled,*	⅛ *tsp. dried thyme*
sliced	

To Cook: In a large skillet, over medium-high heat, sauté the bacon bits until half-cooked. Add the meat pieces and sauté, stirring often, until browned. Add the vegetable slices and stir for 3 or 4 minutes. Turn into the slow-cooker. Pour the stock into the skillet, scrape up the pan juices, add the seasonings, and turn into the cooker. Cover and cook on Low for 6 to 8 hours.

Makes 6 to 8 servings.

DAISY ROLL AND BRAISED SAUERKRAUT
8 to 10 hours

2 *to 3 lb. daisy roll or ham*	1 *cup hot water*
roast	1 *cup white wine*
1 *medium onion, peeled,*	*Braised Sauerkraut (below)*
sliced	

To Cook: If using a daisy roll, remove plastic and mesh casings. Place all ingredients except Sauerkraut in the slow-cooker; cover and cook on Low for 8 to 10 hours. Remove meat from the cooking liquid and serve with Braised Sauerkraut.

Makes 4 to 6 servings.

BRAISED SAUERKRAUT

¼ cup butter or margarine
1 medium onion, peeled, chopped
3 cups drained, canned sauerkraut, rinsed in cold water

2 medium apples, peeled, cored, sliced
2 cups beef stock, or 2 beef bouillon cubes and 2 cups water
1 potato, peeled, grated
1 Tbs. caraway seed

In a large skillet, over medium heat, melt the butter and sauté the onion until translucent. Stir in the well-washed sauerkraut and the apple slices. Add the bouillon, stir well, cover, and simmer for 30 minutes. Add the potato and caraway seed and simmer, stirring constantly, until the mixture has thickened and the potato is cooked.

PORK WITH APRICOTS AND PRUNES
6 to 8 hours

This is a Silesian dish, to make with boneless rolled pork or a daisy roll of ham. We like it with baked sweet potatoes.

2 lb. boneless rolled pork or daisy ham roll (plastic casing removed)
1 cup dried apricots

1 cup dried prunes, pitted
¼ cup firmly packed light-brown sugar
½ cup dry white or rosé wine

To Cook: Place the pork or ham in the slow-cooker with the dried fruits, sugar, and wine. Cover and cook on Low for 6 to 8 hours. Serve the meat sliced with the fruity sauce ladled over it.

Makes 4 to 6 servings.

FRESH HAM WITH SOUR CREAM
8 to 10 hours

3 lb. fresh ham
1 tsp. salt
¼ tsp. pepper
1 tsp. caraway seed
½ cup water

1 large onion, peeled, sliced
   ¼ inch thick
3 whole cloves
1 Tbs. cornstarch
1 Tbs. cold water
1 cup sour cream

To Cook: Season the meat with salt and pepper and press caraway seed all over the top. Place in the slow-cooker; add the water, and arrange the onion rounds on the meat. Add the cloves. Cover and cook on Low for 8 to 10 hours, or until tender.

Before Serving: Remove the meat to a serving platter and keep warm. Skim as much fat as possible from the cooking liquid and remove the cloves. Combine the cornstarch and water. Turn the cooking liquid into a small saucepan, over medium heat; stir in the cornstarch mixture and keep stirring until the sauce simmers clear—3 to 5 minutes. Remove from the heat; stir in the sour cream and reheat, but do not let boil. Add a little salt if needed. Serve sauce with the meat, sliced thinly.

Makes 6 to 8 servings.

DAISY HAM ROLL
8 to 10 hours

The slow-cooker is a good way to handle a daisy roll. Discard the cooking stock or do as I do—use it to make pea soup. Serve the sliced ham with plain boiled new potatoes and butter, and have prepared mustard on the side.

1 daisy ham roll
Water to cover
1 small onion, stuck with
   4 whole cloves
8 peppercorns
1 bay leaf
1 carrot, peeled, broken into
   chunks

1 stalk celery, washed and
   broken into chunks
½ tsp. dried thyme
2 large sprigs fresh parsley,
   or 1 tsp. dried parsley
1 cup firmly packed brown
   sugar
1 cup cider vinegar

To Cook: Remove the plastic casing from the ham roll. Place all the ingredients in the slow-cook pot; cover and cook on Low for 8 to 10 hours. Remove the cotton mesh from the roll before serving. Makes 4 to 6 servings.

SOUTHERN HAM POT
6 to 8 hours

This is a very basic recipe for flavorful ham cooked the slow way.

¼ *cup all-purpose flour*
2 *tsp. salt*
1 *tsp. curry powder*
2 *lb. boneless smoked ham,*
 cut into 1-inch cubes
6 *medium sweet potatoes,*
 peeled and cut into slices
 ¼ *inch thick*

1 *large Bermuda onion, sliced*
 in rings ½ inch thick
1 *package (10 oz.) frozen*
 green peas
¼ *cup pimento-stuffed green*
 olives, sliced in rings
1 *cup boiling water*
2 *Tbs. butter or margarine*

To Cook: In a large bowl, combine the flour, salt, and curry powder. Toss the ham cubes in the mixture. Place one-third of the ham cubes in the slow-cooker and cover with a layer of half the sweet-potato slices, onion, peas, and olives. Repeat these two layers and end with a third layer of ham cubes. Pour the boiling water over the ingredients and dot with butter. Cover and cook on Low for 6 to 8 hours, or until the ham is tender.

Makes 6 servings.

JOE BOOKER STEW
8 to 10 hours

This is a soupy stew that gets its flavor from salt pork. It was famous around Booth Bay Harbor, Maine. It's plain and hearty winter food, good for after cutting ice or chopping trees.

½ lb. salt pork, diced
2 cups lean hamburger or diced stew beef
2 cups diced yellow turnips
2 cups diced potatoes
2 cups diced carrots
1 cup chopped onion

3 cups beef stock, or 3 beef bouillon cubes and 3 cups water
½ tsp. salt
¼ tsp. pepper
3 large sprigs parsley

To Cook: In a large skillet, over medium heat, render the fat from the salt pork. Discard the cracklings. In the same skillet, sauté the beef until well browned. Scrape meat and fat into the slow-cooker. Add the remaining ingredients. Cover and cook on Low for 8 to 10 hours.

Makes 8 servings.

NEW ENGLAND BOILED DINNER
6 to 8 hours

This is a favorite of my family's, simple but hearty, and just right for cold winter nights. Since the slow-cooker does most of the work, I can start the dish in the morning and serve it for supper when I get home. I serve prepared mustard and butter for the vegetables with this.

1 Polish sausage
4 large potatoes, peeled and halved
2 medium carrots, scraped and cut in rounds
1 stalk celery, sliced in rounds
1½ to 2 lb. corned beef
3 cups drained, rinsed sauerkraut

½ tsp. dried marjoram
½ tsp. dried thyme
1 onion, stuck with 4 whole cloves
1 tsp. chopped fresh parsley, or ½ tsp. parsley flakes
About 3 cups water
1 tsp. caraway seed (optional)

To Cook: Place the sausage in the slow-cooker and layer on the potatoes, carrots, and celery. Place the corned beef next and cover it with sauerkraut. Combine the remaining ingredients, except caraway seed, and pour into the cooker; water should reach just below the kraut. Sprinkle the kraut with caraway seed, if desired. Cover and cook on Low for 6 to 8 hours.

Before Serving: Lift the ingredients gently from the cooker and arrange attractively on a large platter. Moisten with a little of the cooking liquid.

Makes 6 to 8 servings.

POLISH SAUSAGE
8 to 12 hours

Polish sausage is great done in a slow-cooker. Follow the recipe for Daisy Ham Roll (page 96) but omit brown sugar and vinegar. Serve with heated sauerkraut and with potatoes and carrots boiled together. Offer butter with the potatoes.

CHICKEN

Most slow-cook chicken recipes give you 5 to 7 hours of free time. Chicken cooks more quickly than most meats and doesn't inherently require electric crock cooking to be perfect. In the oven, you can bake an average roasting chicken in about 2 hours; split broilers can be readied in less than an hour. However, the slow-cooker is a tremendous help in speeding the preparation of chicken casseroles. I use it two ways. One is for making a rice casserole when I'm in a hurry. Chicken with Tomatoes and Rice and Chicken-Breasts-and-Rice Casserole (page 106) take no time at all to get into the cooker in the morning. The second is for helping with preparation of some of the gourmet dishes—party cooking—in Chapter 6.

To make Chicken à la King (page 161) conventionally, you must be near the stove for an hour or two. The dish doesn't require working all that time, but specific things must be done at specific times. With the slow-cooker, you can set the chicken to cook, go away for

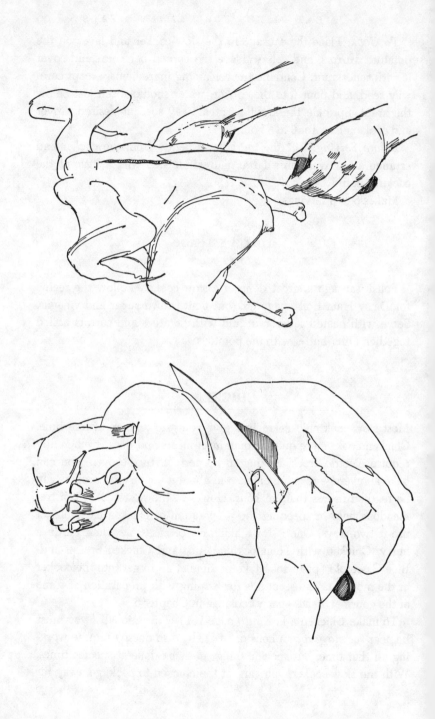

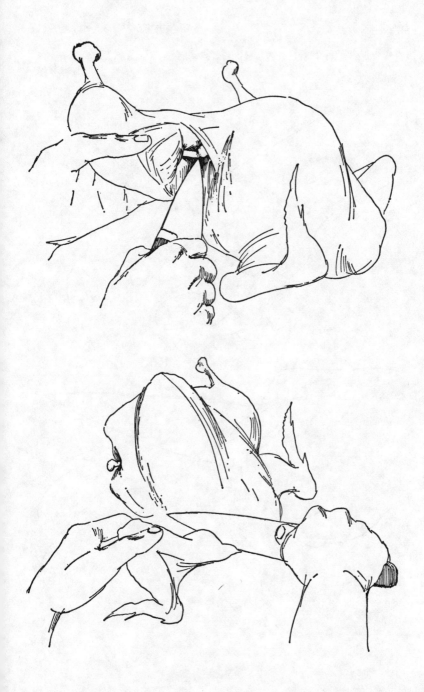

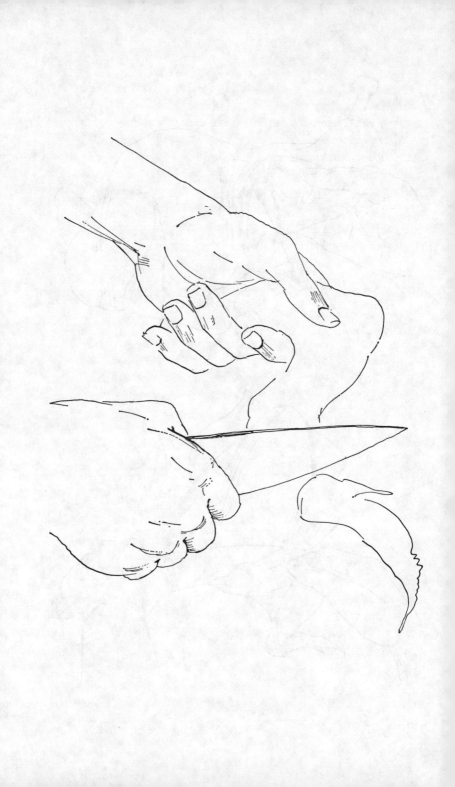

5 to 7 hours, and finish the dish in about 30 minutes. Chicken Caccia-
tore (page 162), a wonderful Italian way with chicken, made in the
conventional manner requires more than an hour to add various ingredients in sequence. When you make it in a slow-pot, you brown
the chicken in a skillet, put it in the slow-cooker with the sauce ingredients, let it cook in your absence, then finish it with a few
sautéed mushroom slices just before serving. Coq au Vin (page
163), chicken cooked with wine—a famous gourmet dish from
France—is made at about the same rhythm.

You can do chicken plain in a slow-pot, too, as in the recipe
Chicken Stuffed with Celery (page 107). Everything goes into the
pot at once, with little preparation, and it's ready to eat 5 to 7 hours
later. Use this timing to create your own variations on the chicken
theme. This dish needs no liquid; the celery and chicken provide all
the juices necessary. With some slow-cookers, however, some liquid must be put in the pot before cooking. Follow instructions for
your model. Thicken the sauce when cooking is over.

Can you overcook a chicken in a slow-cooker? Yes, you can, but it
will still be pretty good. Overbaked chicken generally is stringy and
dry, but a chicken casserole done in a slow-cooker can overcook
quite a bit without getting dry and unpleasantly stringy. I have
heard that a test-kitchen chef working with a slow-cooker forgot a
chicken for 30 hours and found it still edible—if not exactly up to
Cordon Bleu standards.

CHICKEN BARGAINS TO CONSIDER

With the slow-cooker, you can use chicken parts and boiling fowl,
both usually available at low prices. Backs and wings (see Chicken
Wings Marcel, page 160) can be used instead of breast or legs in
many of the recipes here. They are terrific for making soups, of
course, but their tender and tasty bits of meat also can be used in
many slow-cook recipes. When I buy chickens, I store the backs,
wings, and giblets in the freezer until I have enough to make soup
or stock or to cook for salads or aspics.

Boiling fowl isn't always found in city markets, but turns up fairly
regularly in country stores. It is excellent, though stringy if roasted,

delicately flavored, and very nice when poached in a slow-cooker. It can be used instead of broilers in the following recipes. A fowl usually is large, so use half and freeze the rest.

CREATE YOUR OWN CHICKEN RECIPES

Chicken cooked plain, as for Chicken Stuffed with Celery, can be flavored in all manner of ways. You can add curry, for instance, to the cooking liquid, or soy sauce, lemon juice, gravy drippings, sherry, or dry white wine; or simmer the liquid with a little tomato paste—about 2 tablespoons per cup of liquid. Or mince fresh parsley (a handful) and 2 peeled medium garlic cloves; sauté in ¼ cup butter or margarine just long enough to wilt the parsley, and combine with the sauce—a sharp, wonderful aroma comes from the pot and the flavor is grand.

The rice-casserole recipes in this chapter can be used as the basis for almost any flavorings you particularly like. Use the specified amounts of rice, water, and chicken—chicken parts are usually interchangeable—and add your favorite vegetables and condiments.

Slow-cooked-chicken leftovers are wonderful for salads. Minced and mixed with mayonnaise, they make a good sandwich spread.

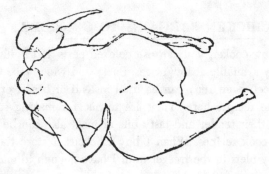

CHICKEN RECIPES

CHICKEN POACHED WITH VEGETABLES AND HERBS
5 to 7 hours

This is an adaptation of a German dish; nice with buttered noodles.

2 *to* 3 *lb. fryer, cut up*
1 *Tbs. all-purpose flour*
1 *tsp. salt*
⅛ *tsp. pepper*
¼ *lb. bacon, minced*
1 *medium onion, peeled, chopped*

1 *medium carrot, peeled, grated*
2 *large tart apples, peeled, cored, cubed*
4 *peppercorns, crushed*
½ *bay leaf*
¼ *tsp. dried thyme*
½ *cup dry rosé wine*

To Cook: Sprinkle the chicken pieces with flour combined with salt and pepper. In a large skillet, over medium heat, stir the bacon bits until crisp. Turn the onion, carrot, and apple into the bacon and sauté until the onion is transparent. Add the peppercorns, bay leaf, and thyme and pat the mixture into the bottom of the slow-cooker. Press the chicken pieces on top and pour the wine over all. Cover and cook on Low for 5 to 7 hours.

Makes 4 to 6 servings.

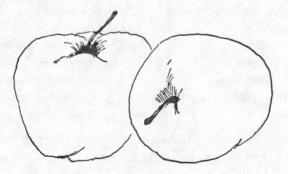

CHICKEN WITH TOMATOES AND RICE
5 to 7 hours

A hurry-up dish that goes into the slow-cooker in the morning and is ready to serve when you get home. It can cook longer without much damage.

2 chicken bouillon cubes
1 cup water
½ tsp. salt
¼ tsp. pepper
½ tsp. oregano
2 large onions, peeled, diced
3 Tbs. butter or margarine
1 cup converted rice
1 16-oz. can whole tomatoes, drained

1 cup tomato juice, drained from tomatoes, or the juice plus water to make 1 cup
2 sweet green peppers, seeded, chopped
1 large clove garlic, peeled, minced
½ tsp. saffron (optional)

To Cook: Place everything in the slow-cooker; cover and cook on Low for 5 to 7 hours.

Makes 6 to 8 servings.

CHICKEN-BREASTS-AND-RICE CASSEROLE
5 to 7 hours

Another mother's-helper to pop into the slow-cooker on mornings when there's no time to fuss. It won't hurt if it cooks longer than indicated.

3 chicken bouillon cubes
2 cups water
½ tsp. salt
¼ tsp. pepper
½ tsp. dried thyme
1 medium onion, peeled, chopped

1 cup converted rice
4 chicken breasts
2 Tbs. butter or margarine
½ cup minced fresh parsley
1 large or 2 medium cloves garlic, peeled, minced

To Cook: Place the bouillon cubes, water, salt, pepper, thyme, onion, rice, and chicken breasts in the slow-cooker. Cover and cook on Low for 5 to 7 hours.

Before Serving: In a small skillet, over medium heat, melt the butter and sauté the parsley and garlic, stirring constantly, about 3 minutes. Sprinkle over the chicken casserole and serve.

Makes 4 servings.

CHICKEN STUFFED WITH CELERY
5 to 7 hours

When you want chicken ready to eat the minute you get home, try it this way in your slow-cooker. For variety, stuff the chicken with fresh basil or tarragon or tomatoes or sliced onions. This is not better than roast chicken—just easier on busy days.

3 lb. chicken, cut in quarters or pieces	1 tsp. salt
½ tsp. curry powder	¼ tsp. pepper
1 small bunch celery, cut into 2-inch lengths (save the leaves)	½ tsp. savory
	2 Tbs. all-purpose flour (optional)

To Cook: Wash and wipe the chicken and rub the skin all over with the curry powder. In the slow-cooker, make a bed of the celery pieces. Place the chicken in the pot, layered with celery leaves, and sprinkle with salt, pepper, and savory. Cover and cook on Low for 5 to 7 hours.

Before Serving: You can serve the chicken plain or turn the cooking liquid into a delicious sauce. Drain the juices from the cooker and skim off and reserve about 1 to 2 tablespoons of chicken fat. Pour the juices into a small skillet; turn the heat to high, and boil down until there is ½ to ¾ cup of stock. In another skillet, over low heat, warm the chicken fat, and stir the flour into it. When you have a smooth paste, pour the cooked-down stock into the skillet, stirring quickly to keep the sauce smooth. Simmer for 3 to 4 minutes, or until thickened. Taste and add salt and pepper if needed. Place the chicken in a serving dish with the celery pieces around it and pour the sauce over all.

Makes 6 to 8 servings.

CHICKEN POT PIE
5 to 7 hours

The basic recipe for Chicken à la King (page 161) makes the beginning of an elegant chicken pie. Freeze extra broth; you'll find many uses for it in recipes in this book.

3 *lb. chicken, quartered*
3 *small carrots, peeled and cut into 1-inch chunks*
½ *cup diced celery*
1 *small onion, stuck with 4 whole cloves*
1 *bay leaf*
¼ *tsp. dried thyme*

2 *tsp. salt*
8 *peppercorns*
1 *cup water*
2 *Tbs. flour*
⅓ *cup dry sherry*
Bisquick (enough for 10 biscuits) or commercial piecrust mix (½ recipe)

To Cook: Into the slow-cooker, put the chicken, carrots, celery, onion, bay leaf, thyme, salt, peppercorns, and water. Cover and cook on Low for 5 to 7 hours.

Before Serving: Remove the chicken to a bowl to cool. Skim ⅓ cup fat from the cooking broth (if there's not enough, add butter). Place the fat in a medium skillet, over medium-low heat. Stir the flour into the fat to make a smooth paste and pour over it all at once 1 cup of hot broth. Beat the broth into the flour, working quickly to make a smooth sauce, and simmer, stirring, for 3 to 4 minutes. Stir in the sherry and simmer another minute. You will have a thick sauce. Skin and bone the chicken and cut the meat into chunks about 1 inch square. Place the chicken and the drained carrots and celery in a deep 9-inch pie tin or in a 1½-quart shallow casserole. Pour the sauce over them. If using Bisquick, prepare enough to make 10 biscuits. Scoop Bisquick mix in dollops over the meat and bake as directed on the package—about 15 minutes. If using piecrust as a topping, prepare ½ recipe for a 2-crust pie. Top the chicken with the raw crust, and bake at 425° F. in a preheated oven for 20 to 30 minutes, just long enough to cook the piecrust through and turn it a deep gold. Brush cold milk over the crust before baking it to make the color better.

Makes 6 to 8 servings.

CHICKEN-AND-HAM CASSEROLE
5 to 7 hours

Save 8 small slices of leftover baked ham in the freezer to make this.

1½ to 2 lb. quartered broiler	½ cup diced celery
8 small slices cooked ham	1 tsp. salt
3 cups water	½ lb. mushrooms, stemmed,
1 small onion, stuck with 4	wiped clean, sliced
whole cloves	Large pinch salt
1 large carrot, peeled, diced	¼ cup all-purpose flour
1 bay leaf	¼ cup dry sherry
¼ tsp. dried thyme	

To Cook: Place the broiler and other ingredients, except mushrooms, pinch of salt, flour, and sherry, in the slow-cooker. Cover and cook 5 to 7 hours on Low. Discard the onion and bay leaf.

Before Serving: Skim 2 tablespoons fat from the cooking liquid into a medium-large skillet and set over medium heat. Add the mushrooms and sauté 5 to 7 minutes. Sprinkle with a pinch of salt and with a slotted spoon remove mushrooms to the serving dish. Add 1 tablespoon fat to the skillet. Stir in the flour. Pour 3 cups cooking liquid into the flour and beat quickly to smooth the sauce. Add the sherry and simmer 5 to 10 minutes. Pour over the meat in the serving dish.

Makes 4 to 6 servings.

LACQUERED CHICKEN
5 to 7 hours

This is Anne Le Moine's economical version of Lacquered Duck, a classic Oriental recipe. It comes to the table enveloped in a gloriously rich, glossy, brown-red coating.

1 Tbs. vegetable oil	1 tsp. salt
2 lb. whole chicken	⅛ tsp. pepper
3 very large onions, peeled,	½ cup water
chopped	1 bouillon cube
5 large tomatoes, chopped	3 heaping Tbs. red-currant,
1 medium orange, unpeeled,	raspberry, or red-grape
seeded, chopped	jelly
1 tsp. sugar	¼ cup sweet sherry

To Cook: In a medium skillet, over medium-high heat, heat the oil and sauté the chicken, turning often, until well browned all over. Remove chicken to a plate. Sauté the onion in the skillet until well browned. Turn into the slow-pot. Place tomatoes, orange, sugar, salt, and pepper in the pot and set the chicken on top. Rinse the skillet with the water and scrape into the cooker. Add the bouillon cube. Cover and cook on Low for 5 to 7 hours.

Before Serving: Remove chicken to a deep serving dish and keep warm. Turn the pot contents into a skillet, set the heat to high, and simmer until thick enough to mound on a spoon. Stir in the jelly and the sherry and cook, stirring, until the sauce boils. Do not overcook, lest the sauce lose its shiny quality. If you wish, add some sugar or sweet sherry to further brighten the taste. If sauce is not shiny enough, bring back to a very brisk boil and quickly stir in some jelly. Pour sauce over chicken.

Makes 4 to 6 servings.

RED-COOKED CHICKEN
7 to 9 hours

For this variation on Walter Fischman's Red-Beef Appetizer (page 57), substitute 1½ pounds boned chicken breast for the beef top round.

CHICKEN STEW, MAINE STYLE
5 to 7 hours

Boiling fowl is usually inexpensive, and it's delicious this old-fashioned way in a thin, chowderlike sauce.

3 *to* 4 *lb. boiling fowl, cut up*	2 *cups water*
4 *potatoes, peeled, sliced*	2 *Tbs. butter or margarine*
2 *medium onions, peeled,*	1 *cup light cream*
sliced thin	6 *hard biscuits*
1 *tsp. salt*	*Cold milk*
¼ *tsp. pepper*	2 *Tbs. minced parsley*

To Cook: Layer the chicken pieces, potato, and onion in the cooker. Add the salt, pepper, and water. Cover and cook on Low for 5 to 7 hours.

Before Serving: Add the butter and cream and heat, covered, on high until simmering. Meanwhile, soak the hard New England biscuits in cold milk. Add to the stew and continue to heat until the biscuits are softened. Sprinkle with parsley, check seasonings, and serve.

Makes 6 to 8 servings.

CHICKEN WITH BEANS
4 to 6 hours

To make this variation on Blanquette de Veau (page 152), use 2 pounds of chicken pieces, with the bone in, in place of the veal. If you are in the mood for savings, skim chicken fat from the cooking broth for use instead of butter in making the sauce, and 1 cup of 1-inch celery chunks, ½ cup of leftover, cooked white beans, and ½ cup of cooked baby limas in place of the mushrooms.

END-OF-THE-MONTH CHICKEN CASSEROLE
5 to 7 hours, or longer

Try this some morning when you have to rush from the house and must have dinner ready when you get home. If you have leftover chicken drippings, remove the fat and add. Noodles, which cook in minutes, are very good with this casserole. Add a green salad and dinner is ready. Freeze leftover cooking liquid for later use in casseroles.

½ chicken, any size	*1 head celery, washed,*
2 packages chicken backs,	*leaves removed, cut*
necks, gizzards	*across the grain*
1 large onion	*in large rounds*
¼ tsp. dried thyme	*1 chicken bouillon cube*
¼ tsp. curry powder	*Water to cover*
1 tsp. salt	*2 Tbs. butter or margarine*
¼ tsp. black pepper	*2 Tbs. all-purpose flour*

To Cook: Place everything except the butter and flour in the slow-cooker. Cover and cook on Low for 5 to 7 hours.

Before Serving: Drain and reserve the stock. In a small saucepan over medium-low heat, melt the butter; stir in the flour to make a smooth paste. Stir in 1½ cups hot cooking stock and stir until sauce is smooth. Turn heat to lowest and let simmer while you remove the meat from the chicken parts. Discard skin and bones. Combine chicken pieces, gizzards, and celery chunks with the sauce.

Makes 3 or 4 servings.

LEFTOVER TURKEY WINGS AND RICE
5 to 7 hours

Years ago, one of Montreal's best restaurants, at the Hotel LaSalle, served this with a crisp lettuce salad embellished with French garlic dressing and a lot of minced parsley. Roasted turkey wings and drumsticks are often so dry by the time the turkey is done that they aren't really edible. Slow-cooked this way, they make a splendid dish, especially if you have a little extra gravy to pour over them before serving. Add a cup of chicken stock to the roasting pan as the turkey finishes cooking—the last hour—and there'll be plenty of gravy.

2 roasted turkey wings	1 tsp. salt
2 roasted drumsticks	⅛ tsp. black pepper
½ cup turkey gravy or pan drippings	½ tsp. curry powder (optional)
1 cup converted rice	1 medium onion, peeled, minced
1½ cups chicken stock or water	2 Tbs. minced parsley

To Cook: Remove the wing tips at the joint and save to make bouillon or soup. Place all the ingredients, except the parsley, in the slow-pot. Cover and cook on Low for 5 to 7 hours. Serve garnished with parsley.

Makes 4 servings.

Chapter 5

Lamb and Variety Meats

LEARN TO SLOW-COOK the lesser cuts of lamb and the variety meats —tongue, for example, and heart; tripe, too—and you can greatly diversify family meals. In this group of recipes I've included corned beef, because its flavor is in the category of variety meats—special. The slow-cooker does it perfectly, with absolutely no tending the pot. The slow-pot can also do superbly the rather tough game meats —lesser cuts of venison, for instance.

LAMB

Leg of lamb isn't good for slow-cooking because it tastes better roasted and because it won't fit whole into a slow-cooker. A small portion of a leg of lamb, bone in, will go in a large cooker, but it will taste like lamb stew—so why not roast it and save the slow-pot for stews?

Stew lamb slow-cooks in about 8 to 10 hours when the cuts are toughish and large. Irish stew is one of the great lamb casseroles. My father's recipe for Irish Stew Marcel is on page 116. Use it as a guide for adapting your favorite lamb recipes. Moussaka (page 165), a wonderfully tasty and inexpensive Greek dish made with ground cooked lamb—leftovers from a leg, for instance—is a good oven dish, but does well enough in a slow-pot and is so easy to put together and so popular in my family that I often slow-cook it.

Lamb necks and breasts are usually a real bargain, and there are several ways to slow-cook them. Leg-of-lamb bones, of course, are the flavor base for Scotch Broth—though you can use uncooked lamb —so don't throw them away. Just turn to Chapter 7 and look up the Scotch Broth recipe.

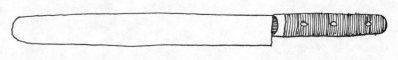

LAMB CUTS SPECIALLY SUITED TO SLOW-COOKING

Blade Lamb Chops: The front part of the shoulder, cut up, and not quite as tender as rib sections. Some shops sell this shoulder cut for roasting, with the bone in or as a rolled roast. The chops have a small, straight bone down the center and are good choices for slow-cooking.

Arm Lamb Chops: Cut from the lower part of the shoulder, these have a series of small bones on one side and a small bone in the center. Good for slow-cooking, especially when cut thick.

Lamb Shank and Lamb Breast: These come in various shapes. They are shoulder cuts and very well suited to slow-cooking recipes.

Foreshank: One of the best lamb cuts for stewing. It is often boned and sold ground.

Lamb Neck: Wonderfully sweet meat, with just a bit of bone in it. Prized for soups and stews, stocks, and many Southern and European specialties. Excellent done in a slow-cooker.

LAMB RECIPES

STUFFED BREAST OF LAMB
Overnight—6 to 8 hours

A festive dish, with tasty spinach stuffing. You can cook the breasts overnight, stuff it in the morning, and have it ready to brown in the oven just before dinner time.

2 to 3 lb. breast of lamb	1 Tbs. minced green pepper
1 tsp. salt	1 Tbs. minced onion
Water to cover	½ tsp. salt
4 Tbs. butter or margarine	¼ tsp. pepper
½ lb. spinach, washed, dried, chopped	2 cups dry bread crumbs
	2 Tbs. butter or margarine
2 Tbs. minced celery	Salt and pepper

To Cook: Place the lamb breast, 1 teaspoon salt, and the water in the slow-cooker; cover and cook on Low overnight, or 6 to 8 hours. Remove meat from the cooker, spread it on a cutting board, and slip the bones from their pockets. Reserve ⅓ cup cooking liquid. In a large skillet, over medium heat, melt 2 tablespoons butter and sauté the spinach, celery, green pepper, and onion, seasoned with ½ teaspoon salt and ¼ teaspoon pepper, about 2 minutes, stirring constantly. Push the spinach aside; melt 2 tablespoons butter and sauté the bread crumbs, tossing them as they cook, about 1 minute. Remove skillet from heat and toss crumbs and vegetables until well combined. Cover the breast with the stuffing; roll it up, tie each end with clean white string or white thread, and place in a buttered baking dish. Spread 2 tablespoons butter over the top; season with salt and pepper; pour reserved cooking liquid into the dish.

Before Serving: Bake at 400° F. until golden brown—20 to 30 minutes.

Makes 4 to 6 servings.

LAMB CURRY, NEW ZEALAND STYLE
5 to 7 hours

Cook this on High, 2½ to 3½ hours, and it's a little better. But it cooks well enough on Low and leaves you more free time. Serve with white rice and chutney.

3 *Tbs. butter or margarine*
2 *lb. boned lamb shoulder,*
  in 1½- to 2-inch cubes
2 *large onions, peeled,*
  chopped
2 *cloves garlic, peeled,*
  minced
2 *Tbs. curry powder*
1 *lemon, unpeeled, sliced,*
  seeded

2 *large tart apples,*
  peeled, cored, chopped
1 *cup chicken stock,*
  or 2 chicken bouillon
  cubes and 1 cup water
2 *tsp. salt*
¼ *tsp. pepper*

To Cook: In a large skillet, over medium-high heat, heat the butter and sauté lamb cubes until well browned. Remove meat to the slow-cooker. Add the onions, garlic, and curry to the skillet; reduce the heat and sauté until onions are translucent—about 5 to 7 minutes. Stir in the lemon slices, apples, stock, salt, and pepper and scrape up the pan juices. Scrape everything into the slow-cooker. Cover and cook on Low for 5 to 7 hours.

Before Serving: If the sauce is thinner than you like, simmer it in a small skillet 5 to 10 minutes to thicken it.

Makes 4 to 6 servings.

LAMB CURRY II

Follow the recipe for Simple Beef Curry (page 56) but use 1 pound of cubed boneless lamb shoulder instead of beef.

IRISH STEW MARCEL
8 to 10 hours

This is my father's recipe for Irish stew and my favorite version. For chicken bouillon, use College Inn brand if you can find it. Or use granules of Steero, dissolved in 2 cups of hot water. The lamb is blanched in water first, then slow-cooked in the bouillon.

3 *lb. boneless lamb shoulder,*
   cut into 1½-inch cubes
2 *quarts boiling water*
2 *cups chicken bouillon*
½ *cup carrots, scraped and*
   cut into ½-inch cubes
½ *cup turnips, scraped and*
   cut into ½-inch cubes

1 *medium onion, peeled,*
   sliced
1 *tsp. salt*
¼ *tsp. pepper*
1 *bay leaf*
¼ *cup all-purpose flour*
1 *tsp. strained lemon juice*

To Cook: Place the lamb cubes in a kettle with the boiling water and simmer for 15 minutes. Discard the water. Place the bouillon, carrots, turnips, onion, salt, pepper, and bay leaf in the slow-cooker and add the blanched lamb. Cover and cook on Low for 8 to 10 hours.

Before Serving: Measure ½ cup cooking liquid; cool it with an ice cube; dissolve the flour in the cooled broth. Add the lemon juice and pour the mixture into the slow-cooker. Turn the heat to High and cook for 10 to 15 minutes—uncovered if the sauce is very thin, covered if thick.

Makes 8 to 10 servings.

LAMB LOAF
5 to 7 hours

You can cook this in the oven as you would beef meat loaf, but on a busy day it is convenient to do it in the slow-pot. If ground lamb isn't available, make the loaf with 2 pounds of shoulder, put through your grinder.

3 *Tbs. butter, margarine,*
   or olive oil
½ *lb. mushrooms, wiped,*
   chopped
1 *Tbs. chopped onion*
2 *Tbs. minced parsley*
2 *slices white bread*
½ *cup whole milk*

2 *lb. ground lamb*
1 *tsp. salt*
⅛ *tsp. pepper*
1 *tsp. dried thyme*
2 *Tbs. lemon juice, strained*
1 *egg*
1 *large sprig fresh parsley*

To Cook: Heat the butter, over medium heat, in a large skillet, and sauté the mushrooms, onion, and minced parsley. Remove from heat. Meanwhile, soak the bread in the milk until saturated; then break into bits with two forks. In a large bowl, toss lightly the lamb, bread, sautéed mixture, salt, pepper, thyme, and lemon juice. Make a well in the center of the mixture; break the egg into it and beat in the egg. Shape into a round loaf and place in a lightly greased slow-cooker. Cover and cook on Low for 5 to 7 hours.

Before Serving: Pour the cooking liquid over the loaf and garnish with parsley sprig.

Makes 4 to 6 servings.

LAMB-NECK STEW
5 to 7 hours

This is a two-step recipe. Set the lamb necks to cooking in the morning. Add the barley an hour or so before dinner and serve when the barley is cooked.

1½ *lb. lamb neck, cut up*	2 *slices lemon, unpeeled*
2 *cups water*	1 *tsp. salt*
2 *cups chopped onion*	⅛ *tsp. black pepper*
1 *cup grated carrot*	¾ *cup barley*

To Cook: Place the neck, water, and everything but the barley in the slow-pot. Cover and cook on Low for 5 to 7 hours, or until the meat is falling off the bones.

Before Serving: Remove the bones from the cooking liquid and skim away surface fat. Add the barley; cover and cook on High for ½ hour, or until barley is completely cooked.

Makes 4 to 6 servings.

LAMB NECKS, SCANDINAVIAN STYLE
5 to 7 hours

This is the dilliest dill dish—good only if you like dill. Nicest with plain boiled potatoes and fresh green beans.

3 *lb. neck of lamb*	2 *Tbs. all-purpose flour*
2 *tsp. dried dill weed, or*	4 *tsp. white-wine vinegar*
4 *sprigs fresh dill*	2 *tsp. sugar*
2½ *cups water*	½ *tsp. salt*
1 *tsp. salt*	2 *egg yolks, slightly beaten*
2 *Tbs. butter or margarine*	3 *Tbs. chopped fresh dill*

To Cook: Place meat, dill weed, water, and 1 teaspoon salt in the slow-pot. Cover and cook on Low for 5 to 7 hours.

Before Serving: Measure the cooking liquid. If it is more than 2 cups, boil it rapidly to reduce. In a medium skillet, over medium-low heat, melt the butter; stir in the flour to make a smooth paste. Beat in the cooking liquid to make a smooth sauce. Add the vinegar, sugar, and ½ teaspoon salt and simmer until thickened—4 or 5 minutes. Pour a little of the hot sauce into the egg yolks; then turn the yolks into the sauce. Remove from heat and stir for 2 or 3 minutes. Add the chopped dill and serve over the hot lamb necks.

Makes 4 servings.

VARIETY MEATS

TONGUE: Beef, pork, lamb, and calf tongues, fresh or smoked, appear from time to time at meat markets. They provide a nice change of pace. Fresh tongue has a special flavor; smoked tongue reminds me of other meats cured in similar fashion—for instance, corned beef. I find the flavor of beef tongue best. Small tongues generally are better flavored and textured than large ones. Scrub tongue well before cooking. Smoked tongue is nicest if it is first parboiled in rapidly boiling water for 5 to 10 minutes. Tongue should be skinned before serving, as the outer casing is unpleasant to eat.

Cooked tongue is excellent with horseradish, raisin sauce, capers, pickled nuts.

HEART AND KIDNEY: Hearts are sometimes available at very good prices in country markets. The flesh is firm and fat-free, which means it is rather dry. So the most popular way to cook a heart is to stuff it with rich, moist ingredients containing some fat. Before you stuff it, wash it well and remove the fat, the tough arteries, veins, and any blood. Beef hearts are larger than calves' hearts. A beef heart weighs between 2 and 5 pounds and will make 6 or more servings. A calf's heart will make 1 or 2 servings, depending on its size.

Only beef and pork kidneys are suitable for slow-cooking, and recipes for them aren't common. I've included one for Beef-and-Kidney Stew (page 125) that I rather like. Soak the kidneys overnight in ice water in the refrigerator, to remove the strong odor, and cut away membranes and excess fat before cooking.

LIVER: Calves' liver is one of the most expensive meats today, and those lucky enough to afford it have loads of ways of cooking it. Baby beef liver, when it is pale, can be cooked like calves' liver, though the flavor won't be quite as delicate. These are not meats to slow-cook. However, if you come across a bargain in baby beef liver that looks as though it did more growing up than the butcher claims, you might try the recipe for Whole Beef Liver, Slow-Pot Style (page 126). Use it to adapt to slow-cooking your own favorite ways of doing half-grown-up beef liver.

HUNTERS' CATCH: If there are hunters in your family, you'll find the slow-pot invaluable for making good stews from strongly flavored game meats. Venison cuts are similar to beef cuts and can be used in recipes for slow-cooked beef. Marinate tough cuts as in the recipe for Braised Shoulder of Venison (page 127) before you start cooking. The Venison Sauce is a good foil for many game meats. This venison recipe can serve as a guide for adapting your favorite game recipes to slow-cooking.

Rabbit and small game can be cooked following beef and chicken slow-cook recipes. The recipe for Lapin Chasseur (page 128) suggests how to adapt small game to slow-cooking.

CORNED BEEF: Corned beef is beef pickled in brine. I think it is best when cooked the slow-pot way. There are many tricks to play with this tasty meat. Our grandparents cooked it with boiling fowl to make Succotash, Pilgrim Style (page 129), and in Vermont it was glazed with maple syrup after cooking. Remember the comic strip Maggie and Jiggs, and how Jiggs loved his corned beef and cabbage? Maggie's main objection was the smell, I'm sure—which seems to cling, even when the dish is cooked in a slow-pot. But it's good.

There's really only one basic way to cook corned beef—slow-cook it in lots of water—so the slow-pot is ideal. What you do with the beef afterward depends on you. I prefer it served with well-buttered boiled potatoes and a little mustard or horseradish sauce. But you can use the recipe for slow-cooked Corned Beef (page 131) to begin the process and finish the dish as you prefer.

Before cooking, rinse corned beef well under cold running water, to remove any pickling brine.

VARIETY MEAT RECIPES

FRESH TONGUE
8 to 10 hours

Tongue simmered in stock flavored with onions and herbs was one of my mother's masterpieces. She served it hot, with boiled potatoes and Mustard Sauce. With leftovers, there was always Vinaigrette Sauce (page 123). The slow-cooker does tongue beautifully.

1 *fresh tongue (about 2 lb.)*	2 *large sprigs parsley,*
1 *large onion, peeled,*	*or 1 tsp. dried parsley*
stuck with 6 cloves	*flakes*
1 *large carrot, peeled, sliced*	1 *bay leaf*
4 *stalks celery, in 2-inch*	*Water to cover*
pieces	*Mustard Sauce (page 80)*

To Cook: Place the tongue in the slow-pot with all the other ingredients except the Mustard Sauce. Cover and cook on Low for 8 to 10 hours. You cannot overcook it. Remove tongue from the stock; discard little bones and peel the skin before slicing. Serve with Mustard Sauce.

Makes 6 to 8 servings.

SMOKED TONGUE
8 to 12 hours

Smoked tongue, if you can get one that fits in your slow-cooker, is great when you prepare it by following the recipe for Daisy Ham Roll (page 96). Serve it with prepared mustard or horseradish sauce and plain boiled potatoes with butter.

STUFFED BEEF HEART
8 to 10 hours

Beef heart is a rich, dark meat with an excellent flavor—and the slow-cooker cooks it to perfection this way.

1 *beef heart* (3 *to* 5 *lb.*)	⅛ *tsp. pepper*
¼ *cup butter*	1 *cup water*
¼ *cup minced onion*	2 *tsp. salt*
¾ *cup lightly packed*	½ *tsp. pepper*
bread cubes or crumbs	1 *tsp. dried marjoram*
½ *tsp. salt*	½ *tsp. dried thyme*
½ *tsp. poultry seasoning*	2 *tsp. strained lemon juice*
1 *tsp. celery seed*	
3 *tsp. minced fresh parsley,*	
or 1½ *tsp. dried parsley*	
flakes	

To Cook: Remove the fat, veins, and arteries from the beef heart and wash heart well. Melt the butter in a medium skillet, over medium heat, and sauté the onion and bread cubes in it with ½ teaspoon salt, the poultry seasoning, celery seed, parsley, and ⅛ teaspoon pepper for 5 or 6 minutes. Remove the stuffing to a bowl. In the same skillet, sauté the beef heart on all sides. Remove from the skillet and stuff with the bread mixture. Pour the water into the skillet and scrape up the pan juices. Place the heart, the sauce in the skillet, and remaining ingredients except the lemon juice in the slow-cooker. Cover and cook on Low for 8 to 10 hours, or until tender.

Before Serving: Remove the heart to a warm serving dish. Turn the cooking liquid into a small skillet; add the lemon juice and simmer until reduced and slightly thickened.

Makes 4 to 8 servings.

SLICED BEEF HEART WITH VINAIGRETTE SAUCE
6 to 8 hours

Slow-cooked beef-heart slices with a strong, tangy sauce.

1 *beef heart* (2 *lb.*)	1 *large onion, peeled, minced*
½ *cup water*	½ *to* 1 *tsp. salt*
2 *carrots, scraped, diced*	½ *tsp. poultry seasoning*
2 *stalks celery, diced*	*Vinaigrette Sauce* (*below*)

To Cook: Prepare the heart as for Stuffed Beef Heart (page 122); then cut it into even slices, across the grain. Place, with remaining ingredients except Vinaigrette Sauce, in the slow-cooker. Cover and cook on Low for 6 to 8 hours, or until tender.

Before Serving: Drain the heart slices; arrange on a platter and serve Vinaigrette Sauce on the side.

Makes 4 servings.

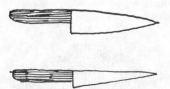

VINAIGRETTE SAUCE

This is excellent with any strongly flavored meat and wonderful with cold meat leftovers—if you like strong flavors.

1 *clove garlic, peeled*	1 *shallot, peeled; or*
½ *tsp. salt*	1 *slice onion, or* 1
⅛ *tsp. pepper*	*small green onion*
½ *cup vegetable oil*	1 *Tbs. minced chives*
1 *Tbs. white-wine vinegar*	1½ *Tbs. minced parsley*
1 *Tbs. tarragon vinegar*	

Combine all ingredients in a blender and blend at low speed about 2 minutes. Chill until ready to serve.

BEEF HEART IN BROWN SAUCE
4 to 6 hours

This is a little more work than the preceding recipes, but you can do it all in the morning. Once the meat is in the slow-cooker, your job is finished—only the cooker has to work.

1 *beef heart* (2 *lb.*)	2 *Tbs. rendered bacon fat,*
½ *cup all-purpose flour*	*or* 2 *Tbs. vegetable oil*
1 *tsp. salt*	¼ *cup red wine, or* ⅛ *cup*
⅛ *tsp. black pepper*	*water and* ⅛ *cup wine*
	vinegar

To Cook: Prepare the heart as for Stuffed Beef Heart (above); then cut it into even slices, across the grain. In a medium bowl, combine the flour, salt, and pepper and toss the heart slices in the mixture. In a large skillet, over medium-high heat, heat the fat until a drop of water spatters in the pan. Then quickly sauté the heart slices on each side until brown. Transfer slices to the slow-cooker; remove the pan from the heat. Pour the wine into the pan and stir, scraping up pan juices. Pour over the heart slices. Cover and cook on Low for 4 to 6 hours.

Makes 4 servings.

BRAISED STUFFED CALVES' HEARTS
6 to 8 hours

These are smaller than beef hearts and are cooked much the same way. Clean and stuff as described for Stuffed Beef Heart (above). You will need 3 calves' hearts to serve 4 to 6 people. Cook the calves' hearts in tomato juice instead of water and cook on Low for 6 to 8 hours, or until tender.

BEEF-AND-KIDNEY STEW
5 to 7 hours

Veal and lamb kidneys are delicious quick-cooked. Beef kidneys, less popular and more strongly flavored, benefit from slow-cooking.

2 lb. boneless beef shin, in 1-inch cubes
¼ cup all-purpose flour
¼ cup butter or margarine
1 cup chopped onion
2 beef kidneys
1 cup beef stock, or 1 cup water and 1 beef bouillon cube

2 Tbs. chopped parsley
1 bay leaf
1 tsp. dried thyme
2 tsp. salt
⅛ tsp. pepper
½ cup finely minced parsley (optional)

To Cook: Roll the beef cubes in the flour. In a large skillet, over medium-high heat, melt the butter and sauté the onion until transparent—2 or 3 minutes. Add the beef cubes and sauté, stirring often, until really well browned on all sides. While the beef is browning, wash the kidneys well under cold running water; remove the outer sacks and fat and discard. Place kidneys in a big bowl of ice water. With scissors, remove remaining fat and tubes; discard. Cut the kidneys into the ice water in thin slices. Drain, and after the beef is browned, sauté kidney slices 2 or 3 minutes, while stirring. Then turn the meats into the slow-cooker. Pour the beef stock into the skillet and scrape up the pan juices. Turn into the slow-cooker with all remaining ingredients except minced parsley. Cover and cook on Low for 5 to 7 hours.

Before Serving: If the sauce is thin, uncover the cooker; turn the heat to High and cook until sauce is thickened. Serve plain or garnished with minced parsley.

Makes 6 to 8 servings.

STEAK-AND-KIDNEY PIE
5 to 6 hours

This is one of my favorites for the slow-cooker. Because the meats cook while I'm at work, all I have to do when I get home is add the topping or crust and bake it while I'm preparing vegetables and setting the table.

6 *lamb kidneys*
¼ *cup all-purpose flour*
1½ *tsp. salt*
½ *tsp. ground ginger*
⅛ *tsp. cinnamon*
1½ *lb. boneless beef round,*
    cut into 1-inch cubes
3 *Tbs. vegetable oil*

1 *tsp. dry mustard*
1 *Tbs. Worcestershire sauce*
½ *Tbs. Tabasco sauce*
6 *small white onions, peeled*
1¼ *cups water*
Bisquick (enough for 10
    biscuits), or commercial
    piecrust mix (½ recipe)

To Cook: Prepare kidneys as in preceding recipe. Cut the kidneys into the ice water in ¼-inch slices. In a medium bowl, combine the flour, salt, ginger, and cinnamon. Drain kidney slices. Toss the beef and kidney pieces in the mixture. In a medium skillet, over medium-high heat, brown the meats in the oil quickly, stirring constantly. Turn the meats into the slow-cooker. Add the mustard, Worcestershire sauce, Tabasco, onions, and water. Cover and cook on Low for 5 to 6 hours.

Before Serving: If using Bisquick, prepare enough to make 10 biscuits. Turn the cooked meats into a 1½-quart ovenproof casserole. If the sauce seems very thin, simmer a few minutes to thicken it. Scoop biscuit mix in dollops over the meat and bake as directed—about 15 minutes. If using piecrust as a topping, prepare ½ recipe for a two-crust pie. Transfer the meat to a casserole or a deep pie dish 8 to 9 inches in diameter; top with the raw crust, and bake at 425° F. in a preheated oven for 20 to 30 minutes, just long enough to turn the crust a deep gold. If you brush cold milk over the crust, it will brown better.

Makes 6 servings.

WHOLE BEEF LIVER, SLOW-POT STYLE
5 to 7 hours

Frozen beef liver isn't wonderful—but fresh beef liver, especially if it is real baby beef liver, is excellent done this way.

1 *beef liver (2 lb.)*
1 *tsp. salt*
⅛ *tsp. pepper*
¼ *tsp. ground sage*
¼ *tsp. dried thyme*

¼ *tsp. ground allspice*
3 *Tbs. butter or margarine*
1 *cup beef stock, or 1 cup*
    water and 2 beef
    bouillon cubes

3 *sprigs fresh parsley, or*
   1 *tsp. dried parsley flakes*
1 *bay leaf*
2 *whole cloves*
1 *small clove garlic, peeled,*
   minced

12 *small white onions, peeled*
1 *cup 1-inch celery chunks*
2 *Tbs. dry sherry*
1 *or 2 Tbs. butter or mar-*
   garine (optional)

To Cook: Wash and dry the liver. Season with salt, pepper, sage, thyme, and allspice. In a large skillet, over medium-high heat, melt 3 tablespoons butter and brown the liver lightly on all sides. Remove the liver to the slow-pot. Pour the beef stock into the skillet and scrape up the pan juices. Turn into the slow-pot and add the remaining ingredients except the optional butter. Cover and cook on Low for 5 to 7 hours, or until tender.

Before Serving: Place the liver on a serving platter; arrange the vegetables around it and keep warm. If the sauce seems very thin, simmer it in a small saucepan until reduced by half. Check seasoning—you might want to add a little salt or sherry. If you like, melt 1 or 2 tablespoons butter in the sauce to make it richer.

Makes 6 to 8 servings.

BRAISED SHOULDER OF VENISON
6 to 8 hours

Shoulder and other tough cuts of venison can be braised successfully in the slow-cooker. I find them best when marinated for several hours or overnight.

Marinade

1 *cup vegetable oil*
½ *cup lemon juice or dry*
   white wine
2 *Tbs. minced parsley*

2 *Tbs. minced onion*
1 *tsp. salt*
⅛ *tsp. pepper*

Combine all ingredients and pour over the meat. Cover and set in a cool room for several hours or overnight.

2 *to 3 lb. venison shoulder*
   roast, boned, marinated
   (as above)

Marinade juices
Venison Sauce (below)

To Cook: Combine marinated meat and marinade juices in the slow-cooker. Cover and cook on Low for 6 to 8 hours. Serve with Venison Sauce.

Makes 4 to 6 servings.

VENISON SAUCE

½ Tbs. butter, margarine,
 or chicken fat
2 Tbs. cider or red wine
1 cup red-currant or grape
 jelly

¼ tsp. salt
½ tsp. ground cloves
½ tsp. cinnamon

In a small skillet, over low heat, melt the butter and stir in the cider. Add the remaining ingredients; simmer until the mixture has slightly thickened. Serve a little over the braised venison and the rest on the side, hot.

LAPIN CHASSEUR
5 to 7 hours

In the South of France, rabbit is cooked this way—with olive oil, mushrooms, and condiments we think of as typical of Italian cooking. Rabbit is as common a meat in Europe as chicken is in this country. In New England, only hare is commonly carried by the butchers. Hare is good for some German dishes, but not for this recipe. I have occasionally found in specialty markets small frozen rabbits, packaged much like frozen vegetables; they are suitable for this recipe. A similar dish from our South is pot-roasted rabbit, in which there is no tomato. Lapin Chasseur is nice with rice and a green salad.

3 lb. rabbit, cut into
 8 pieces
1 tsp. salt
½ tsp. pepper
4 Tbs. olive oil
1 large onion, peeled,
 chopped
2 large green peppers,
 seeded, cut up

3 large tomatoes, peeled,
 cut up
2 large cloves garlic, peeled,
 minced
1 cup dry red wine
½ tsp. dried thyme
½ lb. mushrooms, wiped,
 sliced thin
½ tsp. salt

To Cook: Sprinkle the rabbit with 1 teaspoon salt and the pepper. In a large skillet, over medium-high heat, warm the oil and sauté rabbit pieces until well browned on all sides—8 to 10 minutes. Remove the meat to a plate. Sauté the onion, green peppers, tomatoes, and garlic long enough to wilt the onion and brown the vegetables a little. Scrape into the slow-pot. Place the meat on top. Pour the wine into the skillet; scrape up the pan juices and turn into the slow-pot with the thyme. Cover and cook on Low for 5 to 7 hours.

Before Serving: Skim a little fat from the cooking liquid into a large skillet and, over medium-high heat, sauté the mushroom slices until tender—5 to 10 minutes. Add ½ teaspoon salt, and stir mixture into the rabbit sauce.

Makes 4 to 6 servings.

SUCCOTASH, PILGRIM STYLE
6 to 8 hours plus 1 to 1½ hours

This version of succotash was made by the Pilgrims and was traditionally served in Plymouth, Massachusetts, on Forefathers' Day, December 21. Make it with leftover, cooked navy beans if you have some, or use canned beans.

2 *lb. corned beef*	3 *potatoes, peeled, sliced*
2 to 3 *lb. boiling fowl*	2 *cups cooked or*
3 *cups water*	*canned navy beans,*
2 *tsp. salt*	*mashed*
¼ *tsp. pepper*	3 *cups drained*
1 *small or ½ medium*	*canned or cooked*
yellow turnip, peeled,	*corn kernels*
sliced	

To Cook: Combine the corned beef, fowl, water, salt, and pepper in the slow-cooker. Cover and cook on Low for 6 to 8 hours, or until the meats are very tender.

Before Serving: Remove meats from the cooker; skim the fat from the cooking liquid. Turn the cooker to High and simmer the turnip and potato slices for 1 to 1½ hours, or until tender. When the vegetables are almost done, stir a little of the cooking liquid into the mashed beans; then stir the beans into the cooker. Add the corn kernels and simmer, stirring, as the mixture thickens. Taste and add salt and pepper if needed. Reheat the meats in the oven as the vegetables finish cooking. Serve the meats on a platter and the vegetables in a tureen.

Makes 8 to 10 servings.

CORNED BEEF
8 to 12 hours

Corned beef, cooked ever so slowly in a crockery cooker, is wonderful with rye bread and mustard. A treat as do-your-own sandwiches for a crowd. Or it is wonderful served with fresh green cabbage as a vegetable. Follow the recipe for slow-cooked Daisy Ham Roll (page 96), but omit brown sugar and vinegar.

CORNED BEEF, VERMONT STYLE
10 to 12 hours

Let this cook in the slow-pot during the day; finish in the oven about 30 to 45 minutes before dinner. The cooking liquid can be used to make soup with split green peas.

4 lb. corned beef   1 medium onion, peeled
Water to cover   10 whole cloves
1 bay leaf   ½ cup maple syrup
1 tsp. dried thyme

To Cook: Place the corned beef, water, bay leaf, thyme, and onion in the slow-cooker. Cover and cook on Low for 10 to 12 hours.

Before Serving: Remove meat from the cooker. Stick the cloves into the meat in a diagonal design and pour the syrup over it. Set meat on a rack in an oven preheated to 350° F. Allow 30 to 45 minutes for the meat to glaze; baste frequently.

Makes 6 to 8 servings.

CORNED-BEEF BOILED DINNER
10 to 12 hours

3 lb. corned beef
Water to cover
6 small white onions,
  peeled
1 small onion, peeled, stuck
  with 6 whole cloves
1 large bay leaf
½ tsp. dried thyme
3 parsnips, peeled

6 large carrots, peeled,
  halved
1 small yellow turnip, peeled,
  cut in 3-inch pieces
4 medium potatoes, peeled,
  halved
6 small cooked or canned
  beets
2 Tbs. minced parsley

To Cook: Place everything but the beets and parsley in the slow-pot. Cover and cook on Low for 10 to 12 hours.

Before Serving: Warm the beets. Drain the cooking liquid and save to make split-pea soup. Discard onion stuck with cloves. Place the corned beef in a large, deep serving dish and arrange the cooked vegetables around it. Add the hot beets to the dish and garnish meat and vegetables with the parsley.

Makes 8 to 10 servings.

CORNED BEEF, SLOW-COOKED
10 to 12 hours

4 lb. corned beef
Water to cover
1 medium onion, peeled,
  stuck with 4 whole
  cloves

2 cloves garlic, peeled,
  minced
1 bay leaf
½ tsp. dried thyme
1 large carrot, scraped, sliced

To Cook: Place all ingredients in the slow-pot; cover and cook on Low for 10 to 12 hours.

Makes 8 to 10 servings.

CORNED BEEF AND CABBAGE
10 to 12 hours

Cook corned beef as in Corned Beef, Slow-Cooked (above). When it is done, wash a fresh green cabbage and cut it into slender wedges. Remove the toughest portions of the core from each wedge. Remove beef from the cooking liquid and keep warm. Turn the heat to High, and when the stock is simmering, drop in the cabbage wedges and cook until tender—15 to 20 minutes or more, depending on the wedges' thickness. Drain well. Serve the corned beef in a deep serving dish with the cabbage wedges around it.

Makes 8 to 10 servings.

CHITTERLINGS
10 to 12 hours, or more

Chitterlings are part of the interior workings (intestines) of a pig, and in the Deep South they are part of the soul-food picture. Soak them 24 hours in cold water before using. Slow-cooking is the ideal way to do them.

10 *lb. chitterlings*	1 *stalk celery, with*
1 *clove garlic, peeled*	*leaves*
3 *large onions, peeled*	2 *Tbs. wine vinegar*
1 *bay leaf*	1 *hot red pepper,*
½ *tsp. each dried clove,*	*chopped*
thyme, mace and allspice	*Cold water to cover*

To Cook: Wash the chitterlings under cold running water and remove excess fat. Place all the ingredients in the slow-cooker. Cover and cook on Low for 10 to 12 hours. Drain well before serving.

Makes 4 to 6 servings.

TRIPE
8 to 10 hours

Tripe is an animal's inner stomach, and it is usually partly cooked when you buy it. It's not one of my favorites, but it is considered a delicacy in France and many other places.

2 lb. fresh tripe, in 2-inch
   squares
Boiling water to cover
2 Tbs. salt
2 Tbs. vegetable oil
1 medium onion, peeled,
   minced
2 medium cloves garlic,
   peeled, crushed

1 can (14 oz.) whole tomatoes
2 green peppers, seeded,
   chopped
6 peppercorns
½ tsp. dried thyme
1 tsp. dried oregano
1 bay leaf
1 tsp. salt
⅛ tsp. pepper

To Cook: Put the tripe in the slow-cooker; cover with boiling water; add 2 tablespoons salt. Cover and cook on Low for 8 to 10 hours.

Before Serving: Drain the tripe. In a large skillet, over medium heat, warm the oil and sauté the remaining ingredients until the green pepper is cooked through. Add the well-drained tripe; heat thoroughly. Taste and add salt and pepper if needed.

Makes 6 to 8 servings.

PART THREE

SLOW-COOK DISHES FOR PARTIES

Chapter 6

Gourmet Foods with the Help of a Crockery Cooker

THE SLOW-COOKER IS a real help when you are entertaining. It is true that some casseroles shouldn't be cooked for hours on end and that many luxury foods are best fast-cooked—lobster, for instance, and fine fillets of beef. Nevertheless, loads of things good for parties can be done in a slow-cooker, and it can do some of the preliminary work for many other dishes and free you from pot watching.

This chapter contains main-dish recipes. You'll find that many other slow-cooked foods are fine for entertaining. Several soups, vegetable dishes, and desserts that are easy to make in the slow-pot are excellent party fare.

CASSEROLES

These are about the most convenient foods to serve at parties. Almost any dish that has meat and vegetables in a sauce is called a casserole. However, there are three types of casserole. Some include luxury foods that should be cooked quickly. Others are best when the meat is cooked slowly and the vegetables quickly, and they are combined in a sauce made with the meat's cooking liquid. Blanquette de Veau (page 152) is one of these. For the third type, all the ingredients cook together, and the sauce is made just before the meal is served. You can make all three types in your slow-cooker.

The casserole recipes here are a cross-section of dishes I can make well in my slow-cooker. For some of them, I combine everything, cook it all day, and have very little more to do before the dish is served. For others, I use the slow-cooker to get the meat and cooking liquid ready during the day and then spend up to an hour finishing the dish and preparing the rest of the food.

As you work with the recipes here, you'll see how you can adapt some of your party casseroles to slow-cooking.

BUFFET DISHES

Nothing sets off a buffet quite as glamorously as an aspic—shimmering jellied meat or fish stock with wonderful tidbits imprisoned in its molded form. Aspics made with gelatin are popular and quick to make, but they can't touch the flavor of a true aspic made with cooking stock. True aspics take time, but with a slow-cooker they are simple to make, and the result is far superior to the hurry-up kind.

Aspics not only are beautiful, but are among the most economical of dress-up dishes because they can be made with bony meat odds and ends. Veal Knuckle in Aspic (page 151), made with veal knuckles, and Brandied Chicken Aspic (page 159), made with boiling fowl, are examples. Using any of the three basic aspic recipes here (meat, chicken, and fish) to make jellied stock, you can concoct all sorts of fancy aspics. The recipe for Shrimp in Aspic (page 169) shows how jelly from slow-cooked fish oddments can produce an economical but impressive dish. Chicken-Neck Aspic (page 159) is one of my poor-day recipes. I get a kick out of using chicken necks to make something really nice.

Tureens, daubes, headcheeses, and pâtés are variations on the aspic theme. A tureen relies on a little jellied cooking liquid—usually reduced—to set the meat, but it also includes fat. This is a pretty mold to turn out on a bed of parsley or watercress, and it's wonderful as a cocktail spread for crackers or as an elegant sandwich filling. The ingredients for tureens and pâtés, like those for many of the aspics, are budget savers—very welcome these days.

FOODS FROM OTHER LANDS

One of the fun things is serving party guests out-of-the-ordinary foods. By now, things like Coq au Vin (page 163) and Boeuf Bourguignon (page 144) are so commonplace in even moderately good restaurants that we take them for granted. But some dishes seen only occasionally in elegant eating places also can be made in the slow-cooker. One that must be slow-cooked is the Italian specialty Osso Bucco (page 153), cross-sections of veal-shank bone cooked so the marrow can be eaten. Served with Gremolata Sauce, it's a conversation piece. Another dish that can be made in a slow-cooker, though it needn't be, is Dolmas (page 165), stuffed vine leaves. If you look over my small collection of slow-cook specialties, it will remind you of other things that might be easier to handle at party time if slow-cooked.

FREEZE-AHEAD FOODS FOR PARTIES

Another way my slow-cooker makes entertaining simpler is by preparing foods I can freeze. You can, of course, successfully freeze many casseroles. However, for a casserole to be fine enough for a party, the vegetables must not be frozen. In other words, you can slow-cook and freeze any casserole that doesn't include vegetables (except those for flavoring).

You can also make ahead and freeze stocks. And if you are fond of Oriental cooking, you can slow-cook chopped pork and freeze cup-size lots, to be used later in stir-fry dishes. I once wrote a cookbook that is essentially Chinese—*Oriental Cooking the Fast Wok Way*—and I was always running out of the ½ or 1 cup of chopped pork so many recipes called for. Mornings when I have a little time to spare, I set stock and sometimes an inexpensive pork cut to simmering in the slow-cooker, and when I get home at night, I measure ½- or 1-cup lots into little plastic freezer containers and label them. They're a wonderful resource if you like to entertain with Chinese food at the drop of a hat.

BEEF DISHES

DAUBE GLACÉE, CREOLE STYLE
Overnight plus 10 to 12 hours

A gourmet dish for very special buffets, Daube Glacée is beef in a delicious aspic jelly made from bones and pig's feet. A slow-cooker makes the big job of preparing this more appealing, since you can do half the cooking overnight and finish the daube the next day. The pig's feet are discarded by some cooks, but my family enjoys them warm and served with cold Vinaigrette Sauce (page 123), bread, and a tossed green salad.

6 Tbs. vegetable oil	4 sprigs fresh parsley
4 lb. beef shinbones, in 1-inch pieces	Water to cover (about 2 quarts)
4 lb. veal shinbones, in 1-inch pieces	4 lb. beef bottom round or top round, cut in half
3 medium onions, peeled, chopped	3 medium carrots, scraped, grated
2 medium stalks celery, chopped, with leaves	3 large cloves garlic, peeled, minced
2 large carrots, peeled, chopped	1 tsp. cayenne pepper
2 lb. pig's feet (front feet if possible)	2 tsp. salt
	1 lemon, washed, dried
	Fresh sprigs parsley

To Cook: The night before, in your largest skillet, over medium-high heat, heat the oil and sauté the bones, stirring often, until well browned all over. Remove bones to the slow-pot. Pour off the fat, leaving a little in the skillet, and brown the onion, celery, and chopped carrots lightly, stirring constantly. Add to the slow-cooker with the pig's feet, washed and dried, 4 parsley sprigs, and the water. Cover and cook on Low overnight, or 10 to 12 hours.

Remove and discard bones; pig's feet may be eaten or discarded. Strain the stock through a sieve and return to the slow-pot. Press vegetables through the sieve into the stock and discard any pulp too coarse to go through the sieve. Skim a little fat from the stock; put it in a medium-large skillet and, over medium-high heat, brown the beef on all sides. Place the beef in the slow-cooker. Cover and cook on Low for 10 to 12 hours.

Remove the beef; let stock and beef cool. Then, with 2 forks, pull the beef into shreds about ¼-inch wide and 2 inches long. Turn them into a large bowl; add the grated carrots, garlic, cayenne pepper, and 2 teaspoons salt, and toss well. Cover and cool in refrigerator. Skim fat from the stock and refrigerate stock until the fat on its surface sets. Remove and discard all the fat. Pour the stock into a saucepan and soften it over low heat. Add salt to flavor, if needed. Pour a ¼-inch layer of stock into 2 (9-by-5-by-3-inch) bread-loaf pans; refrigerate until it has jelled. Cut the lemon into 6 thin, round slices. Dip them into the soft stock and arrange 3 slices in each pan. Let chill until jelled. Pour remaining stock over the chilled beef mixture; mix well; then ladle into the loaf pans. Cover with foil and refrigerate overnight, or at least 12 hours, before serving.

Before Serving: Warm the pan bottoms briefly in warm water, and unmold on serving platters. Garnish with parsley sprigs.

Makes 2 (9-by-5-by-3-inch) daubes, enough for 10 to 12 servings.

BOEUF EN DAUBE
8 to 10 hours

This is the French version of braised beef as I do it in a slow-pot. It is marinated in the refrigerator 3 to 4 days before cooking, so you must do some advance planning. Use a strong, very dry red wine for the marinade—such as Mountain Red.

3 to 4 lb. top or bottom round
    or chuck shoulder pot
    roast
2 cups dry red wine
4 medium cloves garlic,
    peeled, minced
1 cup peeled, sliced onion,
    chopped
1 cup peeled, sliced carrots
1 Tbs. salt
2 bay leaves

4 whole cloves
6 peppercorns
½ tsp. dried thyme
2 cardamom seeds, peeled
4 tomatoes, fresh or canned,
    drained, chopped
3 Tbs. olive oil or vegetable oil
¼ cup all-purpose flour
Salt
1 cup beef stock or bouillon, hot

To Cook: Marinate the beef in a mixture of the wine, garlic, onion, carrots, 1 tablespoon salt, bay leaf, cloves, peppercorns, thyme, cardamom, and tomatoes in a large bowl, covered, in the refrigerator for 3 to 4 days. Remove meat from the marinade and tie the herbs in a small cheesecloth bag. Drain the vegetables, reserving the marinade. Under the broiler, at medium-high heat, brown the meat on all sides, turning often. Meanwhile, in a medium-large skillet, over medium heat, heat the oil and brown the vegetables lightly, stirring often. Add the flour, turn down the heat, and stir until the flour is a rich brown. Remove from the heat and at once stir in reserved marinade, beating quickly to make the sauce smooth. Return to the heat; add ½ teaspoon or more salt, and, still stirring, bring to a simmer. Turn vegetables and sauce into the slow-pot; add the browned meat, the cheesecloth bag, and the hot stock. Cover and cook on Low for 8 to 10 hours.

Before Serving: If the sauce seems too thin, turn it into a small saucepan and simmer until reduced to a thicker consistency. Taste the sauce and add salt if needed.

Makes 6 to 8 servings.

CARBONNADES À LA FLAMANDE
8 to 10 hours

This is a Belgian dish, beef stewed in beer, and world famous. Serve with it boiled young carrots and boiled quartered potatoes garnished with finely minced parsley. As a substitute for the fresh onions called for here, you may prefer to use ½ cup onion flakes soaked in ⅓ cup water for 10 minutes.

3 *lb. boneless chuck roast, cut into 2-inch cubes*
½ *Tbs. vegetable oil*
½ *Tbs. salt*
1 *tsp. pepper*
⅛ *cup butter or margarine*
4 *cups peeled, sliced onion*
2 *large cloves garlic, peeled and minced*
1 *can (12 oz.) light beer*

2 *Tbs. light-brown sugar, firmly packed*
1½ *Tbs. salt*
2 *large sprigs parsley, or 1 Tbs. dried parsley flakes*
1 *large bay leaf*
½ *tsp. dried thyme*
1½ *Tbs. cornstarch*
2 *Tbs. white vinegar*

To Cook: In a large skillet, over medium heat, sauté the meat in the oil until well browned on all sides. Remove the meat to a bowl and season with ½ tablespoon salt and the pepper. In the same skillet, melt the butter and sauté the onion, stirring often, until medium brown. A minute before the onion is done, stir in the garlic. Turn the onion and garlic into the slow-cooker. Add the browned meat and juices from the bowl. To the still-hot skillet add the beer,

sugar, 1½ tablespoons salt, the parsley, bay leaf, and thyme. Scrape up the pan juices and turn into the cooker. Cover and cook on Low for 8 to 10 hours.

Before Serving: Pour the cooking liquid into a measuring cup. If you have more than 2 cups of liquid, cook in a skillet, over high heat, until reduced. Thicken these 2 cups of sauce by simmering with cornstarch dissolved in vinegar for 3 to 4 minutes, stirring constantly. Place the onion in the serving dish; set the meat cubes on top, and spoon the sauce over all.

Makes 6 to 8 servings.

BOILED BEEF WITH GREEN SAUCE
5 to 7 hours

This is a crockery-cooker variation on Bolliti Misti, an Italian dish for those who love the flavor of anchovy and capers. The sauce is made in the blender just before serving.

2 *lb. boneless bottom round of beef, cut into* 1½*-inch cubes*	1 *large leek, chopped*
	1 *tsp. salt*
1 *lb. boneless veal*	½ *tsp. dried thyme*
10 *Italian sausages, hot or sweet*	½ *tsp. dried marjoram*
	⅛ *cup water*
1 *to* 2 *lb. broiler chicken, quartered*	½ *cup chopped fresh parsley*
	2 *anchovy fillets*
1 *large onion, peeled*	1 *tsp. capers*
1 *clove garlic, peeled and minced*	1 *medium clove garlic, peeled and halved*
2 *large carrots, peeled and coarsely chopped*	½ *cup olive oil*
	1 *Tbs. strained lemon juice*

To Cook: Place the beef, veal, sausages, chicken, onion, minced garlic, carrots, leek, salt, thyme, and marjoram in the slow-cooker and pour the water over them. Cover and cook on Low for 5 to 7 hours.

Before Serving: Just before serving, combine the remaining ingredients in the blender and blend on low until the sauce is smooth. Turn the meats and cooking juices into a deep serving dish and serve the green sauce in a sauce boat.

Makes 8 to 10 servings.

BOEUF BOURGUIGNON IN A NOODLE RING
8 to 10 hours

A treat served in a noodle ring. To make the ring, just cook a 12-ounce package of broad noodles as directed on the package and turn them into a 2-quart ring mold. As they cool, they'll jell into the ring shape. You unmold it and fill the center with the Boeuf Bourguignon. Make this with dry white wine, too; it's great!

¼ *lb. strip fatty pork, cut into ½-inch pieces, or butter*

4 *lb. boneless chuck or round beef, cut into 2- to 2½-inch cubes*

3 *Tbs. all-purpose flour*

1½ *cups dry red wine*

½ *cup beef bouillon, or ½ cup water with 1 beef bouillon cube*

1 *tsp. salt*

½ *tsp. pepper*

1 *bay leaf*

½ *tsp. ground thyme*

½ *tsp. ground savory*

2 *Tbs. butter or margarine*

1 *small onion, peeled and minced*

1 *lb. mushrooms, wiped clean, caps and stems separated and cut on a slant*

3 *cloves garlic, peeled and minced*

4 *sprigs parsley, chopped*

To Cook: In a large skillet, over medium heat, sauté the pork to render the fat. Remove and reserve the pork bits. Raise the heat to high and thoroughly brown the beef pieces, a few at a time. As they finish cooking, lift them into the slow-cooker. Remove skillet from heat, and stir the flour into the drippings, working rapidly. Stirring all the time, add the wine and the bouillon. The sauce should be as thick as heavy cream; if it isn't, simmer a little longer. Add the salt, pepper, bay leaf, thyme, savory, and pork bits. Make sure you have scraped up all the pan juices and turn the sauce into the cooker. Cover and cook on Low for about 6 hours, or until almost tender.

Before Serving: In a medium skillet, over medium-high heat, melt the butter and sauté the onion until translucent. With a slotted spoon, lift the onion bits into the slow-cooker. Sauté the mushrooms in the skillet, stirring, for 2 minutes. Add the garlic and parsley; cook, stirring, for 1 minute. Skim any fat from cooking liquid in the slow-cooker and spoon a little liquid into the skillet. Scrape up the pan juices; then scrape mushrooms and juices into the cooker. Cover and cook on Low for 1 or 2 hours.

Makes 10 to 12 servings.

FLANK STEAK WITH SABLAISE STUFFING
8 to 10 hours

The difference between this and Flank-Steak Pot Roast (page 67) is in the stuffing. Follow all the directions for the Flank-Steak Pot Roast, but substitute the following stuffing.

3 *Tbs. butter or margarine*	1 *whole egg, slightly beaten*
½ *lb. mushrooms, minced fine*	1 *tsp. grated lemon rind*
1 *large clove garlic, peeled*	*Salt*
and minced	*Pepper*
1 *cup minced onion*	*Ground thyme*
½ *cup minced parsley*	

To Cook: In a large skillet, over medium heat, melt the butter and sauté the mushrooms for about 2 minutes. Add the garlic and the onion and sauté for 1 or 2 minutes—until onion becomes translucent. Add the parsley and sauté, stirring constantly, about 1 minute, or until parsley turns dark green. Immediately stir in the egg; it acts as a binder only and shouldn't cook more than 1 minute —just enough so the white is congealed and is no longer transparent. Remove skillet at once from heat and add salt, pepper, and ground thyme to suit your taste.

Makes 4 or 5 servings.

BEEF À L'ESTOUFFADE
10 to 12 hours

This dish is associated with the romance of French peasant life. It is served at family dinners right from the cooking pot and accompanied by big chunks of crusty French bread. Since it cooks for a very long time, it's a good way to prepare lesser cuts of meat. The original recipe calls for canned truffles. Since truffles are hard to come by and worth their weight in gold, I use a mixture of mushroom stems and grated lemon rind to approximate truffle flavoring.

½ cup minced fresh mushroom stems

½ tsp. grated lemon rind

1 large clove garlic, peeled and sliced

2 pork hocks

6 small carrots, scraped and sliced

½ lb. mushrooms, wiped and stemmed

1 green pepper, seeded, peeled, and thinly sliced

4 oz. pitted green olives

1 large bay leaf

¼ tsp. ground thyme

4 whole cloves

4 peppercorns

2 tsp. salt

1 large sprig parsley, or ½ tsp. dried parsley flakes

4 lb. top round of beef, cut in a square

2 cups dry red wine

To Cook: In a small bowl, preferably one with a rough surface, such as wood, mash the mushroom stems, lemon rind, and garlic to make a paste. Place the pork hocks, carrots, mushroom caps, green pepper, olives, bay leaf, thyme, cloves, peppercorns, salt, and parsley in the slow-cooker. Set the beef on top and cover with the mushroom paste. Pour the wine into the cooker. Cover and cook on Low for 10 to 12 hours.

Before Serving: The sauce will be rather thin. If you would like it richer, pour it into a small skillet and simmer until thickened.

Makes 10 to 12 servings.

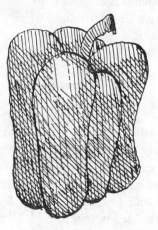

PAUPIETTES DE BOEUF
5 to 7 hours

This takes time to prepare before it is ready for the slow-cooker. It's a really delicious and distinctly different French gourmet dish, nice with Beaujolais wine.

2 Tbs. butter or margarine

2 medium onions, peeled and finely minced

½ lb. fresh mushrooms, wiped and minced

1 Tbs. grated lemon rind

2 Tbs. unflavored bread crumbs

½ cup minced fresh parsley

1 tsp. salt

¼ tsp. pepper

2 eggs, slightly beaten

1 lb. bottom round of beef, cut into 16 thin slices, each 4 inches square

Salt

Pepper

Ground thyme

All-purpose flour

4 Tbs. butter or margarine

1 cup warm water

2 medium cloves garlic, peeled and crushed

2 Tbs. prepared mustard, preferably Maille or white Dijon

To Cook: In a heavy skillet, over medium-low heat, melt 2 tablespoons of butter and sauté the onion and mushrooms until onion is translucent. Stir in the lemon rind, bread crumbs, parsley, 1 teaspoon salt, and ¼ teaspoon pepper. When the parsley has wilted—about 1 minute after you add it to the skillet—quickly stir in the eggs to bind the mixture and remove skillet from the heat at once. Set aside. With a rolling pin or a wooden mallet, flatten the beef pieces until each is very thin and about twice its original size. As you finish each piece, season it with a little salt, pepper, and a pinch of thyme. At the widest end of each beef slice, place 1 teaspoon of breadcrumb mixture from the skillet. Roll up the meat, sausage-shape, and secure it with a wooden toothpick through the center. Roll each piece in flour. In a very large skillet, over medium-high heat, melt 4 tablespoons of butter and brown the pieces of beef. As you finish, place them in the slow-cooker. Pour the water into the skillet; scrape up the pan juices and add. Turn the sauce into the cooker. Cover and cook on Low for about 5 hours.

Before Serving: About half an hour before serving, mix the garlic and mustard into the sauce around the beef; cover; turn heat to High, and cook for 30 minutes. If the sauce seems less flavorful than you like, about 5 minutes before serving add a dab of prepared mustard and a little salt. If the sauce seems thin, leave the cover off during this second cooking period.

Makes 6 to 8 servings.

SHORT RIBS OF BEEF PARISIENNE
8 to 10 hours

Short ribs are delicious if they are cooked slowly and at length—and they're among the less expensive cuts of beef.

2 Tbs. vegetable oil	1 cup fresh mushrooms, wiped
2 tsp. salt	and sliced thin
4 lb. short ribs of beef, cut	⅛ tsp. salt
into 3-inch pieces	1 cup dairy sour cream
½ tsp. black pepper	2 Tbs. minced fresh chervil or
3 cups sliced onion	parsley
¼ cup water	

To Cook: Set a large skillet over medium-high heat. When it is sizzling hot, sprinkle it with 2 teaspoons salt, and at once add the meat pieces. Brown well on all sides. Season the meat with pepper, and turn into a bowl. Add the oil to the skillet and sauté the onion for 2 to 3 minutes; then turn into the slow-cooker. Swirl the water in the still-hot skillet and scrape up the pan juices. Turn into the slow-cooker with the meat. Cover and cook on Low for 8 to 10 hours, or until the meat is very tender.

Before Serving: In a medium skillet, over medium-high heat, sauté the mushroom slices in 1 or 2 tablespoons of fat skimmed from the cooking liquid; stir constantly. In about 5 minutes, the slices will be tender and the moisture will have evaporated. Add ⅛ teaspoon salt. Arrange the short ribs on a heated serving platter and turn the cooking liquid into the mushroom skillet. Simmer, scraping up the pan juices, until the sauce is as thick as heavy cream. Remove skillet from the heat. Stir in the sour cream; return to the heat just long enough to thoroughly warm the sauce. Then pour over the meat and sprinkle with chervil.

Makes 6 to 8 servings.

GOURMET'S CURRY
6 to 8 hours

You need lots of Indian cooking spices for this version of curry. Wonderful with rice or noodles. For a very rich curry, use 1 cup evaporated milk instead of the bouillon.

1 *large onion, peeled and chopped*	1 *Tbs. ground coriander*
1 *large clove garlic, peeled and minced*	½ *tsp. ground turmeric*
	½ *tsp. ground cumin*
3 *Tbs. butter, margarine, or vegetable oil*	½ *tsp. red-pepper flakes*
	⅛ *tsp. ground ginger*
1 *lb. bottom round of beef, cut in 1-inch cubes*	2 *cups beef bouillon, or 2 cups water with Steero beef granules*

To Cook: In a large skillet, over medium-high heat, sauté the onion and garlic in the butter until the onion is beginning to turn dark gold. Add the meat cubes and spices and sauté until the cubes are brown on all sides. Turn the meat into the slow-cooker. Add the bouillon to the skillet, scrape up the pan juices, and turn the sauce into the cooker. Cover and cook on Low for 6 to 8 hours, or until the meat is tender.

Before Serving: If the sauce seems a little thin, turn it into a skillet and cook, over high heat, for a few minutes until it thickens. Taste and add salt if needed.

Makes 4 to 6 servings.

COCIDO
8 to 10 hours

This is an adaptation of a recipe for Spanish Cocido, which is best made with Spanish olive oil, if you have it. It is made with chickpeas (garbanzos), leftover ham, and chicken parts—a splendid dish when economy is an objective. The beans must soak overnight before cooking. You can buy canned garbanzos in many areas. If these are used, do not add the quart of water called for below.

¼ cup olive or vegetable oil

2 lb. boneless stew beef, cut into 1½-inch cubes

1 quart water

1 lb. dried chickpeas, soaked overnight

3 large onions, peeled and sliced

2 medium cloves garlic, peeled and minced

2 large tomatoes, stemmed, peeled, and quartered

½ cup minced fresh parsley

1 cup small cubes leftover ham

1 ham bone

4 chicken wings, or 2 wings plus neck and backbone

2 tsp. salt

½ tsp. pepper

4 medium carrots, peeled and diced

To Cook: In a large skillet, over high heat, heat the oil and brown the beef on all sides. Lift into a bowl. Pour 1 cup of the water into the skillet while it is still hot and scrape up the pan juices. Turn this liquid into the slow-cooker, along with remaining ingredients and top with the beef. Cover and cook on Low for 8 to 10 hours, or until the chickpeas are tender. If they have absorbed all the liquid (how they cook depends on their age and other variables) and aren't tender, add ½ cup water and continue to cook. Usually there's plenty of rich sauce when the cooking is done.

Before Serving: Remove and discard the ham bone. Dice the meat from the chicken bones into the Cocido and discard the bones. If the sauce seems thin, pour it into a small skillet and simmer, over medium-high heat, stirring, until thickened.

Makes 8 servings.

VEAL DISHES

BASIC MEAT ASPIC
8 to 10 hours, or more

With this recipe, you can make the flavorful meat jelly that is the base of aspics. Veal makes the nicest meat aspic, to my mind. You can add to it diced meats of all kinds, hard-cooked eggs, canned asparagus, and decorate with sliced olives, parboiled slices of celery, green pepper, carrots, cucumbers. With green onions, boiled limp, you can make all sorts of designs and graceful patterns. Since the purpose of this recipe is to render enough gelatin from the bones for the cooking liquid to set when chilled, you can hardly overcook it. If you cook it overnight, in the morning you can chill the liquid and during the day finish the aspic dish. Veal aspics are nice served with lemon wedges.

1 *or* 2 *veal knuckles, cut up*	¼ *tsp. black pepper*
½ *medium onion, peeled*	⅛ *tsp. dried thyme*
½ *carrot, peeled, sliced*	1 *small bay leaf*
6 *stalks celery, with leaves*	2 *large sprigs parsley*
1 *tsp. salt*	*Water just to cover*

To Cook: Combine all ingredients in the slow-pot; cover and cook on High. When the mixture begins to boil, quickly skim away the froth and cover again. When it boils again, skim once more. The more you skim, the clearer the jelly. Turn the heat to Low; cover and cook 8 to 10 hours. Taste the broth and add salt and pepper if needed. If it still seems a little tasteless, boil it down to intensify the flavor.

Before Serving: Strain the cooking liquid through 4 thicknesses of wet cheesecloth to make it as clear as possible; then chill it in the refrigerator. Discard the bones. Save the meat to include in the aspic, or serve it hot in a little stock. When the stock has set, remove any fat congealed on it.

Makes 6 to 8 servings.

VEAL KNUCKLE IN ASPIC
4 to 6 hours

When you can find a veal knuckle, take time to make this unusual aspic, a delicious, delicate dish for a buffet or a gala summer luncheon. Serve slices of crusty bread and butter with it.

1 *veal knuckle, cut into 3 or 4 pieces*
1 *lb. veal shoulder*
1 *medium onion, peeled, sliced*
6 *peppercorns*
2 *bay leaves*
1 *tsp. ground thyme*
2 *tsp. salt*
1½ *quarts cold water*
2 *tsp. finely minced fresh parsley*
1 *hard-cooked egg, sliced in rounds*
¼ *cup pimento-stuffed olives, sliced in rounds*
1 *lemon, cut in wedges*
1 *bunch fresh parsley*

To Cook: Place the knuckle pieces, veal, onion, peppercorns, bay leaves, thyme, salt, and water in the slow-cooker. Cover and cook on Low for 4 to 6 hours, or until the meat is very tender.

Remove the meat, discard the bones, and put the meat through a food chopper, using the medium blade. Or, with 2 forks, pull the meat into fine shreds. Strain the cooking liquid and in a medium saucepan, over high heat, boil it down to about 2½ to 3 cups. To ½ cup of the liquid, add the minced parsley and chill in the freezer. Pour into a 1½- or 2-quart mold; refrigerate until slightly thickened. Garnish with egg and olive slices. I use the egg slices as the centers of daisies and the olive slices as petals. Pour a little more of the cooking liquid over the garnish; refrigerate until it sets. Combine remaining liquid with the meat and turn into the mold. Cover with foil; refrigerate until set, or overnight. Serve with lemon wedges on a bed of parsley.

Makes 6 to 8 servings.

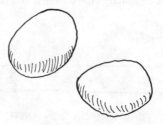

BLANQUETTE DE VEAU
4 to 6 hours

Veal is a luxury meat and not one, as a rule, that benefits from lots and lots of cooking. However, you can make this veal casserole in your slow-cooker. The second step—cooking the onions and mushrooms and making the sauce after the veal and stock are cooked—takes about half an hour.

2 *lb. boned veal shoulder,* *cut in 2-inch pieces*	1 *tsp. salt*
1 *quart water*	¼ *cup butter or margarine*
1 *small onion, peeled and* *stuck with 4 whole cloves*	1 *lb. small white onions,* *peeled (about 15)*
5 *carrots, scraped and* *quartered*	½ *lb. small fresh mushrooms,* *wiped and stemmed*
1 *bay leaf*	2 *Tbs. butter or margarine*
⅛ *tsp. dried thyme*	¼ *cup all-purpose flour*
½ *cup diced celery*	2 *egg yolks*
4 *peppercorns*	2 *Tbs. strained lemon juice*
	1 *Tbs. minced parsley*

To Cook: In the slow-cooker, place the veal, water, onion stuck with cloves, carrots, bay leaf, thyme, celery, peppercorns, and salt. Cover and cook on Low for 4 to 6 hours.

Before Serving: When the veal has finished cooking, or about ¾ hour before you intend to serve dinner, melt ¼ cup butter in medium skillet; turn the onions into the butter and cover. Simmer at low heat for 15 minutes, or until the onions are cooked through. Don't let them color (they will if the heat is too high). Remove to a warm serving dish. In the same skillet, sauté the mushroom caps, uncovered, for 5 minutes. Then scoop them into the serving dish. Melt 2 tablespoons butter in the skillet, over low heat; stir in the flour. Measure 3½ cups of the cooking liquid into the skillet, and stir quickly to make a smooth sauce. Place the egg yolks in a cup; beat slightly; mix in the lemon juice, and stir in ¼ cup of the hot sauce. Stir this mixture into the skillet of sauce. Heat, without boiling, for 3 or 4 minutes. Lift the veal and vegetables from the slow-cooker, drain well, and turn into the serving dish. Pour the sauce over the meat; garnish with parsley and serve. If you reheat this dish at any point, don't let it boil.

Makes 6 to 8 servings.

OSSO BUCCO
8 to 10 hours

This is best when cooked slowly until the meat falls off the bones, and a slow-cooker is the best utensil to make it in. Since the delicacy here is the marrow, select young veal shanks. They should weigh about 1½ pounds each. Serve Gremolata Sauce on the side—if your family approves of garlic.

¼ cup all-purpose flour
½ tsp. salt
¼ tsp. pepper
6 lb. veal shanks, cut
    into 2-inch pieces
½ cup vegetable oil
1 medium onion, peeled
    and minced
1 medium carrot, scraped
    and minced
1 stalk celery, minced

2 cloves garlic, peeled
    and minced
½ cup dry white wine
½ cup beef bouillon,
    or ½ cup water with
    1 beef bouillon cube
1 can (12 oz.) whole tomatoes,
    drained and chopped
½ tsp. dried basil
½ tsp. dried rosemary
Gremolata Sauce
    (below; optional)

To Cook: Mix the flour, salt, and pepper in a large bowl and toss the veal shanks in the mixture until well coated. In a large skillet, heat half the oil over medium-high heat. A few pieces at a time, brown the veal on all sides until deeply colored and crusty-looking. In another skillet, over medium heat, sauté the onion, carrot, celery, and garlic in remaining oil 3 to 4 minutes. Turn the vegetables into the slow-cooker. Arrange the veal on top; stand it so the marrow will stay in the bone when it begins to tenderize. Pour the wine into one of the skillets and scrape up the pan juices. Pour the bouillon into the other skillet, and scrape up the pan juices. Pour both over the ingredients in the slow-cooker and add the tomatoes, basil, and rosemary. Cover and cook on Low for 8 to 10 hours.

Before Serving: If the sauce seems thin, simmer in a skillet until thickened. Check seasoning and add salt and pepper if needed.

Makes 6 to 8 servings.

GREMOLATA SAUCE

6 cloves garlic, peeled
    and minced

2 Tbs. grated lemon peel
½ cup chopped fresh parsley

Combine all ingredients and mix well. Serve on the side with Osso Bucco.

Makes enough for 6 to 8 servings.

PORK DISHES

CASSOULET
20 to 24 hours

A French version of baked beans, this is a wonderful dish for a party. Cook the beans overnight in the slow-cooker; then you can begin to put the dish together in the morning.

4 oz. salt pork
4 cups dried white beans
12 cups water
1 bay leaf
1 tsp. dried thyme
4 peppercorns
2 medium carrots, scraped and halved
1 medium onion, peeled and stuck with 8 whole cloves
2 tsp. salt
2 Tbs. vegetable oil
2 lb. boned pork loin, cut into 2-inch cubes (save the bones)

2 lb. boned shoulder of lamb, cut into 2-inch cubes (save the bones)
2 onions, peeled and chopped
2 cloves garlic, peeled and minced
1 cup canned tomato purée
1 big garlic sausage
Salt and pepper
1 cup beef bouillon, or 1 cup water and 1½ beef bouillon cubes
1 cup unflavored bread crumbs
Freshly ground black pepper

To Cook: The night before the dish is to be cooked, cover the salt pork with water; bring to a boil and simmer for 5 minutes; then drain and dice. Place in the slow-cooker, along with the beans, 12 cups water, bay leaf, thyme, peppercorns, carrots, onion stuck with cloves, and 2 teaspoons salt. Cover and cook on Low for 12 to 14 hours.

In the morning, remove the bay leaf, peppercorns, onion, and any remaining water. In the oil in a large skillet over medium-high heat, brown the pork and lamb cubes and the bones. Stir in the chopped onion and garlic and cook 2 minutes. Stir in the tomato purée. Prick the sausage all over with a fork and brown in another skillet. Remove the sausage to a paper towel and cut into ½-inch slices. Place the bones in the slow-cooker. Combine the meat cubes and cooked beans. Taste and add salt and pepper as needed. In the cooker, alternate layers of bean-and-meat mixture with sausage slices, ending with sausage slices. Pour the bouillon over all and top with bread crumbs and a grinding of fresh pepper. Cover and cook on Low for 8 to 10 hours. Remove the bones before serving.

Makes 12 to 16 servings.

PORK CHOPS, FRENCH STYLE
8 to 10 hours

This can stand for hours before being served. Fine for a big family meal and good enough to serve at a party. A take-along dish most people really enjoy. If your slow-pot is small, halve the recipe.

10 *shoulder pork chops*	4 *medium cloves garlic,*
1½ *tsp. salt*	*peeled*
¼ *tsp. pepper*	1 *bay leaf*
10 *new potatoes, scraped*	½ *tsp. dried thyme*
5 *large carrots, scraped,*	½ *tsp. ground cloves*
quartered	3 *Tbs. all-purpose flour*
5 *medium onions, peeled,*	*(optional)*
quartered	*Salt and pepper*
¾ *cup dry white vermouth*	2 *Tbs. minced parsley*

To Cook: Cut extra fat from the chops and use it to grease a large skillet. Heat the skillet on medium-high heat and brown the chops quickly on both sides. Season them with 1½ teaspoons salt and ¼ teaspoon pepper. Place the potatoes in the slow-cooker. Arrange the chops and carrot and onion quarters in layers on the potatoes. Pour the vermouth into the skillet and scrape up the pan juices. Add the garlic, bay leaf, thyme, and cloves and pour over the cooker contents. Cover and cook on Low for 8 to 10 hours, or until the meat is very tender.

Before Serving: Place the chops and vegetables in a deep serving dish. If you wish to thicken the sauce, skim 2 tablespoons fat from the cooking liquid into a medium skillet, over moderate heat. Stir in flour to make a smooth paste. Pour in the cooking liquid, beat until smooth, and simmer a few minutes. Add salt and pepper, if needed, to thin or thickened sauce and pour over the meat and vegetables. Garnish with parsley.

Makes 8 to 10 servings.

STUFFED CABBAGE CATALAN
5 to 7 hours

Leftover chicken or ham is used to stuff the cabbage, and the whole is cooked in white wine or, if you want to go overboard, in champagne. You will get a different flavor but an excellent dish by substituting light beer for the wine. Use College Inn chicken bouillon or bouillon made with Steero granules.

1 *medium leafy green cabbage*	1 *medium onion, peeled and sliced*
½ *lb. fresh ground pork*	4 *carrots, scraped and diced*
½ *cup minced cooked chicken or ham*	1 *bay leaf*
1 *medium onion, peeled and minced*	½ *tsp. dried thyme*
	4 *whole cloves*
1 *tsp. salt*	8 *whole peppercorns*
¼ *tsp. pepper*	½ *cup dry white wine or champagne*
⅛ *tsp. ground allspice*	½ *cup chicken bouillon, or ½ cup water with chicken Steero granules*
2 *slices white bread, crusts removed, soaked in ½ cup milk*	

To Cook: Place the cabbage in boiling water for a minute. Drain and let cool. In a bowl, mix the pork, chicken or ham, minced onion, salt, pepper, allspice, and bread. Place the cabbage on a cutting board and part the leaves gently until you reach the center. Working from the center outward, spread a little stuffing on each leaf, pressing them back into place until the cabbage resumes its original shape. Then tie it toward the top with string. Place the sliced onion, carrots, bay leaf, thyme, cloves, and peppercorns in the slow-cooker and set the stuffed cabbage on top. Pour the wine mixed with chicken bouillon over the top. Cover and cook on Low for 5 to 7 hours, or until the cabbage is tender. Remove the string and the bay leaf, cloves, and peppercorns before serving with the cooking liquid.

Makes 6 to 8 servings.

HAM IN CIDER
8 to 10 hours

Slow-cookers do ham wonderfully. However, not all cookers are large enough to handle the average ham, half ham, or even smaller cuts. Measure the diameter of your cooker and shop for a ham that fits. Then try this recipe.

Ham that fits your cooker
Sweet cider or apple juice to
    cover (about 4 cups)
1 cup light-brown sugar,
    firmly packed

2 tsp. dry mustard
1 tsp. ground cloves
2 cups white seedless raisins

To Cook: Place the ham and cider in the slow-cooker and cook on Low for 8 to 10 hours.

Before Serving: Remove the ham from the cider. Turn the oven to 375° F. Make a paste of the sugar, mustard, cloves, and a little hot cider—a scant tablespoon usually moistens the paste. Remove outer skin from the ham, if there is one, and smear ham with the paste. Place in a baking pan and pour in 1 cup of the cider, along with the raisins. Bake in the preheated oven ½ hour, or just until the paste has turned into a glaze. The cider will have reduced enough to make a flavorful raisin sauce.

The number of servings depends on the size of the ham.

CHICKEN DISHES

BASIC CHICKEN ASPIC

Follow the recipe for making Basic Meat Aspic (page 150), but use 2 pounds of chicken or 2 quarts of chicken parts, not including liver and giblets, instead of the veal knuckle bones.

BRANDIED CHICKEN ASPIC
7 to 9 hours

4 or 5 lb. boiling fowl, cut up	1½ tsp. salt
¼ cup brandy	¼ tsp. pepper
1 cup chicken stock or water	1 Tbs. curry powder
1 large onion, peeled, sliced	1 cup heavy cream

To Cook: Pull a blob of fat from the chicken vent and heat in a large skillet, to render it. Over high heat, brown the chicken parts well, turning often—about 7 to 10 minutes. Warm the brandy in a ladle or a small saucepan; light with a match and pour over the chicken. Ladle over the chicken until the flames die. Remove the chicken to the slow-cooker. Pour the stock into the skillet; scrape up the pan juices; turn into the cooker. Add remaining ingredients except cream. Cover and cook on Low for 7 to 9 hours, or until the meat is falling off the bones.

Before Serving: Remove chicken from the pot; skin and bone it. Arrange the pieces in a 3-quart mold. Skim fat from the cooking liquid. Measure the liquid into a saucepan. There should be 1½ cups; if there is more, boil to reduce it. Add the cream and heat until just below boiling. Taste; add salt and pepper if necessary; then strain over the chicken pieces. Chill until set. Unmold to serve.

Makes 6 to 8 servings.

CHICKEN-NECK ASPIC
8 to 10 hours

You don't have to make this with chicken necks; you can use backs and wings. But the meat in necks is flavorful, and it's fun to find a way to use them.

12 *chicken necks*
½ *medium onion, peeled*
1 *medium carrot, peeled*
4 *stalks celery, with leaves*
1 *tsp. salt*
⅛ *tsp. pepper*
½ *tsp. dried thyme*
1 *small bay leaf*

3 *whole cloves*
2 *large sprigs parsley*
Water just to cover
½ *cup sliced pimento-stuffed*
   olives
½ *cup minced cooked veal or*
   pork
2 *hard-cooked eggs, sliced*

To Cook: Follow instructions for slow-cooking Basic Meat Aspic (page 150), omitting the last 3 ingredients. When the cooking is done, remove and discard skins from the necks (my dog and cat love them). Pick the meat from the necks; this will be the main ingredient in the aspic. Follow instructions for making Canned-Shrimp Aspic (page 169), using the chicken-neck meat, the vegetables from the cooking liquid, drained, the olive slices, minced veal, and egg slices to complete the aspic.

Makes 6 servings.

CHICKEN WINGS MARCEL
4 to 5 hours

This is a family recipe. It is easy, once the chicken is cooked, and that's where the slow-cooker is a great help. The dish must be served the very minute it is finished. Have everything ready to pop into the skillet; just before the guests sit down at the table, finish the cooking. Use the leftover chicken broth to make chicken soup; or freeze it in 1-cup lots and use it for cooking. The parsley for this must be fresh; don't use dried flakes.

18 *chicken wings*
Water to cover (about 3 or 4
   cups)
1 *small onion, stuck with 4*
   whole cloves
1 *bay leaf*
½ *tsp. dried thyme*

6 *peppercorns*
3 *large sprigs fresh parsley*
2 *tsp. salt*
4 *Tbs. butter*
2 *large cloves garlic, peeled*
   and finely minced
1 *cup finely minced fresh*
   parsley

To Cook: Cut off the wing tips (the skinny, bony section) and place with larger wing pieces in the slow-pot, along with water to cover them, the onion, bay leaf, thyme, peppercorns, parsley sprigs, and salt. Cover and cook on Low for 4 to 5 hours.

Before Serving: You can leave the chicken wings in the cooking liquid for many hours if you turn the heat off and remove the cover. Drain the wings, discard wing tips, and place the wings near the stove. Set a large skillet (the biggest you have) over medium-high heat and melt the butter in it. As soon as it is melted and before it begins to color, add the wings and sauté to golden brown. Keep them all in the skillet, all browning evenly; it will take 4 to 5 minutes. This dish is especially nice if the wings crisp a little. Add the garlic and sprinkle the minced parsley into the skillet. With a spatula, toss and sauté the wings with the parsley and garlic, working quickly. This should take about 2 minutes—just long enough for the parsley to turn bright green and the dish to give off a strong odor of garlic. Serve the wings the minute they are finished.

Makes 6 servings.

CHICKEN À LA KING
5 to 7 hours

This is a two-step dish. The slow-cooker will ready the chicken while you are away, and you can finish the sauce just before serving. If you have leftover broth, freeze it for future use.

3 *lb. frying chicken, quartered*	⅓ *cup dry sherry*
8 *small onions, peeled*	⅛ *cup canned pimento, cut into 1-inch pieces*
1 *bay leaf*	½ *lb. fresh mushrooms, wiped, sliced; or 1 can (10 oz.) mushrooms, sliced*
2 *tsp. salt*	
¼ *tsp. pepper*	
1 *cup water*	
⅓ *cup all-purpose flour*	2 *Tbs. butter or margarine*
1 *cup light cream or whole milk*	½ *tsp. salt*

To Cook: Into the slow-cooker put the chicken, onions, bay leaf, 2 teaspoons salt, the pepper, and water. Cover and cook on Low for 5 to 7 hours.

Before Serving: Remove the chicken to a bowl to cool. Skim ⅓ cup fat from the cooking liquid (if you can't get that much, use butter to make up the difference). Place the fat in a medium skillet, over medium-low heat. Stir in the flour to make a smooth paste and pour over it all at once 1 cup of hot chicken broth. Beat the broth into the flour, working quickly to keep the sauce smooth, and simmer, stirring, for 3 or 4 minutes. Stir in the cream and the sherry, and simmer for 1 or 2 minutes. Add the pimentos. In another skillet, over medium-high heat, sauté the mushroom slices in the butter for about 5 minutes, or until all the moisture has gone from the skillet and the mushrooms are tender. Season the mushrooms with ½ teaspoon salt. Skin and bone the chicken and cut the meat into large chunks. Place them in a warm serving dish. Add the mushrooms and onions and pour the cream sauce over all.

Makes 6 to 8 servings.

CHICKEN CACCIATORE
4 to 5 hours

This is a favorite Italian dish. Serve it with spaghetti. I usually have grated Parmesan cheese on the side, though that isn't the way it is served by most Italians.

3 *lb. frying chicken, in pieces*	1 *tsp. salt*
½ *cup olive or vegetable oil*	¼ *tsp. pepper*
2 *medium-large onions,*	1 *tsp. dried basil*
peeled and chopped	¼ *cup dry red wine, or white*
2 *large cloves garlic, peeled*	½ *cup sliced fresh mushrooms,*
and minced	*or 1 can (4¼ oz.) mush-*
2 *cans (8 oz.) tomato sauce*	*rooms, sliced*
1 *Tbs. chopped parsley*	⅛ *tsp. salt*

To Cook: In large skillet, over medium-high heat, sauté the chicken pieces in the oil until well browned on all sides. Remove the pieces to the slow-cooker. Add the onion, garlic, tomato sauce, parsley, 1 teaspoon salt, pepper, basil, and wine to the skillet. Stir to scrape up the pan juices and pour over the chicken. Cover and cook on Low for 4 to 5 hours or more if you like.

Before Serving: Remove the chicken pieces to a warm serving dish. Skim 2 or 3 tablespoons of fat from the cooking liquid and place it in a medium skillet. Over medium-high heat, sauté the mushroom slices until they are tender and the moisture has dried from the skillet. Season the mushrooms with ⅛ teaspoon salt and place with the chicken. Pour the cooking liquid into the skillet and simmer rapidly, stirring often, until the sauce has become very thick. Pour over the chicken.

Makes 6 to 8 servings.

CHICKEN-AND-SHRIMP PILAF
4 to 6 hours

Rice dishes work wonderfully well in your slow-cooker. This pilaf will give you an idea of how to adapt your favorite pilaf recipes to a slow-cook pot.

1 tsp. vegetable oil	¼ tsp. cinnamon
1 stick (¼ lb.) butter or margarine	⅛ tsp. ground cardamom
	⅛ tsp. ground mace
1 large Bermuda onion, chopped	1 tsp. ground cloves
	⅛ tsp. pepper
½ lb. cut-up boneless chicken pieces	2 cups converted rice
	2 cups chicken bouillon
1 tsp. salt	½ tsp. ground saffron, dis-
3 cloves garlic, peeled and minced	solved in 1 Tbs. water
	1 lb. raw shrimp, shelled and
3 Tbs. dark, seedless raisins	deveined

To Cook: In a medium skillet, heat the oil over medium heat; melt the butter in it and sauté the onion until crisp. Add the chicken pieces; salt them and sauté 1 minute. Add the garlic, raisins, cinnamon, cardamom, mace, cloves, and pepper, and sauté until the chicken begins to brown—about 5 minutes. Add the rice and sauté 3 minutes. Add the bouillon, scrape up the pan juices, and turn into the slow-cooker. Cover and cook on Low for 4 to 6 hours.

Before Serving: Mix the saffron dissolved in water into the cooker. Bury the shrimp in the rice; cover and cook another 20 minutes, or until the shrimp are pink and completely cooked.

Makes 6 to 8 servings.

COQ AU VIN
7 to 9 hours

The flavor of this French classic is very rich, so plan to serve with it plain-cooked vegetables and a light dessert.

12 small white onions, peeled
4 lb. roasting chicken, cut up;
    or 4 lb. chicken thighs
½ tsp. salt
¼ tsp. black pepper
¼ cup brandy or cognac
2 cloves garlic, peeled and
    crushed
¼ tsp. ground thyme

1 bay leaf
1½ cups dry, strong red wine
5 Tbs. all-purpose flour
1 cup chicken bouillon
¾ lb. fresh mushrooms, wiped
    and stemmed
1 Tbs. butter or margarine
¼ tsp. salt
1 Tbs. chopped fresh parsley

To Cook: Place onions in the slow-cooker. Remove the fat from the vent of the chicken (or cut bits of fat from the chicken thighs), and dice it. In a large skillet, over medium heat, heat the fat until it is rendered. Discard the shriveled bits and sauté the chicken until well browned. Season with ½ teaspoon salt and the pepper. Warm the brandy in a ladle or a small saucepan; light it with a match, and pour it over the chicken. When the flames die, lift the chicken into the slow-cooker and add the garlic, thyme, and bay leaf. Pour the wine into the hot skillet and scrape up the pan juices. Dissolve the flour in the bouillon, turn into the skillet, and bring to simmering, stirring briskly to prevent lumps. Turn into the slow-cooker. Cover and cook on Low for 7 to 9 hours.

Before Serving: About 10 minutes before serving, in a medium skillet, sauté the mushrooms in the butter over medium-high heat. In about 5 minutes, they will be tender, and the moisture will have evaporated from the skillet. Season with ¼ teaspoon salt and add to the chicken casserole. If the sauce seems thin, simmer it in the mushroom skillet long enough to thicken to the consistency of heavy cream. Garnish the Coq au Vin with parsley before serving.

Makes 8 to 10 servings.

LAMB DISHES

DOLMAS
3 to 5 hours

Stuffed vine leaves, Turkish style, with a lamb filling. Chill them and serve as appetizers. Vine leaves, ready to roll, are sold canned in specialty shops.

3 *Tbs. olive oil*	½ *tsp. salt*
1 *large onion, peeled, minced*	1½ *cups ground lamb*
6 *Tbs. converted rice*	30 *vine leaves*
4 *Tbs. pine nuts or slivered almonds*	*Hot water*
	½ *cup dry white wine*
2 *Tbs. finely minced parsley*	1 *cup chicken stock*
2 *Tbs. minced fresh dill*	*Lemon wedges*

To Cook: In a large saucepan, over medium-low heat, warm the oil and sauté the onion until translucent. Add the rice and sauté until pale gold—3 to 4 minutes. Add the pine nuts, parsley, dill, and salt; toss well; remove from heat. Combine with the ground lamb and add a little salt if needed. Soak the vine leaves for 1 minute in very hot water, to soften them. Then spread the leaves flat and put 1 tablespoon of the meat mixture in the center of each leaf. Fold in the ends and roll into finger-shape bundles. Arrange in the slow-cooker; add the wine and stock. Cover and cook on Low for 3 to 5 hours. Remove the cover, turn heat to High, and cook until the liquid is just about gone. Chill, and serve with lemon wedges.

Makes 8 to 10 servings.

MOUSSAKA
5 to 7 hours

A good way to use leftover cooked lamb. Or use ground raw lamb or even ground round steak, sautéed until brown in 1 or 2 tablespoons olive oil.

5 *lb. small eggplants*
¼ *tsp. cornstarch*
¼ *cup beef bouillon, or ¼ cup*
water with ½ tsp. Steero
beef granules
2 *Tbs. olive oil*
2½ *cups ground cooked lamb*
⅔ *minced onion, sautéed in 1*
Tbs. olive oil

⅛ *tsp. pepper*
2 *tsp. salt*
½ *tsp. dried thyme*
½ *tsp. dried rosemary*
1 *small clove garlic, peeled and*
crushed
3 *Tbs. tomato paste*
3 *large eggs, well beaten*

To Cook: Cut the eggplants in half lengthwise and bake in the oven at 350° F. until tender—about 30 minutes. Scoop the meat into a large mixing bowl; discard the skins. Dissolve the cornstarch in the bouillon, and beat it, along with the remaining ingredients, into the eggplant pulp. Turn into the slow-cooker. Cover and cook on Low for 5 to 7 hours.

Makes 6 to 8 servings.

LAMB OMAR KHAYYAM
8 to 10 hours

Try this when you want something different, with the Peanut Ring Mold. Or serve the lamb with rice.

2 *lb. boneless lamb shoulder,*
cut into 2-inch cubes
1 *Tbs. vegetable oil*
1 *carton (8 oz.) plain yogurt*
½ *cup chicken bouillon, or ½*
cup water with Steero
chicken granules
¼ *cup white wine*

⅓ *cup tomato paste*
1 *Tbs. Worcestershire sauce*
1 *tsp. salt*
1 *tsp. curry powder*
1 *bay leaf*
½ *cup white wine*
2 *Tbs. all-purpose flour*
Peanut Ring Mold (below)

To Cook: In a large skillet, over medium-high heat, brown the lamb cubes in the oil. Remove cubes to the slow-cooker. Remove skillet from heat and add the yogurt, bouillon, ¼ cup wine, tomato paste, Worcestershire sauce, salt, curry powder, and bay leaf. Scrape up the pan juices and turn the sauce into the cooker. Cover and cook on Low for 8 to 10 hours.

Before Serving: In a small saucepan, boil ½ cup wine until reduced by half. Cool quickly with an ice cube, discard the cube and stir in the flour. Remove the lamb cubes from the cooker to a warm serving dish. Turn the cooker to High; stir in the flour mixture and cook until the sauce has thickened. Combine with the lamb and spoon into the Peanut Ring Mold.

Makes 6 servings.

PEANUT RING MOLD

4 cups enriched-bread cubes	*⅓ cup butter or margarine,*
⅓ cup chopped peanuts	* melted*
1 tsp. salt	*2 eggs*
¼ tsp. pepper	*¾ cup whole milk*
½ cup chopped celery	*3 Tbs. shortening*
¼ cup chopped onion	*1 Tbs. flour*

In a large bowl, stir together the bread cubes, peanuts, salt, and pepper. In a medium skillet, over medium heat, sauté the celery and onion in the butter until the onion is translucent. Combine with the bread mixture. Beat the eggs and milk together and, working to keep the mixture fluffy, combine with the bread mixture. In a small bowl, cream the shortening and stir the flour into it. Spread the shortening mixture over the bottom and sides of an 8-inch ring mold. Spoon the bread mixture into the mold, packing it enough to remove air pockets. Refrigerate for about 1 hour; then bake in a preheated oven at 350° F. for 40 minutes.

NAVARIN PRINTANIER
8 to 10 hours

This famous French dish is at its best when the vegetables are spring's early crops. Even in spring, fresh peas can be hard to find, so I usually plan to use frozen.

4 Tbs. butter or margarine

4 small onions, peeled and
   sliced

4 lb. boneless lamb shoulder
   or breast, cut into 2-inch
   cubes

2 lb. small new potatoes,
   scraped

8 baby carrots, scraped

8 baby turnips, peeled

3 Tbs. all-purpose flour

1 cup beef bouillon, or 1 cup
   water with 1 beef bouillon
   cube

1 tsp. salt

¼ tsp. pepper

2 sprigs fresh or ⅛ tsp. dried
   rosemary

1 clove garlic, peeled

1 bay leaf

1 package (10 oz.) frozen
   green peas

To Cook: In a large skillet, over medium heat, melt the butter and sauté the onion until golden. Add the lamb pieces and sauté until golden brown on all sides. Place the potatoes, carrots, and turnips in the slow-cooker. Place lamb pieces on vegetables. Add the flour to the skillet and stir until it turns light brown. Beat in the bouillon and stir continuously until the sauce becomes smooth. Turn the sauce into the cooker, along with the salt, pepper, rosemary, garlic, and bay leaf. Cover and cook on Low for 8 to 10 hours, or until the meat is completely tender.

Before Serving: About 10 minutes before you are ready to serve, add frozen peas to the cooker, turn the heat to High, and cook until the peas are tender—about 10 minutes. If the sauce seems thin, cook uncovered; if it seems thicker than a cream soup, cover for these last moments of cooking.

Makes 10 to 12 servings.

SEAFOOD DISHES

BASIC FISH ASPIC
4 to 6 hours

You can use the fish ingredients here to make good fish stock that will gel, or you can use the heads of almost any kind of fish—if they are truly fresh, not more than a day old. Summers on Cape Cod, we sometimes buy a whole fresh cod from a local fisherman, poach it, head and all, for 20 or 30 minutes in just enough water to cover. We serve the body at dinner, boil the backbone and head in the cooking liquid until it is reduced to 1 or 2 quarts, and from this make a wonderful—and so economical—jellied stock. Bits of cooked shrimp, lobster, canned crab, tomatoes, hard-cooked eggs, parboiled green onions, parsley sprigs can be jelled in the stock for a really handsome buffet dish. Serve with lemon wedges.

2 lb. fresh fish, fish heads and bones, gills, and other trimmings
1 onion, thinly sliced
4 sprigs parsley
½ tsp. salt

1 cup dry white wine (optional)
½ tsp. dried thyme
1 bay leaf
1 medium carrot, peeled, cut in rounds
Water to cover

To Cook: Follow the instructions for Basic Meat Aspic (page 150), but slow-cook for only 4 to 6 hours.

Makes 6 to 8 cups aspic jelly.

CANNED SHRIMP IN ASPIC

Instead of shrimp, you can use leftover poached fish or bits salvaged from a feast of boiled lobsters, or canned lobster or crabmeat. Hard-cooked eggs combined with fish products make a good aspic. This dish is not made in the slow-cooker—I include it to suggest ways to use the basic aspic jellies.

2½ cups Basic Fish Aspic (above)
½ carrot, peeled, sliced thin
1 stalk celery, sliced thin, with leaves
1 large, thin sliced onion

¼ cup dry sherry
2 cups canned shrimp, well rinsed
3 hard-cooked eggs, sliced
Bunch parsley sprigs
1 lemon, cut in wedges

To Cook: In a saucepan, over medium-high heat, cook the Basic Fish Aspic with the carrot and celery until the vegetables are tender. Add the onion and sherry and cook until the onion is limp. Add the shrimp; cook 1 minute; then remove from heat. Pour ½ inch of the cooking liquid into a 1½-quart mold and chill 5 to 10 minutes. Refrigerate remaining stock mixture until the jelly layer has set. Lift some of the shrimp, the onion ring, carrot pieces, and celery chunks and leaves from the stock and arrange in a pretty pattern on the jelly layer. Complete the design with some of the egg slices. Pour a little stock over the pieces. Coat some egg slices with stock and press against the mold sides. Chill until set once more. Refrigerate the balance of the stock. When the second layer has jelled, pour remaining stock into the mold and add rest of shrimp and egg slices. Cover and chill overnight. Unmold on a bed of parsley and garnish with lemon wedges.

Makes 6 to 8 servings.

BOUILLABAISSE
5 to 8 hours

The seafood soup/stew called Bouillabaisse comes from the southern shores of France, where it is the custom to add all the day's catch, whatever it is, to the simmering kettle. This formalized version can include cod, flounder, haddock, red snapper, sea bass, or perch. The fish must be very fresh. If you catch it yourself, fillet it and save the trimmings—the heads and bones. Shellfish suited to Bouillabaisse are crab, lobster, lobster or crayfish tails, mussels, clams, and scallops.

4 *lb. fish fillets*	2 *cloves garlic, peeled*
2 *lb. shellfish*	6 *cups water*
16 *to* 24 *mussels, scallops, or*	*Fish trimmings (page* 169)
steamer clams	1 *medium carrot, peeled*
½ *cup olive oil*	*and halved*
½ *cup chopped leeks or*	1 *bay leaf*
onion	½ *Tbs. salt*
2 *large tomatoes, peeled,*	⅛ *tsp. pepper*
seeded, cut up; or 1 *cup*	⅛ *tsp. ground saffron*
cut-up canned, drained	8 *to* 10 *slices stale French*
whole tomatoes	*bread*

To Cook: Cut the large fish fillets on a slant into slices about 2 inches wide. If you are using lobster, split it; if crab, lift the tail flap. Clean the mussels or clams. Refrigerate the fish and shellfish. In a large skillet, over medium heat, heat the oil and sauté the leeks until translucent—about 5 minutes. Swish the tomatoes around in the skillet and turn skillet contents into the slow-cooker. Add the garlic, water, fish trimmings, carrot, bay leaf, salt, pepper, and saffron. Cover and cook on Low for 5 to 8 hours.

Before Serving: Remove the fish trimmings from the slow-pot. Turn the heat to Medium High or, if your cooker has no in-between setting, to High. Add the shellfish to the stock; cover; return to a boil and simmer for 10 minutes. Add firm-fleshed fillets (snapper, bass, perch); cover and simmer for 5 minutes. Add the soft-fleshed fish (cod, flounder, haddock) and the mussels, scallops, or clams. When the soup returns to a boil, simmer for 5 minutes. To serve the Bouillabaisse, place in each bowl a slice of stale French bread and a portion of each type of shellfish and fish.

Makes 8 to 10 generous servings.

PART FOUR
THE HOSPITALITY POT

Chapter **7**

Great Soups and Stocks; Soups with Leftovers

When you look at your slow-cooker, think hospitality—think variety —think economy—think soup. In putting together the recipes in this chapter, I was tempted to include almost every soup and stock I know because slow-cooking is the best way to do so many of them.

I say "Think hospitality" because stewy soups—rich, thick concoctions of meat and vegetables, including leftovers—are almost infinitely expandable. If a member of the family wants a friend to stay for dinner, you can add to a simmering slow-pot soup canned or frozen vegetables, sautéed bits of steak or chicken, or cut-up leftover meat. Or just add pieces of stale French bread sautéed in a little butter. Then the soup will serve one, two, three, or four more people. Bake a batch of biscuits, add a dessert, and you can feed everyone a memorable meal on a potluck basis.

If you think soup is too simple for guests, think again. Among the most fashionable—and successful—places for light suppers are elegant restaurants called La Soupière and La Potagerie, where large bowls of hearty, steaming vegetables and meats in wonderfully thick broths are coupled with big chunks of crusty French bread and butter. Cheese, a small green salad, and fresh fruit complete the meal.

USING LEFTOVERS

Soup is one of the best ways to use treasured leftovers—meaty ham and lamb bones, beautifully browned roasted or pan-fried beef bones, rich chicken bones. Also, leftovers work wonders for soup flavors. The recipes here show how I've worked leftovers into soups for my family for years. I don't think there's any leftover I haven't found a use for. But my leftovers often are the result of the kind of cooking I do. You may have quite different ones. Even so, what I do with mine will suggest how you can use yours.

Bones of roasted or baked (but not charcoal-broiled) meats add flavor to soup. So do bits of gravies saved from the drippings of beef and other roasts. Store bones in the freezer; they remain fresh for months. When you have enough, make stocks, bouillons, and soups.

Bones from leg-of-lamb roast and other bone-in lamb cuts also can be used to make soup and stocks, and so can veal bones, which can be used interchangeably with chicken bones. Veal bones impart a flavor specially their own, so delicate that it blends well in any soup made with chicken stock or bouillon.

Though I save beef, veal, lamb, and ham bones (the last for pea and lentil soup), I don't save chicken bones for soup or bouillon or stock. The wing tips, necks, and backs cooked in a slow-pot make excellent chicken stock. Packaged separately from a whole chicken, they can simply be popped into the freezer and kept until you have enough for a particular recipe.

TO MAKE SOUP

Many other kitchen discards are useful for soup. Celery leaves, carrot peels, the cooking water from fresh vegetables, and gravies (as mentioned) are some that make good stocks and soups. Drying remnants of pork products, prosciutto, ripe olives, leftover salad, meat sauce, tag ends—all are flavor accents you can add to a bubbling slow-cooker.

So why not let the slow-pot salvage odds and ends, instead of discarding them? Using them in soups gives one a virtuous feeling —and gives the soups a great deal of flavor.

STOCKS, BROTHS, AND BOUILLONS

Bouillon is a strong stock—that magic ingredient gourmet recipes call for. In the old days, stock was made by simmering collected meat bones and other scraps for hours. In modern kitchens not equipped with slow-pots, making stock has drawbacks. It uses a lot of gas or electricity and keeping water simmering all day fills the kitchen with steam and heat. But in the slow-cooker, which lets no steam escape, stock or bouillon can simmer all day or all night without demanding your attention, without filling the room with moisture—and for pennies, much less than the cost of canned bouillon.

CLEAR-THE-FRIDGE SOUP
10 to 12 hours

The base for this soup is leftover meat or tomato sauce from spaghetti. All sorts of vegetable odds and ends can be added. The ones I've suggested are those I usually find in my crisper.

½ to 1 cup Meat Sauce for Spaghetti (page 72)

2 to 4 chicken necks, wing tips, or backs

1 large onion, peeled, chopped

1 or 2 coarse outer stalks celery, with leaves

½ cup light-red kidney beans or other beans

2½ quarts beef broth, or 4 beef bouillon cubes and 2½ quarts water

½ cup leftover rice, spaghetti, or macaroni

3 sprigs parsley, minced; or 3 Tbs. minced parsley stems

1 large clove garlic, peeled, minced

⅓ cup grated Parmesan or Swiss cheese, or cottage cheese

To Cook: Combine all ingredients except the cheese in the slow-cooker. Cover and cook on Low for 10 to 12 hours. Taste and season with salt and pepper if needed. Add some cheese to each serving.

Makes 6 to 8 servings.

HODGEPODGE SOUP
8 to 10 hours

This soup makes use of everything but the pig's squeal, all the odds and ends of pork products you may have on hand—ham bone, ham-roast tidbits, dried salami or hot-dog leavings, bits of roast pork, pork-roast drippings, or breakfast sausage. The meat is for flavoring. You can toss in tag ends of white wine or beer, use up cheese such as Parmesan or Swiss, and serve the soup over hard crusts of French bread—to make it the perfect refrigerator cleaner-outer. And what flavor! So filling, it makes a meal all by itself.

Pork-product leftovers (see above)

2 carrots, peeled, shredded

2 small white turnips, peeled, shredded

2 parsnips, peeled, shredded

2 medium potatoes, peeled, shredded

3 large onions, peeled, shredded

4 to 8 outer leaves of a winter cabbage, shredded

½ cup white wine or beer

2 tsp. salt

¼ tsp. black pepper

4 sprigs fresh parsley, or 2 tsp. dried parsley flakes

4 cups water

Crusts of French bread (optional)

Grated cheese (optional)

To Cook: Layer the pork and vegetables in the slow-cooker in the order in which they are listed. Add everything except the bread and cheese. Cover and cook on Low for 8 to 10 hours. If you wish, place one or two hard crusts of French bread and a tablespoon of grated Parmesan or other cheese into each bowl before ladling in the soup.

Makes 8 to 10 servings.

DUTCH SOUP WITH BREAD
8 to 10 hours

This uses up stale bread and all sorts of leftovers. I start with bones from steak and beef roasts I have saved in the freezer. A half dozen T-bones (not from steaks broiled over charcoal, please!) or the bones from a medium rib roast will do.

Beef bones (see above)
1 bay leaf
½ tsp. dried thyme
1 medium onion, stuck with 4 whole cloves
1 tsp. dried parsley flakes
2 tsp. Steero beef granules, or 2 beef bouillon cubes
3½ cups water
2 tsp. salt

¼ tsp. pepper
½ cup finely chopped onion
3 tsp. butter or margarine
6 slices dried-out whole-wheat bread
½ cup canned beets, shredded
½ tsp. caraway seed
2 cups shredded fresh green cabbage
1 cup whole milk

To Cook: Place the beef bones, bay leaf, thyme, onion stuck with cloves, parsley, beef granules, water, salt, and pepper in the slow-cooker. Cover and cook on Low for 8 to 10 hours.

Before Serving: Discard the bones. In a large skillet, over medium heat, simmer the chopped onion in the butter until golden brown. Add the bread slices, 2 cups of stock from the cooker, the beets, and the caraway seed, and simmer for 15 minutes. Add the cabbage and simmer for 10 minutes. Stir in the milk and heat through. Add mixture in skillet to slow-pot, stir well, and serve.

Makes 6 to 8 servings.

ONION SOUP WITH PUFFY CHEESE CROUTONS
8 to 10 hours

Make this onion soup with saved-up chicken parts and beef bones.

8 to 10 *wing tips, 4 to 6 necks,*
and 2 or 3 backs of
chicken

2½ *cups water*

1 *medium onion, peeled and*
chopped

2 tsp. *Steero chicken*
granules, or 2 chicken
bouillon cubes

1 *bay leaf*

½ tsp. *dried thyme*

2 tsp. *salt*

¼ tsp. *pepper*

3 *whole cloves*

Bones from beef rib roast and
steaks

4 *cups thinly sliced onion*

¼ *cup butter or margarine*

2 Tbs. *all-purpose flour*

3½ *cups water*

Puffy Cheese Croutons (below)

To Cook: Place the chicken and the next 9 ingredients in the slow-cooker. Cover and cook on Low for 8 to 10 hours.

Before Serving: Discard the meat bones, chicken parts, bay leaf, and cloves. In a large skillet, over medium-low heat, sauté the onion slices in the butter, but do not brown them. Lower the heat. Stir in the flour to make a smooth mixture. Add 2 cups of the broth from the cooker all at once and beat quickly to smooth the roux. Turn the sauce into the slow-cooker; add 3½ cups water; cover and cook on High for about 10 minutes. Serve the soup topped with Puffy Cheese Croutons.

Makes 4 to 6 servings.

PUFFY CHEESE CROUTONS

¼ *cup butter or margarine*

1 Tbs. *whole milk*

1 *cup shredded, aged*
*Cheddar cheese (*¼ *lb.)*

2 *egg whites*

French bread cut into bite-size
pieces

Set the oven at 400° F. Melt butter in the top section of a double boiler over hot, but not boiling, water or in a small saucepan over very low heat. Add milk; stir in cheese, stirring constantly until the cheese is melted. Remove from heat. Beat the egg whites until stiff but not dry. Gently fold beaten egg whites into the cheese mixture. Dip bread pieces into the egg-cheese mixture and place on ungreased baking sheet. Bake in preheated oven 10 to 15 minutes, or until slightly browned. Remove immediately. Serve with the Onion Soup above.

Makes enough for 4 to 6 servings.

ONION SOUP SUPREME
6 to 8 hours

Another onion soup made good by using chicken parts you often discard.

8 to 10 *wing tips*, 4 to 6 *necks, and* 2 *or* 3 *backs of chicken*	1 *tsp. dried thyme*
	2 *tsp. salt*
	¼ *tsp. pepper*
1 *medium onion, peeled and chopped*	2 *cups thinly sliced onion*
	2 *Tbs. butter or margarine*
2½ *cups water*	3 *Tbs. all-purpose flour*
2 *tsp. Steero chicken granules, or* 2 *chicken bouillon cubes*	½ *tsp. dry mustard*
	3 *cups whole milk*
	½ *tsp. ground coriander*
1 *bay leaf*	¼ *tsp. paprika*

To Cook: Place the chicken parts in the slow-cooker, along with the chopped onion, water, chicken granules, bay leaf, thyme, salt, and pepper. Cover and cook on Low for 6 to 8 hours.

Before Serving: Discard the chicken parts and bay leaf. In a medium skillet, over medium-low heat, sauté the sliced onion in the butter until the onion is golden. Blend in the flour and the dry mustard, and at once add 1 cup of hot stock from the pot. Stir to smooth the mixture; then add the milk and coriander. Stir this into the stock in the cooker; turn the heat to High for 1 or 2 minutes; then pour into a tureen. Garnish with paprika.

Makes 4 to 6 servings.

IMPERIAL CARROT SOUP
6 to 8 hours

A hearty chicken soup with—surprise—a carrot flavor. It is made with chicken discards you can save up in the freezer.

8 to 10 *wing tips, 4 to 6*
    necks, and 2 or 3 backs
    of chicken
1 *medium onion, peeled and*
    chopped
2½ *cups water*
2 *tsp. Steero chicken*
    granules, or 2 chicken
    bouillon cubes
1 *bay leaf*
½ *tsp. dried thyme*

2 *tsp. salt*
¼ *tsp. pepper*
3 *whole cloves*
2 *Tbs. butter or margarine*
3 *cups thinly sliced carrots*
¼ *tsp. ground coriander*
    (optional)
1 *cup whole milk or half-*
    and-half
1 *tsp. freeze-dried chives*

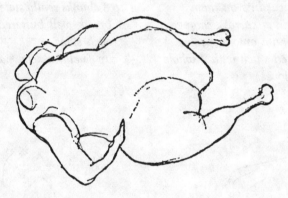

To Cook: Place the chicken parts in the slow-cooker, along with the onion, chicken granules, bay leaf, thyme, salt, pepper, and cloves. Cover and cook on Low for 6 to 8 hours.

Before Serving: Discard the chicken parts, bay leaf, and cloves. In a large skillet, over low heat, melt the butter and sauté the carrot slices. Scoop a little chicken stock from the pot into the skillet and mix. Add the coriander if desired and turn skillet contents into the pot. Turn the cooker to High and cook for about 10 minutes, or until the carrots are very tender. Add the milk. Reserve a few slices of carrot. Using a blender on low, blend the soup, 2 cups at a time. Turn into a tureen and garnish with carrot slices and chives.

Makes 4 to 6 servings.

PARSLEY SOUP, PEASANT STYLE
10 to 12 hours

This is a family favorite. The chunks of stale French bread are well buttered before we put them into the soup plates, and they soften as they absorb liquid, until they are just right to eat—and deliciously filled with broth.

2½ tsp. salt
1 lb. stew beef, cut into 1-inch cubes
8 cups water
2 quarts beef bones with meat bits on them
2 medium carrots, scraped
2 medium onions, peeled and stuck with 6 whole cloves

2 sprigs fresh parsley, or 1 tsp. dried parsley flakes
½ tsp. dried thyme
2 medium cloves garlic, peeled
¼ cup dry red wine
4 to 8 chunks really stale French bread, well buttered on each side
¼ cup finely minced parsley

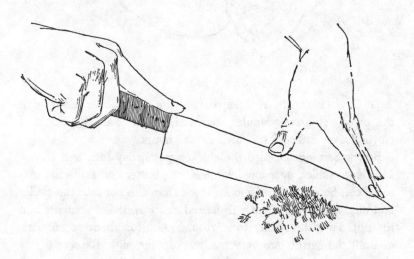

To Cook: In a large skillet, over medium-high heat, sprinkle the salt, and brown the beef on all sides. Brown it really well. Pour 1 cup water into the skillet, scrape up the pan juices, and turn the whole thing into the slow-cooker. Add the rest of the water and all the other ingredients except the wine, bread, and minced parsley. Cover and cook on Low for 10 to 12 hours. Discard bones.

Before Serving: Mix the wine into the hot bouillon; turn the heat to High and simmer, uncovered, for 3 to 4 minutes. Place the bread chunks in the serving bowls; divide the parsley among the bowls; pour in the soup and serve at once.

Makes 4 to 6 servings.

SPLIT-PEA SOUP
8 to 10 hours

This is another favorite. I make it with a leftover ham bone, and the slow-pot cooks it to perfection. You can sauté the onion first in butter, but the easiest, hurry-up way is the one described below.

2 Tbs. butter or margarine	1 ham bone
1 cup minced onion	1 cup finely minced celery
8 cups water	1 cup diced carrots
2 cups green split peas, washed (1 lb.)	⅛ tsp. dried savory
	⅛ tsp. dried marjoram
4 whole cloves	1 Tbs. salt
1 bay leaf	¼ tsp. pepper

To Cook: Place all the ingredients in the slow-cooker. Cover and cook on Low for 8 to 10 hours.

Before Serving: I like this soup to be really thick, and after the first long-cook period, I generally simmer it down to a consistency that almost lets you stand a matchstick in it. If you want to try it that way, uncover the soup, turn the heat to High, and simmer, stirring occasionally, until the desired consistency is reached. The peas may stick to the pot bottom during this second cooking period, so do not forget to stir occasionally. If you want the finished soup thinner instead of thicker, thin it with milk—it's delicious. Remove the ham bone, cloves, and bay leaf before serving and dice any meat from the bone and return it to the soup.

Makes 6 to 8 servings.

LENTIL SOUP WITH A HAM BONE
8 to 10 hours

I usually make this soup with a ham bone I've saved, but it is almost as good made instead with the broth left over from the cooking of a Daisy Ham Roll (page 96). So if you don't have a ham bone and want lentil soup, plan to make the Daisy Ham Roll the day before you make the soup.

2 Tbs. butter or margarine	1 cup finely minced celery
1 cup minced onion	1 cup diced carrots
8 cups water	⅛ tsp. dried savory
2 cups lentils, washed (1 lb.)	⅔ tsp. dried marjoram
4 whole cloves	1 Tbs. salt
1 bay leaf	¼ tsp. pepper
1 ham bone	

To Cook: Place all the ingredients in the slow-cooker. Cover and cook on Low for 8 to 10 hours.

Before Serving: Remove the ham bone, cloves, and bay leaf. Dice the meat and fat from the bone and return to the soup.

Makes 6 to 8 servings.

CHICKEN-AND-BEEF SOUP
10 to 12 hours

1 lb. lean stew beef	2 carrots, peeled, diced
1 quart beef bones from a roast or from 3 or 4 pan-fried steaks	1 leek, washed, minced
	4 canned and drained or fresh Italian tomatoes
1 lb. chicken necks and backs, or 4 to 6 necks, 3 or 4 backs	3 quarts water
	1 tsp. salt
1 stalk celery, diced	¼ tsp. pepper
3 sprigs parsley	¼ tsp. dried thyme

To Cook: Place all the ingredients in the slow-cooker. Cover and cook on Low for 10 to 12 hours. Strain; check seasoning and add salt and pepper to taste.

Makes 6 to 8 servings.

BEEF BROTH, ITALIAN STYLE
10 to 12 hours

Another soup that gets its flavor from saved-up bones and pan drippings from a beef roast or pan-fried steaks.

2 *lb. lean stew beef*	3 *sprigs parsley*
2 *quarts beef bones with bits*	1 *tsp. tomato paste*
of meat on them	1 *tsp. salt*
2 *carrots, peeled, diced*	⅛ *tsp. pepper*
1 *small turnip, peeled, diced*	⅛ *tsp. dried rosemary*
2 *leeks, well washed, minced*	3 *quarts water*
1 *stalk celery, diced*	

To Cook: Place all the ingredients in the slow-cooker. Cover and cook on Low for 10 to 12 hours. Strain before serving; check seasoning as you may need more salt and pepper. Dice meat from the bones and return to the soup.

Makes 6 to 8 servings.

FRANCESCA MORRIS'S SCOTCH BROTH
6 to 8 hours

When Francesca has a leftover lamb bone, she makes this soup with it. You'll have to break the bone to fit it into the slow-cooker. If you want to start from scratch, use shoulder.

3 *lb. lamb shoulder, bone in,*	1 *large onion, peeled and diced*
or a leftover lamb bone	1½ *tsp. salt*
with meat	⅛ *tsp. pepper*
6 *cups cold water*	1 *cup raw barley*
1 *bay leaf*	2 *Tbs. butter or margarine*
1 *cup diced carrots*	2 *Tbs. all-purpose flour*
1 *cup diced celery*	2 *Tbs. finely chopped parsley*
1 *cup sliced, washed leeks*	
(cut in small slices)	

To Cook: Cut the meat into 2-inch cubes and place, with the bone, in the slow-cooker. Place the remaining ingredients except the butter, flour, and parsley in the cooker. Cover and cook on Low for 6 to 8 hours.

Before Serving: In a small saucepan, over low heat, melt the butter and stir the flour into it. Pour 1 cup of hot soup from the cooker into the flour and stir quickly to make a smooth sauce. Mix this back into the soup. Cook, uncovered, on High for about 5 minutes, stirring occasionally. Remove the bay leaf and bone; garnish with parsley and serve.

Makes 10 to 12 servings.

EGG-DROP SOUP

This is a favorite with those who love Chinese food, and since its basis is Chicken Stock or Bouillon, Chinese Style, I include it here. It's light—not a soup that makes a complete supper. Let the slow-cooker make the basic chicken stock overnight or while you are away. Finish the soup, as below, just before serving dinner.

4 to 5 cups Chicken Stock or
*   Bouillon, Chinese Style*
*   (page 192)*
1 Tbs. cornstarch
½ tsp. soy sauce
3 Tbs. cold Chicken Stock or
*   Bouillon, Chinese Style*
*   (page 192)*

½ tsp. salt
2 eggs
1 scallion, minced
1 tsp. minced Chinese parsley
*   (optional, but don't use*
*   regular parsley)*

To Cook: Heat the 4 or 5 cups chicken stock to a simmer in a large kettle, over medium heat. Mix the cornstarch and soy sauce in a small container and add 3 tablespoons cold chicken stock. Add the salt, stir thoroughly, and pour the mixture into the soup. Stir until the soup has thickened and cleared (it will cloud when you add the cornstarch). Break the eggs into a bowl; mix just a little, and in a thin stream pour the eggs slowly—*slowly*—into the soup.

Remove the soup from the heat and stir it once. Divide the scallion and the parsley among the soup plates and ladle on the soup.

Makes 4 to 6 servings.

COLD CUCUMBER SOUP
10 to 12 hours, or overnight

This is a soup to be served cold on a hot day. It begins by the overnight cooking of Classic White Stock or Chicken Stock or Bouillon. Then make as directed below.

¼ lb. butter or margarine

1 small onion, peeled and minced

4 young cucumbers, peeled and thinly sliced

3 Tbs. all-purpose flour

6 cups hot Chicken Stock or Bouillon (page 191) or Classic White Stock (page 189)

¼ tsp. pepper

1 Tbs. dry sherry

1 cup heavy cream

2 egg yolks, slightly beaten

3 Tbs. minced parsley

To Cook: Melt the butter in a medium saucepan and sauté the onion and cucumber until wilted. Stir in the flour; then beat in the hot broth, stirring constantly until mixture is smooth. Bring to a simmer; add the pepper; lower the heat and simmer 10 minutes. Purée in the blender 2 minutes. Stir the sherry and cream into the yolks. Beat a little of the broth into the egg-yolk mixture; then beat back into the broth and return to just below boiling. Chill, covered, several hours or overnight in the refrigerator. Serve garnished with parsley.

Makes 6 to 8 servings.

CONSOMMÉ MADRILÈNE

You'll find this on menus in fine restaurants everywhere, and it's easy to make once you have used your slow-pot to turn out a supply of Classic Brown Stock or Beef Stock or Bouillon (pages 188, 189). For each cup of stock, add 1 tablespoon of madeira or dry sherry; stir in a pinch of cayenne pepper and some minced fresh herbs, such as parsley, chervil, or whatever you wish. Madrilène can be served chilled (it is then stiff, like a jelly, and is stirred into small chunks before serving) or hot.

CONSOMMÉ JULIENNE THE EASY WAY

Another consommé found on all good menus, this is a breeze when you have good beef stock (see below) on hand. For 6 cups of stock, use a *small* can of julienne vegetables or 1 cup of finely diced leftover vegetables (preferably mixed). Drain the vegetables well and sauté for 1 minute in butter. During the sautéing, add a pinch of sugar and some finely minced herbs of your choice. Stir vegetables into the stock; heat, and serve.

CLASSIC BROWN STOCK
10 to 12 hours

When your gourmet recipes call for brown stock, use this. Use it also for any recipes in this book calling for beef broth or stock. The bones should have a little meat clinging to them.

2 lb. beef and veal bones	2 large stalks celery, diced
2 Tbs. melted butter, margarine, or beef-fat drippings	2 tsp. salt
	4 sprigs parsley
	¼ tsp. black pepper
2 medium carrots, peeled, diced	2 quarts water
	1 tsp. dried thyme
2 medium onions, peeled, minced	1 bay leaf
¼ lb. pork rind	1 large clove garlic, peeled, chopped

To Cook: Brush the bones with butter, then place with carrots, onion, and rind in a baking dish and brown in a 450° F. oven for about 40 minutes, turning them often. Turn bone mixture and pan juices into the slow-cooker, along with the remaining ingredients. Cover and cook on Low for 10 to 12 hours. Strain.

Makes about 2 quarts.

CLASSIC WHITE STOCK
10 to 12 hours

When your gourmet recipes call for white stock, use this. You can also use plain veal stock or plain chicken stock, but this is the classic recipe, and it is best made in a slow-cooker. You can use saved-up chicken wing tips and/or necks.

1½ lb. veal bones	1½ tsp. salt
1 to 2 lb. chicken wing tips and/or necks (4 cups)	3 sprigs parsley
	2 cloves
1 medium onion, peeled, sliced	1 bay leaf
	½ tsp. dried thyme
1 large carrot, peeled, sliced	2½ quarts water
1 large stalk celery, sliced	

To Cook: Place all the ingredients in the slow-cooker. Cover and cook on Low for 10 to 12 hours. Strain.

Makes about 2½ quarts.

BEEF STOCK OR BOUILLON
10 to 12 hours

This is an excellent basic bouillon with which you can make all sorts of delicious soups and stews and casseroles. Add some to the pan in which beef has baked or roasted, just before it finishes cooking; scrape up the pan juices, and you'll have a delicious gravy. Save and freeze roasted beef bones with bits of meat on them to make this.

2½ tsp. salt	2 sprigs fresh parsley, or 1 tsp. dried parsley flakes
1 lb. stew beef, cut into 1-inch cubes	2 medium carrots, scraped
10 cups water	2 medium onions, peeled and stuck with 6 whole cloves
2 quarts beef bones with meat bits on them	½ tsp. dried thyme
	2 medium cloves garlic, peeled

To Cook: In a large skillet, over medium-high heat, sprinkle the salt and brown the beef on all sides. Brown it really well. Pour a cupful of the water into the skillet; scrape up the pan juices, and

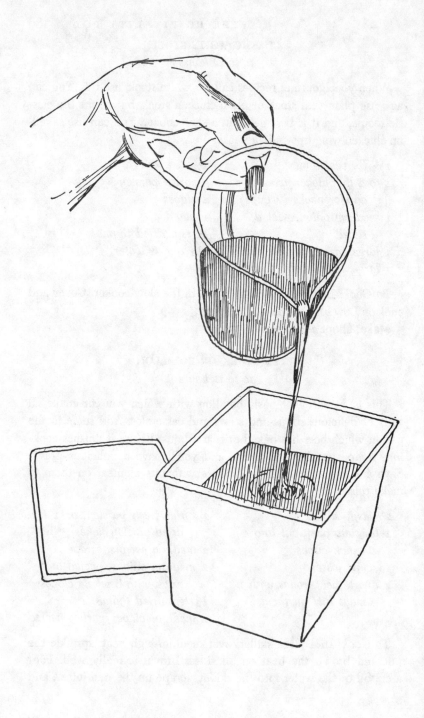

turn the whole thing into the slow-cooker. Add remaining water and all the other ingredients. Cover and cook on Low for 10 to 12 hours. Strain.

Makes about 10 cups.

CHICKEN STOCK OR BOUILLON
10 to 12 hours

This is a basic recipe for making chicken bouillon to serve as soup. Serve the chicken, cut from the bones if you like, in soup plates filled with broth. Add croutons to dress it up for special occasions. Save broth left over and freeze it in 1-cup lots; any casserole or stew made with a bouillon will turn out a great deal better than one made with plain water.

2½ *lb. chicken, cut up, or*
chicken necks, backs,
wing tips
1 *small onion, peeled*
1 *medium carrot, scraped*
1 *medium parsnip, peeled*
2 *medium cloves garlic,*
peeled

6 *black peppercorns*
2 *sprigs fresh parsley, or 1 tsp.*
dried parsley flakes
1 *bay leaf*
½ *tsp. dried thyme*
2 *tsp. salt*
8 *cups water*

To Cook: Place all the ingredients in the slow-cooker. Cover and cook on Low for 10 to 12 hours. If the flavor seems a little pale, add salt and pepper at the end. Strain stock or bouillon before serving.

Makes 8 to 8½ cups.

CHICKEN STOCK OR BOUILLON, ITALIAN STYLE
10 to 12 hours

Serve the cooked chicken meat in a little broth, or remove it from the bones, combine it with a little leftover Meat Sauce (page 72) and serve with spaghetti on the side.

2½ lb. chicken, cut up, or
   chicken necks, backs,
   wing tips
1 small onion, peeled
1 medium carrot, scraped
1 medium clove garlic, peeled
6 black peppercorns

2 sprigs fresh parsley, or 1 tsp.
   dried parsley flakes
1 bay leaf
½ tsp. dried thyme
1 tsp. dried rosemary
8 cups water

To Cook: Place all the ingredients in the slow-cooker. Cover and cook on Low for 10 to 12 hours. If the flavor seems a little pale, add salt and pepper at the end. Strain.

Makes 8 to 8½ cups.

CHICKEN STOCK OR BOUILLON, CHINESE STYLE
10 to 12 hours

Use the cooked chicken to make Oriental stir-fried dishes including cooked chicken. Or serve it for dinner in a little broth seasoned with soy sauce, and offer with it a Chinese vegetable dish.

2½ lb. chicken, cut up, or
   chicken necks, backs,
   wing tips
1 small onion, peeled
1 medium carrot, scraped
1 medium parsnip, peeled
2 medium cloves garlic,
   peeled
6 black peppercorns
2 sprigs fresh parsley or 1 tsp.
   dried parsley flakes

1 bay leaf
½ tsp. dried thyme
1 tsp. soy sauce
2 slices fresh ginger, ½ inch
   thick; or 1 tsp. ground
   ginger
2 tsp. salt
8 cups water

To Cook: Place all the ingredients in the slow-cooker. Cover and cook on Low for 10 to 12 hours. If the flavor seems a little pale, add salt and pepper at the end. Strain.

Makes 8 to 8½ cups.

Chapter 8

Soups That Make One-Dish Dinners

A LIGHT BUT filling meal at the end of the day is soup—and it makes very good sense nutritionally. At supper time, the energy that burns calories is in least demand. Our biggest meal should be breakfast, a fact we've all known for ages and generally ignore.

A compromise is to serve for supper, at least once in a while, one of the hearty soups in this chapter. Most of them include meat, but they are lighter and easier to digest than the usual meat-and-potatoes meal if only because the liquid is so filling you want—and eat—less meat. Since meat is one of the most expensive food items, soup meals are economical, and for most of us today that's a consideration.

THE SUPPER SOUPS

The soups grouped here—and some of those in Chapter 7—are hearty enough to be meals all by themselves. Add a tossed green salad and dessert—no one will want more. Beef-Gumbo, Baked-Bean Soup, and Beef-and-Cabbage Soup (pages 196, 201, 197) are typical of soups that make a satisfying meal when served with some kind of bread. Sweet and hot rolls and biscuits dripping with melted butter (this is not a diet book) make the meal memorable and as easy on the cook as on the budget.

But you don't need meat for a soup fit for a king (or queen). You can make meal-in-one soups with just vegetables and grains. A big bowl of Corn Chowder (page 207)—with or without the luxury of a few oysters—is a full meal. If the diners have room to spare, serve a pastry dessert. The vegetable-soup recipe on page 208 is my mother's. When I was a child, it was one of my favorite dishes; I always had two servings and never wanted anything more except a piece of fruit. Francesca Morris's Scotch Broth (page 185) is another family favorite. Francesca makes it when she has a bone from a roast leg of lamb. There's little meat on the bone, but the vegetables and barley (a wholesome, nutritious grain) make the soup as filling as a three-course meal.

Soups aren't interesting only as budget trimmers. Vichyssoise (page 209) is one of the most delightful—and sophisticated—dishes you can serve for lunch, and Egg-Drop Soup (page 186), a Chinese favorite, is a conversation piece. Clam Chowder (page 207) is another lunch dish everyone loves and gourmets treasure. Chilled soups—like Cold Cucumber Soup (page 187)—are fine for hot-weather luncheon parties.

HAM-HOCK SOUP, CREOLE STYLE
10 to 12 hours

2 cups light-red kidney beans	1 tsp. salt
1½ lb. smoked ham hocks	¼ tsp. pepper
2 large onions, peeled, chopped	3 quarts water
	¼ cup dry red wine
1 cup chopped celery and leaves	2 egg yolks, slightly beaten
	2 scallions, sliced in rounds
1 large bay leaf	2 lemons, sliced into thin rounds

To Cook: In the slow-cooker, combine the beans, hocks, onion, celery, bay leaf, salt, and pepper with the water. Cover and cook on Low for 10 to 12 hours.

Before Serving: Remove the ham hocks. Discard half the skin. Place the other half, cut into small pieces, in the blender with a little cooking liquid and blend 2 or 3 minutes. Strain the beans and vegetables and purée in the blender with a little cooking liquid for 1 or 2 minutes. Place the puréed hock skin, vegetables, cut-up hock meat, and the cooking liquid in a medium casserole and heat to simmering. Add the wine and bring to a boil. Beat a little of the broth into the egg yolks; then return to the casserole, stirring quickly and constantly. Remove from heat without letting the broth boil again. Serve, garnishing each plate with scallion and lemon rounds.

Makes 8 to 10 servings.

CALIFORNIA CHICKEN-GUMBO FOR A MOB
10 to 12 hours

Feed a multitude with this hearty soup and bread or rolls and butter. It's grand for outdoor parties.

¼ cup butter, margarine, or chicken fat
¼ cup diced ham
½ cup diced celery
1 cup chopped onion
½ cup diced sweet pepper
¼ cup converted rice
4 Tbs. all-purpose flour
2½ quarts chicken stock or bouillon

1 cup drained sliced okra, fresh or canned
1 cup chopped tomatoes
2 Tbs. diced pimento
½ cup cut-up cooked chicken
⅓ cup dried beans (black-eyed peas, baby limas, light-red kidneys)
2 tsp. salt
½ tsp. pepper

To Cook: Warm the butter in a large skillet, over medium heat, and sauté the ham, celery, onion, and sweet pepper until the onion is translucent. Add the rice and sauté, stirring constantly, 5 minutes. Stir in the flour. Add a little chicken broth, scrape up the pan juices, and turn the skillet contents into the slow-cooker. Add remaining broth and all the other ingredients to the cooker. Cover and cook on Low for 10 to 12 hours.

Makes 12 to 14 servings.

CREAM OF LIMA SOUP
10 to 12 hours, or overnight

A soup my grandmother used to make on the back of the stove. She used ¾ cup of heavy cream. You might prefer light cream. I make this the night before and reheat it at dinner time.

1 cup dried baby limas	¾ cup cream
3 cups water	2 Tbs. butter (optional)
1 tsp. salt	Sprigs of fresh parsley

To Cook: Put the beans, water, and salt into the slow-pot and cook on Low 10 to 12 hours or overnight. The beans should be mushy soft. Strain the beans and purée in the blender with a little cooking liquid. Add salt if needed. Mix purée and cooking liquid. Reheat before serving and add the cream at the end. Place a dab of butter and a parsley sprig in each soup plate before serving.

Makes 4 to 6 servings.

TRIPOLINI IN BROTH

Tripolini are the small egg-noodle bows sold in Italian specialty shops. Heat 4 cups of Beef Stock or Bouillon or Chicken-and-Beef Soup (pages 189, 184). Cook ¾ cup of tripolini in 1 quart of salted water 10 to 12 minutes, drain and combine with soup. Sprinkle with grated Parmesan to taste.

Makes 4 servings.

BEEF-GUMBO
6 to 8 hours

This is a hearty meat-and-vegetable soup that makes a complete meal. Serve a good portion of meat in each soup plate.

2 to 3 lb. cross-cut beef shanks, cut 2 inches thick	1 cup diced peeled potato
	½ cup diced celery
1 Tbs. butter or margarine	1 can (16 oz.) whole tomatoes
1 quart water	1 package (10 oz.) frozen lima beans
1 Tbs. salt	
¼ tsp. pepper	1 package (9 oz.) frozen cut green beans
1 bay leaf	
1 medium onion, peeled and quartered	1 can (16 oz.) whole-kernel corn
6 medium carrots, peeled and diced	¼ head green cabbage, sliced fine
	1 can (16 oz.) okra, drained

To Cook: In a large skillet, over medium-high heat, brown the shanks in the butter. Place the shanks in the slow-cook pot with the water, salt, pepper, bay leaf, onion, carrots, potato, celery, and tomatoes. Cover and cook on Low for 6 to 8 hours.

Before Serving: Turn the heat to High and add the lima beans, green beans, corn, and cabbage. Simmer, uncovered, for 20 to 30 minutes. Add the okra and heat thoroughly.

Makes 6 to 8 servings.

BEEF-AND-CABBAGE SOUP
6 to 8 hours

A hearty soup. Serve with bread to make a complete meal.

1½ lb. top round or sirloin tip, cut into 2-inch cubes
2 Tbs. vegetable oil
4 cups water
1 Tbs. soy sauce
4 cups shredded cabbage
1 cup chopped onion
¼ lb. bacon, minced
1 large clove garlic, peeled and minced
2 tsp. salt
½ tsp. pepper
½ tsp. dry mustard
2 large white potatoes, peeled and diced
2 large sweet potatoes, peeled and diced
2 Tbs. catsup or chili sauce

To Cook: In a medium skillet, over medium heat, sauté the beef cubes in the oil until dark brown on all sides. Add the water, the soy sauce, 3 cups of the cabbage, the onion, bacon, garlic, salt, pepper, mustard, potatoes (both kinds), and catsup. Cover and cook on Low for 6 to 8 hours.

Before Serving: Uncover; turn the heat to High; add the remaining cabbage; simmer until tender—about 15 minutes.

Makes 6 to 8 servings.

CURRY SOUP
8 to 10 hours

This is especially good if you have a really good curry powder to make it with.

1 *lb. boneless lamb or veal, cut into 2-inch cubes*	6 *cups water*
2 *Tbs. vegetable oil*	6 *tsp. Steero chicken granules, or 6 chicken bouillon cubes*
1 *cup thinly sliced onion*	1 *apple, peeled, cored, and diced*
½ *cup thinly sliced carrot*	
½ *cup thinly sliced white turnip*	1 *bay leaf*
	⅛ *tsp. dried thyme*
2 *tsp. curry powder*	1 *cup converted rice*
¼ *cup butter or margarine*	1 *tsp. strained lemon juice*

To Cook: In a large skillet, over medium heat, sauté the lamb in the oil until lightly browned on all sides. Remove to the slow-cooker. Add the onion, carrot, turnip, and curry powder to the skillet. Sauté in butter for 3 or 4 minutes. Pour the water and chicken granules into the skillet, scrape up the pan juices, and turn contents into the cooker. Add the apple, bay leaf, thyme, and rice. Cover and cook on Low for 8 to 10 hours.

Before Serving: Stir the lemon juice into the soup and serve.

Makes 8 to 10 servings.

CHICKEN CHOWDER, MARTHA'S VINEYARD STYLE
7 to 9 hours

4 to 5 lb. boiling fowl, cut up	¼ lb. salt pork
2 quarts water	2 medium onions, peeled,
1 bay leaf	minced
¼ tsp. dried thyme	8 cups diced potatoes
3 whole cloves	4 cups scalded milk
1 tsp. salt	2 Tbs. butter or margarine

To Cook: Place the fowl, water, bay leaf, thyme, and cloves in the slow-cooker with 1 tsp. salt. Cover and cook on Low for 7 to 9 hours, or until very tender. Skin the chicken pieces and mince the meat. Discard the bones. When the cooking liquid has cooled, skim off the fat and discard.

Before Serving: In a large kettle, over medium heat, render the fat from the salt pork; discard the cracklings. Add the onion and cook until light brown. Add the cooking liquid from the chicken and then the potatoes and simmer, uncovered, until the potatoes are tender—about 20 minutes. Add the minced chicken and simmer 10 minutes. Add the milk and butter and heat until the butter has melted.

Makes 12 servings.

CHICKEN SOUP WITH RICE
10 to 12 hours

2½ lb. cut-up chicken	6 black peppercorns
1 small onion, peeled, chopped	2 sprigs fresh parsley, or 1 tsp. dried parsley flakes
1 medium carrot, scraped and cut into 1-inch pieces	1 bay leaf
1 medium parsnip, peeled and cut into 1-inch pieces	½ tsp. dried thyme
	1 cup raw converted rice
2 medium cloves garlic, peeled	2 tsp. salt
	8 cups water

To Cook: Place all the ingredients in the slow-cooker. Cover and cook on Low for 10 to 12 hours. Remove the chicken pieces from the soup, skin and bone the meat, cut into small cubes, and return to the soup. If the flavor seems a little pale, add salt and pepper.

Makes 8 to 9 servings.

HEARTY CREAM OF CHICKEN SOUP
10 to 12 hours

This is a variation of Chicken Soup with Rice. Kids love it.

2½ lb. cut-up chicken
1 small onion, peeled
1 medium carrot, scraped and
    cut into 1-inch pieces
1 medium parsnip, peeled
    and cut into 1-inch pieces
2 medium cloves garlic,
    peeled
6 black peppercorns

2 sprigs fresh parsley, or
    1 tsp. dried parsley flakes
1 bay leaf
½ tsp. dried thyme
1 cup raw converted rice
2 tsp. salt
8 cups water
3 Tbs. all-purpose flour

To Cook: Place all the ingredients except the flour in the slow-cooker. Cover and cook on Low for 10 to 12 hours. Remove the chicken pieces from the soup, skin and bone the meat, cut into small cubes, and return to the soup. If the flavor seems a little pale, add salt and pepper.

Before Serving: Skim 2 tablespoons of fat from the soup and place it in a medium skillet, over medium-low heat. Stir in the flour; then beat in, all at once, a cup or so of the soup. Work quickly to keep the sauce smooth. Allow it to simmer for 5 or 6 minutes; then turn it into the slow-cooker. Raise the heat to High and simmer for 2 or 3 minutes.

Makes 6 to 8 servings.

BEANS-AND-HAM SOUP
18 to 20 hours

This soup combines beans with a small ham shank and makes a complete and very hearty meal for a crowd. Start it the night before.

1 lb. dried white beans
    soaked in water
1 small smoked ham shank
8 cups water
2 cups chopped onion
1 cup chopped celery

1 cup shredded carrots
¼ cup minced parsley
2 cloves garlic, peeled and
    minced
2 to 3 tsp. salt
1 tsp. pepper

To Cook: The night before, measure the beans and place them in the slow-cooker. Measure 3 times as much water as beans and add to the pot. Cover and cook on Low overnight—about 12 hours. In the morning, drain off any water. Add the ham and remaining ingredients to the cooker. Cover and cook on Low for 6 to 8 hours.

Before Serving: Remove the ham to a cutting board. Remove the bone and dice the meat. While you are doing this, simmer the soup on High if it seems thin. Return the diced meat to the soup.

Makes 8 to 10 servings.

BAKED-BEAN SOUP
18 to 20 hours

This is an overnight job. Start the beans the night before and let the soup finish cooking the next day. A nice way to use up left-over ham.

1 *cup dried navy beans*
3 *cups water*
1 *cup diced ham*
2 *Tbs. chopped onion*
2 *Tbs. bacon drippings or drippings from ham*
1 *can (16 oz.) whole tomatoes*

1 *Tbs. tightly packed light-brown sugar*
2 *Tbs. vinegar*
1 *tsp. salt*
2 *Tbs. chili sauce or taco sauce*

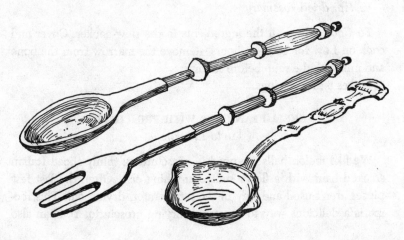

To Cook: The night before, place the beans and the water in the slow-cooker. Cover and cook on Low overnight—about 10 to 12 hours. In the morning, sauté the ham and the onion in the bacon drippings in a small skillet. Add them and the tomatoes, sugar, vinegar, and salt to the slow-pot. Cover and cook on Low until the beans are tender—6 to 8 hours.

Before Serving: Mash the beans a little to thicken the soup, but leave some of them whole to give it body. If the soup seems too thick, thin with a little boiling water. Check for seasoning; it may need salt. Flavor with a dash of chili sauce in each soup plate.

Makes 4 to 6 servings.

BEAN SOUP WITH MARROWBONE
10 to 12 hours

When you have ripe olives left over from a cocktail party, consider this soup as a way to use them up. Beans can take longer than you expect; if they do, turn the heat to High for the last few hours.

1 *cup dried navy beans*	2 *Tbs. tomato paste*
1 *beef marrowbone, 5 inches long*	1 *cup converted rice*
	1½ *tsp. salt*
2 *cloves garlic, peeled, minced*	¼ *tsp. pepper*
	4 *to 6 ripe olives (optional)*
4 *sprigs parsley, chopped*	3 *quarts water*
⅓ *tsp. dried rosemary*	

To Cook: Place all the ingredients in the slow-cooker. Cover and cook on Low for 10 to 12 hours. Remove the marrow from the bone and mix with the soup before serving.

Makes 6 to 8 servings.

SHELL-BEAN SOUP WITH PROSCIUTTO
10 to 12 hours

We like melon balls wrapped in prosciutto, a thinly sliced Italian smoked ham with a flavor unlike anything else. Often the last few pieces aren't used and stay in the refrigerator, drying out. This recipe is a delicious way to cope with drying prosciutto. You can also make it with leftover slices of baked ham, but it won't be the same.

5 Tbs. olive oil

1 or more slices prosciutto or
  leftover ham, minced

½ medium onion, peeled,
  minced

1 medium clove garlic, peeled

¼ cup minced celery

¼ tsp. dried basil

1 cup chopped peeled Italian
  tomatoes or drained
  canned Italian tomatoes

4 cups fresh shell beans or
  dried navy beans

3 quarts water

1½ cups chopped macaroni

1½ tsp. salt

¼ tsp. pepper

½ cup grated Parmesan
  cheese

To Cook: Heat the olive oil in a medium skillet, over medium heat, and sauté the prosciutto, onion, and garlic (whole) until the garlic turns light brown. Discard the garlic. Add the celery, basil, and tomatoes and sauté until the celery turns bright green. Scrape the skillet contents into the slow-cooker. Add the beans, water, macaroni, salt, and pepper. Cover and cook on Low for 10 to 12 hours. Before serving, add the cheese.

Makes 6 to 8 servings.

YANKEE SUCCOTASH CHOWDER
10 to 12 hours

Here's an old recipe that calls for cranberry beans, but this can be made with other types as well—for instance, pintos. It uses fresh corn and is a handy recipe when the corn in your garden is a little too ripe for eating on the cob.

¼ lb. salt pork

10 ears sweet corn

3 cups cranberry beans

12 cups water

1 large onion, peeled,
  chopped

1 quart whole milk

4 Tbs. butter or margarine

1 tsp. salt

⅛ tsp. pepper

To Cook: Dice the salt pork and cut the corn from the cobs. Reserve the kernels. Place the cobs with the salt pork, beans, water, and onion in the slow-pot. Cover and cook on Low for 10 to 12 hours.

Before Serving: Remove the cobs from the slow-cooker and press any kernels from them. Place these and the reserved kernels in the cooker with the milk, butter, salt, and pepper. Turn to High, cover, and simmer 10 to 15 minutes. Old recipes recommend that this soup stand a day before serving.

Makes 12 to 14 servings.

RED-KIDNEY-BEAN SOUP
10 to 12 hours

1 *cup light-red kidney beans*	¾ *cup heavy cream*
1 *medium onion, peeled,*	1 *egg yolk, slightly beaten*
minced	1 *tsp. salt*
1 *carrot, peeled, grated*	¼ *tsp. pepper*
6 *cups Beef Broth, Italian*	
Style (page 185); or	
6 *beef bouillon cubes*	
and 6 cups water	

To Cook: Combine the beans, onion, carrot, and broth in the slow-cooker. Cover and cook on Low for 10 to 12 hours.

Before Serving: Drain the beans and vegetables. Put them in the blender with a little of the broth and blend at low speed for 1 or 2 minutes. Turn purée and broth into a medium kettle and bring to a slow boil. Combine the cream and egg yolk with salt and pepper in a small bowl and beat in ½ cup of the broth. Pour into the broth, stirring quickly and constantly. Remove from the heat as soon as all the egg mixture is stirred in.

Makes 6 to 8 servings.

ONION SOUP WITH CHEESE

Make this with Beef Stock or Bouillon. You need ovenproof tureens or pyrex cups in 8- to 10-ounce size. It is a very popular soup, wonderful to serve at after-skating or after-ski parties and for casual group suppers. Followed by a home-baked pie, it is all you need for a meal.

8 onions, peeled, sliced thin
3 Tbs. butter or margarine
5 cups Beef Stock or Bouillon
   (page 189)
4 Tbs. dry white wine
1½ tsp. salt
¼ tsp. pepper
2 oz. Swiss cheese, slivered
8 small slices stale French
   bread
8 Tbs. grated Swiss cheese

To Cook: In a large, heavy kettle, simmer the onion slices in the butter until they are lightly browned. Stir in the beef stock, wine, salt, and pepper and simmer for 30 minutes.

Before Serving: Divide the slivered cheese among 8 ovenproof small soup bowls, cups, or ceramic soup tureens or custard molds. Break each slice of bread into 2 or 3 pieces and place in the bowls. Spoon on the soup. When the bread chunks rise to the surface, sprinkle them with the grated cheese. Bake in a 325° F. oven for about 20 minutes; then set briefly under the broiler, on high, to brown the cheese.

Makes 8 servings.

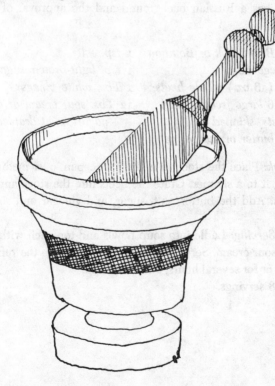

LENTIL SOUP, ITALIAN STYLE
12 to 14 hours

Lentils can be slower to cook than indicated; if necessary, turn the heat to High the last few hours.

1 cup dried lentils	1 Tbs. tomato paste
2½ quarts water	1 tsp. salt
⅛ lb. salt pork, diced	⅛ tsp. pepper

To Cook: Combine lentils with remaining ingredients in the slow-cooker. Cover and cook on Low for 10 to 12 hours.

Makes 6 servings.

BORSCHT, HOT OR COLD

Wonderful cold for summer luncheons or hot for winter nights, this soup has a Russian background and the approval of most of the world.

8 cups Beef Stock or Bouillon (page 189)	1 tsp. salt
	1 tsp. light-brown sugar
2 cans (16 oz.) whole beets; or 6 large fresh-cooked beets, skinned	1 Tbs. white vinegar
	12 Tbs. sour cream or diet yogurt, well drained
1 Tbs. butter or margarine	

To Cook: Place the stock in a large saucepan, over medium heat, and bring it to a simmer. Grate the beets into the stock and simmer 5 minutes. Add the butter, salt, sugar, and vinegar and simmer 10 minutes.

Before Serving: Ladle into soup bowls and top each with 1 tablespoon of sour cream. Serve hot; or chill, covered, in the refrigerator overnight or for several hours, and serve cold.

Makes 8 servings.

MINESTRONE MILANESE
10 to 12 hours

3 Tbs. butter or margarine
⅓ cup diced salt pork
1 medium onion, peeled,
   chopped
2½ quarts beef broth, or 6
   beef bouillon cubes combined with 2½ quarts
   water
1 large carrot, peeled, diced
⅓ cup diced celery

2 small zucchini, diced
1 cup light-red kidney beans
1 cup converted rice
3 sprigs parsley, minced
1 medium clove garlic, peeled,
   minced
¼ tsp. dried basil
¼ tsp. dried thyme
⅓ cup grated Parmesan
   cheese

To Cook: In a medium kettle, over medium heat, warm the butter and sauté the salt pork and the onion until the onion is transparent. Scrape into the slow-cooker. Rinse the skillet with the beef stock and add to the cooker with all ingredients except the cheese. Cover and cook on Low 10 to 12 hours. Taste and add salt if needed. Before serving, add the cheese.

Makes 8 servings.

CORN CHOWDER
6 to 8 hours

This is one of my personal favorites, but it isn't really right unless you make it with salt pork. Bacon, which many cooks use as a substitute for salt pork, won't taste the same.

⅛ lb. salt pork, cut in ½-inch
   cubes
1 large onion, diced
3 cups diced potatoes
1½ cups water
1 can (12 oz.) whole-kernel
   corn

2 tsp. salt
⅛ tsp. pepper
⅛ tsp. paprika
⅛ medium green pepper,
   diced
2 cups whole milk

To Cook: In a medium skillet, over medium-high heat, sauté the salt pork until crisp and brown. Remove the bits, drain on a paper towel, and put aside. Add the onion, potatoes, water, and corn to the slow-cooker, with the salt, pepper, and paprika. Cover and cook on Low for 6 to 8 hours.

Before Serving: Turn the cooker to High and add the green pepper to the soup. Simmer for 5 to 10 minutes, or until the pepper is tender. Add the milk and warm it through. Place the pork bits in the serving bowls and ladle the soup over them.

Makes 6 servings.

MOTHER'S VEGETABLE SOUP
6 to 8 hours

One of my favorite memories is eating this soup for a late, light supper, with plain bread and butter.

1 *large onion, peeled and chopped*	3 *large potatoes, peeled and diced*
1 *Tbs. butter or margarine*	2 *large sprigs fresh parsley, minced*
5 *cups water*	
4 *carrots, peeled and diced*	1 *cup diced celery*
½ *medium yellow turnip, peeled and diced*	2 *tsp. salt*
	¼ *tsp. pepper*

To Cook: In a medium skillet, over medium heat, sauté the onion in the butter until translucent—about 4 or 5 minutes. Pour a little of the water into the skillet and scrape the water and onion into the slow-cooker. Add remaining water and all the other ingredients to the cooker. Cover and cook on Low for 6 to 8 hours.

Makes 4 to 6 servings.

LEEK SOUP
5 to 7 hours

This is a classic recipe, from which all sorts of variations can be made. The most famous is Vichyssoise (below). Add milk to Leek Soup, and the flavor changes. Dress it with a dab of curry, and the flavor changes. Mince ½ cup of parsley very finely and sprinkle it over the hot soup after serving, and you have a whole new soup.

It's a hearty soup and with crisp French bread, butter, cheese, and dessert makes a complete meal.

4 large or 6 small leeks
2 Tbs. butter or margarine
1 small onion, peeled and
    chopped
1 quart water

3 cups diced peeled medium
    potatoes
½ tsp. salt
1 Tbs. butter or margarine

To Cook: Washing the leeks is important. Any sand left will make the soup a lot less fun to eat, especially when you get to the bottom of the pot. Cut the leeks in half and remove yellowed or wilted outer leaves. Fill the sink with water and wash each leek leaf until absolutely clean. Rinse under cold running water. In a medium skillet, over medium heat, melt 2 tablespoons butter and sauté the onion until translucent. Don't let it brown. Pour a little of the water into the skillet and turn the skillet contents into the slow-pot. Place remaining water, leeks, and rest of ingredients except the 1 tablespoon of butter in the pot. Cover and cook on Low for 5 to 7 hours.

Before Serving: Mash the ingredients in the soup to make a smooth cream. If you'd like the soup thinner, add a little milk. Add a dab of butter to each serving.

Makes 4 to 6 servings.

VICHYSSOISE
5 to 7 hours

This is the fancy version of Leek Soup. It's lovely hot and divine cold. To serve it cold, let it cook all night; chill it, covered, all day in the refrigerator; add cream, chives, and serve. It's a wonderful summer luncheon dish, served with a small green salad and hot biscuits.

5 large or 8 small leeks
2 Tbs. butter or margarine
1 very small onion, peeled
    and minced
1 quart chicken bouillon,
    or 4 cups water with
    Steero chicken granules

3 cups diced, peeled old
    potatoes
1 Tbs. salt
1 cup heavy cream
2 Tbs. chopped chives

To Cook: Wash the leeks carefully. Cut them in half and remove spoiled or wilted outer leaves and the green portions of the other leaves. Wash leaves one at a time in a sinkful of cold water. When all sand is gone, rinse under cold running water. In a medium skillet, over medium heat, melt the butter and sauté the onion until golden and translucent. Don't let the onion brown at all. Pour a little of the chicken bouillon into the skillet and turn the skillet contents into the slow-pot. Add the remaining bouillon, the potatoes, salt, and leeks. Cover and cook on Low for 5 to 7 hours.

Before Serving: In a blender on low, blend the soup 2 cups at a time. Taste and add salt if needed. Combine with cream and serve hot, garnished with chopped chives. Or chill for several hours; then combine with cream and garnish each serving with chives.

Makes 4 to 6 servings.

CLAM CHOWDER
4 to 5 hours

Quahogs are great big hard-shell clams. If these aren't available, use small hard-shell clams or steamers.

1 *quart shucked clams or quahogs; or 2 dozen hard-shell clams, shucked, or steamers*	3 *medium potatoes, peeled and sliced thin*
¼ *lb. salt pork, diced*	½ *tsp. salt*
1 *large onion, peeled and finely minced*	⅛ *tsp. pepper*
4 *cups water*	4 *cups whole milk*
	6 *large, hard, cracker-barrel crackers, split*
	2 *Tbs. butter or margarine*

To Cook: Drain the clams, reserving the liquid. Remove the tough neck portion from each clam. Separate the belly, or soft part, from the firm part. Chop the firm parts and put the soft parts in the refrigerator, covered. In a medium skillet, over medium heat, sauté the salt pork until crisp and golden. Drain on paper towel. Sauté the onion until translucent. Add the water and clam liquid to the skillet and scoop the skillet contents into the slow-cooker. Add the potatoes, salt, pepper, salt-pork bits, and the chopped firm parts of the clams. Cover and cook on Low for 4 to 5 hours.

Before Serving: Add the milk, cover, and turn the heat to High. When the milk is simmering, turn off the heat; add the soft portions of the clams; cover, and let stand for 15 to 20 minutes before serving. Place the crackers in the serving bowls; add a bit of butter to each and ladle the chowder over them.

Makes 6 to 8 servings.

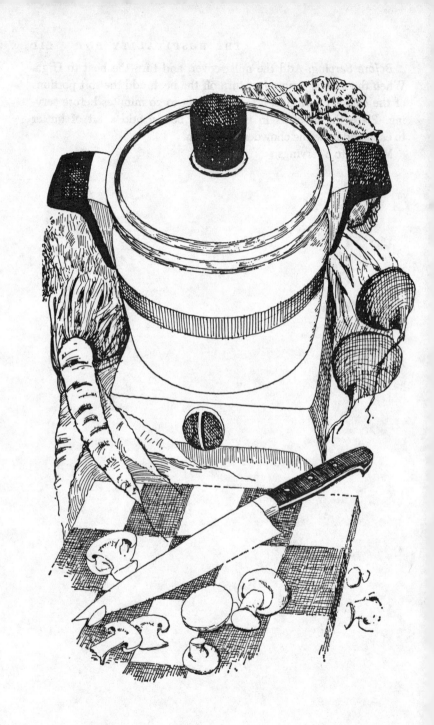

PART FIVE

VEGETABLES AND SIDE DISHES

Chapter 9

Vegetable Casseroles; Sauces and Fondues

THE SLOW-COOKER OPENS up a world of vegetable casseroles and sauces to the absentee cook—but I can't recommend it for all garden-fresh vegetables. What I mean is, garden peas and beans and corn are a travesty when cooked for hours, while sauces and casseroles of vegetables (like Madame Bertrand's Ratatouille, page 221), work out wonderfully well.

Garden-fresh vegetables that can be slow-cooked successfully include the firm root vegetables, potatoes, celery, and leeks. Carrots, yellow turnips, potatoes, and leeks change color when cooked for hours in a slow-pot, but their flavor is all right. I think carrots and turnips, if they are to be slow-cooked, are best in casseroles, such as Turnip-and-Carrot Pot (page 220). Celery and leeks braised in a little beef stock in the slow-cooker are very good.

Potatoes already baked when you arrive home come in handy, and they go well with cold cuts and salads or fish dishes. Wrap the potatoes loosely in foil, so steam and drips from the slow-cooker's cover won't make them soggy. Bake them on a trivet. If you don't have a trivet, you can improvise one from Pyrex custard cups, as described in Chapter 11. In a slow-cooker, potatoes don't bake crisp, but they taste good.

Casseroles combining vegetables that have a good deal of moisture are excellent slow-cooked, though you may have to boil away liquid before serving. Ratatouille, a classic fresh-vegetable casserole of Southern France, combines tomatoes, eggplant, sweet peppers, zucchini, and onions. You can invent your own ratatouille, guided by vegetables in your garden or plentiful at the market. Be sure to include a vegetable to provide moisture, such as tomato. If the dish is watery after cooking, simmer it on the stove top. A good combination is tomatoes and green beans or shell beans of any kind. Tomatoes and onions, flavored with oregano and a little basil, can be the base for a slow-pot casserole that could include almost any vegetables you have. Add a little sugar, and the flavor will be gentler.

Dishes combining moisture-holding vegetables with dry ingredients work out well in a slow-cooker—Stuffed Cabbage Rolls (page 217), for example. Stuff cabbage or lettuce leaves with your own favorite mixture of bread crumbs or rice and meat.

You can make vegetable puddings in the slow-cooker. A vegetable pudding is a little like a soufflé. The slow-cooker must be large enough for the baking mold, and the mold—a soufflé dish is fine, too—must sit on a trivet and should be covered. Use the Corn Pudding recipe (page 249) to adapt your recipe to slow-pot cooking.

PLANNING MEALS AROUND VEGETABLE CASSEROLES

When you serve a vegetable casserole, the rest of the meal can be simple and quick to prepare. The hearty casserole supplies all the down-home flavor the meal needs. Add cold leftover meat of any kind—even cold cuts from the delicatessen—and a salad, and you've got it made. Or serve any fast-cooked pan-fried or grilled meat— hamburger, minute steak, veal steaks, veal scallopini.

Vegetable casseroles also go very well with egg dishes, notably omelettes and fried eggs, and with fish and fish sticks.

SLOW-POT SAUCES AND FONDUES

The slow-cooker is ideally suited to making sauces that require long cooking. They have a wonderfully rich flavor. There are several sauces in the meat chapters. The recipes in this chapter are vegetable based (mainly tomato) and will make a celebration of a simple grilled hamburger, baked beans, an egg dish, or baked fish. I use the Spanish Sauce (page 231) with shredded lettuce. Or use sauces to dress pastas, rice, or beans.

If you have a vegetable garden, plant plenty of tomatoes and make sauces to freeze for later use. Packed into sturdy plastic freezer containers, they keep all winter.

The slow-cooker can also be used to make fondues. Although fondues are easily made over a low flame in a sterno container, they often are burned or overheated. Made slowly in the crockery cooker, they are delicious. You can serve fondues or sauces right from the cooker because they remain gently warmed for hours and never overcook or dry out.

VEGETABLE CASSEROLES

ANNE LE MOINE'S BAYRISCHE KRAUT
6 to 8 hours

A traditional Bavarian dish that uses up all sorts of pork tidbits. The pork is for flavoring and can include ham leftovers, a ham bone, ends of hot dogs, drying salami, bits of roast pork, pork-roast drippings, dried-up cold cuts, sausages, old bacon. The whole thing cooks for hours and tastes marvelous. It can also be made without the meat. Then serve it with white meat, such as veal, pork, or chicken.

1 *small winter (white) cabbage, shredded*	1 *to 2 tsp. sugar*
4 *to 6 large onions, shredded*	1 *to 2 tsp. salt*
2 *Tbs. finely chopped parsley*	2 *heaping Tbs. dried currants (optional)*
1½ *tsp. cumin or caraway seed*	*Pork-product leftovers (optional; see above)*
1 *to 2 Tbs. white vinegar*	

To Cook: Measure the shredded cabbage; then measure an equal amount of shredded onion. Place both in the slow-cooker with the remaining ingredients. Cover and cook on Low for 6 to 8 hours. Drain excess cooking liquid before serving.

Makes 6 to 8 servings.

RED-CABBAGE CASSEROLE
6 to 8 hours

In the old days, this cooked at the back of the stove for hours and hours, the lid sealed steamproof with a heavy stone. The slow-cooker makes it to perfection. Very good with pork or any fatty-meat dish.

½ *medium red cabbage,* *shredded*	1 *big bay leaf*
1 *very big apple, peeled,* *cored, shredded*	2 *Tbs. wine vinegar*
	¼ to ½ *cup sugar*
	1 *tsp. salt*

To Cook: Place all the ingredients in the slow-pot. Cover and cook on Low for 6 to 8 hours.

Before Serving: If there is a lot of cooking liquid, drain it off (use it in borscht) before serving.

Makes 4 to 6 servings.

STUFFED CABBAGE ROLLS WITH TOMATO SAUCE
8 to 10 hours

A wonderful dish for the family on a cold night. The preparation is a little tedious because you have to make the cabbage rolls, but they can cook all day and be ready whenever you are.

1 *medium green cabbage*	1 *medium carrot, peeled and* *grated*
1 *lb. chopped cooked beef,* *veal, or pork (2 cups)*	1 *tsp. salt*
¼ *cup raw converted rice*	¼ *cup malt vinegar*
1 *egg, slightly beaten*	½ *cup light-brown sugar, firmly* *packed*
1 *medium onion, peeled and* *grated*	1 *cup canned tomato sauce*

To Cook: Drop the cabbage into a large kettle of boiling water and cook for 4 to 8 minutes, or until the outer leaves come off easily. Drain and cool. Remove 8 of the large outer leaves. Discard the tough inner core and chop the rest of the cabbage. Spread the chopped cabbage over the bottom of the slow-cooker. In a bowl, combine the meat, rice, egg, onion, carrot, and salt. Spread some of this mixture in the center of each large cabbage leaf, leaving a generous flap on either side. Roll up the leaves, sausage fashion. Place the rolls in the slow-cooker, tucking in the flap ends neatly. In a small bowl, combine the vinegar, sugar, and tomato sauce and pour over the rolls. Cover and cook on Low for 8 to 10 hours.

Makes 4 to 6 servings.

CABBAGE-AND-POTATO CASSEROLE
3 to 4 hours

A hearty dish for winter dinners, this uses up leftover mashed potatoes—and it's good, besides.

2 Tbs. butter or margarine	2 Tbs. sugar
2 medium onions, peeled, chopped	2 tsp. salt
	¼ tsp. pepper
1 small white cabbage, shredded	2 cups chicken bouillon, or Steero granules in 2 cups hot water
2 green apples, thinly sliced	
1½ tsp. white vinegar	½ cup leftover mashed potatoes

To Cook: In a large skillet, over medium heat, melt the butter and simmer the onion until golden brown. In the slow-cooker, make alternate layers of cabbage and apple. Add the onion, vinegar, sugar, salt, and pepper. Mix the bouillon into the mashed potatoes to make a thin sauce and pour it over the cabbage. Cover and bake on High for 3 to 4 hours.

Makes 6 or 7 servings.

CASSEROLE OF ROOT VEGETABLES
6 to 8 hours

This takes a long time to cook, and the vegetables won't be a very pretty color when they're finished, but they taste very good with pork roasts and game dishes.

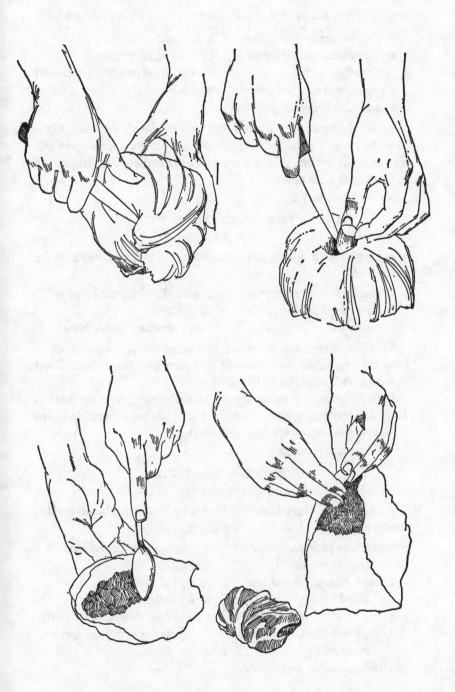

1 *Tbs. butter or margarine*
2 *cups diced peeled white
   turnips*
2 *cups diced scraped carrots*
2 *cups diced peeled potatoes*

2 *tsp. salt*
¼ *tsp. black pepper*
½ *tsp. dried oregano (optional)*
1 *cup water*

To Cook: Butter the bottom and side of the slow-cooker. Combine the diced vegetables with the salt and pepper and oregano and turn into the cooker. Add the water. Cover and cook on High for 6 to 8 hours, or until tender.

Makes 6 to 8 servings.

TURNIP-AND-CARROT POT
6 to 8 hours

A long-cooking winter dish that makes a fine accompaniment for roast duck.

3 *Tbs. butter or margarine*
2 *cups diced peeled white
   turnips*

2 *cups diced scraped carrots*
¼ *tsp. salt*
1 *tsp. strained lemon juice*

To Cook: Butter the sides and bottom of the slow-cooker. Combine the vegetables with the salt and turn into the cooker. Cover and cook on Low for 6 to 8 hours.

Before Serving: If there's liquid in the cooker, turn the heat to High and cook, uncovered, until the liquid has gone. Sprinkle lemon juice over the vegetables, toss well, and serve.

Makes 4 to 6 servings.

VEGETABLE MARMITE
8 to 10 hours

A mélange of vegetables that gives off a wonderful home-cooking aroma and is almost effortless to prepare.

6 *medium potatoes, peeled
   and thinly sliced*
1 *small turnip, peeled and
   diced*
1 *cup fresh or frozen peas*
2 *large tomatoes, skinned and
   quartered*
1 *onion, peeled and thinly
   sliced*

¼ *cup raw converted rice*
1 *tsp. salt*
⅛ *tsp. pepper*
⅛ *tsp. allspice*
2 *cups beef bouillon, or Steero
   granules in 2 cups water*

To Cook: In the slow-pot, layer the vegetables; end with the rice and seasoning. Pour the bouillon over the vegetables. Cover and cook on Low for 8 to 10 hours.

Makes 6 servings.

MADAME BERTRAND'S RATATOUILLE
6 to 8 hours

When I lived in Southern France, my landlady taught me to make this as she did, in a crockery saucepan on the back of a wood-burning stove. The crockery cooker is the only utensil that gets it just right in a modern kitchen.

⅓ *cup olive oil*
3 *large cloves garlic, minced*
4 *large, firm tomatoes, peeled, cut into 2-inch chunks*
1 *medium eggplant, peeled and cut into 2-inch cubes*
2 *red or green sweet peppers, seeded and cut in large strips*

2 *medium zucchini, unpeeled, cut into 4-inch pieces*
3 *medium onions, peeled and quartered*
2 *tsp. salt*
¼ *tsp. pepper*
½ *tsp. dried oregano*
½ *tsp. dried thyme*

To Cook: In a large skillet, heat the oil and sauté the garlic for about 2 minutes. In a large bowl, gently combine the vegetables with the seasonings and herbs. Turn the garlic and oil into the slow-cooker; add the vegetables. Cover and cook on Low for 6 to 8 hours.

Before Serving: If there's a lot of liquid in the ratatouille after everything in it is cooked soft, turn the heat to High and simmer, uncovered, until the liquid has gone.

Makes 10 to 12 servings.

MÉLANGE OF GREENS—GARBURE
6 to 8 hours

This is another of Anne Le Moine's long-cook food-saver recipes. To make it, you need a savoy cabbage (that's the crinkle-leaved, dark-green type) and 4 other leafy greens (spinach, broccoli, turnip greens, mustard greens, collard greens, etc.). Leftovers can be frozen. With the addition of chicken stock, or half chicken stock and half milk, this will make a delicious thick, creamy soup, to be served with croutons. The nutty-flavored Garbure can be served with just butter and nutmeg, or mixed half-and-half with mashed potatoes and a little butter. Delicious.

1 *savoy cabbage, shredded finely*	⅛ *tsp. pepper*
Equal amount of 4 other leafy greens (as above)	3 *Tbs. butter or margarine*
	¼ *tsp. grated nutmeg*
1 *tsp. salt*	*Milk or cream (optional)*

To Cook: Measure the shredded cabbage in packed cupfuls and shred and measure an equal amount of each of the other leafy greens. Place in the slow-cook pot, with salt and pepper. Cover and cook on Low for 6 to 8 hours.

Before Serving: Drain the liquid from the greens (save it for soup stock) and purée the greens in the blender. Serve with butter, a sprinkling of nutmeg, and milk or cream if you wish.

Makes 10 to 12 servings.

ANNE LE MOINE'S CASSEROLE ORLÉANS
6 to 8 hours

A French vegetable casserole that relies on leftover chicken, with or without canned white tuna, for its unusual flavor.

2 *cups diced cooked chicken, or 1 cup diced chicken and 1 cup flaked, drained canned tuna*	½ *cup white wine*
	1 *tsp. salt*
	⅛ *tsp. pepper*
	2 *Tbs. cold water*
2 *large carrots, peeled, sliced*	1 *Tbs. cornstarch*
2 *large stalks celery, diced*	*Juice of ½ lemon, strained*
1 *large parsnip, peeled, sliced*	2 *Tbs. minced fresh parsley*
1 *large onion, peeled, diced*	¼ *tsp. grated nutmeg*
4 *large potatoes, peeled, halved lengthwise*	2 *Tbs. heavy cream (optional)*
1 *cup chicken stock, or 1 chicken bouillon cube and 1 cup water*	

To Cook: Place chicken, carrots, celery, parsnip, onion, potatoes, stock, wine, salt, and pepper in the slow-pot. Cover and cook on Low for 6 to 8 hours.

Before Serving: Pour the cooking liquid into a small saucepan and set over medium heat. Combine the water and cornstarch and stir into the hot liquid. Stir until the liquid clears and thickens. Stir in the lemon juice, parsley, and nutmeg, and cook 1 minute more. If you wish, stir in the heavy cream. Pour over the vegetables, mix gently, and serve. Divide the potatoes when serving.

Makes 6 to 8 servings.

PIG IN A POTATO
6 to 8 hours

You need big Idaho potatoes. They will taste just as good fast-cooked (about 50 minutes) in a 375° F. oven, but are good slow-cooked, too. This is an adaptation of an old Maine recipe from the *Book of Dorcas Dishes.*

6 *large Idaho potatoes*   6 *small sausages*

To Cook: Wash and wipe the potatoes. Make a tunnel through each with an apple corer; the tunnels must be large enough to hold the sausages. Push the sausages into the tunnels. Wrap in foil and place in the slow-pot. Cover and cook on Low for 6 to 8 hours.

Makes 6 servings.

POTATO-ONION CASSEROLE
4 to 6 hours

Cape Cod fishermen called this Scootin'-'Long-the-Shore. In Maine, a similar dish is called Very Poor Man's Dinner.

½ *cup bacon drippings or fat*   8 *cups thinly sliced potatoes*
skimmed from ham-roast   2 *cups thinly sliced onion*
drippings   ½ *tsp. pepper*

To Cook: In a very large skillet, melt the fat and add the potatoes, onion and pepper. Toss well until vegetables are completely coated with fat. Transfer to the slow-cooker. Cover and cook on Low for 4 to 6 hours.

Makes 10 to 12 servings.

PAPA'S SCALLOPED POTATOES
3 to 4 hours

4 Tbs. butter or margarine	2 tsp. salt
4 large potatoes, peeled and	¼ tsp. pepper
sliced ¼ inch thick	½ cup light cream or whole milk

To Cook: Butter the bottom and sides of the slow-pot. Arrange a layer of sliced potatoes, season with ½ the salt and pepper, and add ½ the remaining butter. Repeat. Add the cream. Cover and cook on High for 3 to 4 hours.

Makes 4 servings.

PARSNIPS
6 to 8 hours

Parsnips are one of the root vegetables I especially like done in the slow-cooker. Here's how:

8 to 10 medium parsnips,	1 tsp. salt
peeled and quartered	3 Tbs. butter or margarine
¼ cup water	½ tsp. strained lemon juice

To Cook: Place the parsnips in the slow-cooker with the water and salt. Cover and cook on Low for 6 to 8 hours.

Before Serving: Uncover and turn the heat to High to cook away any moisture in the pot. Add the butter and lemon juice. When the butter is melted, serve the parsnips.

Makes 5 or 6 servings.

GREEN-PEPPER CASSEROLE
6 to 8 hours

Make this with leftover veal or lamb. Or a tag end of raw hamburger works well.

2 Tbs. olive oil	2 large tomatoes, peeled,
2 medium onions, peeled,	chopped
chopped	1 clove garlic, peeled and
1 cup ground cooked veal or	minced
lamb	1 tsp. salt

⅛ tsp. pepper
1 bay leaf, crushed
½ tsp. dried thyme
1 cup raw converted rice
2 Tbs. butter or margarine

8 large green peppers, seeded
   and sliced into 1-inch
   strips
1 cup canned tomato sauce
½ tsp. minced fresh basil, or ¼
   tsp. dried basil

To Cook: In a large skillet, over medium-high heat, heat the oil and sauté the onion until golden brown. Mix in the meat and brown it a little, stirring constantly. Stir in the tomatoes, garlic, salt, pepper, bay bits, thyme, and rice. Sauté another couple of minutes until the rice begins to look opaque. Smear the butter over the bottom and sides of the slow-cooker. Layer the green-pepper strips and the tomato mixture in the cooker, ending with green pepper. Pour the tomato sauce over all and sprinkle with basil. Cover and cook on Low for 6 to 8 hours.

Makes 8 servings.

TOMATO CASSEROLE
6 to 8 hours

Tastes like stuffed tomatoes, but the texture is different.

2 Tbs. butter or margarine
1 medium onion, peeled and
   minced
1 clove garlic, peeled and
   minced
½ lb. sausage meat
1 tsp. salt
2 tsp. sugar
¾ cup unflavored bread
   crumbs

3 Tbs. water
1 Tbs. soy sauce
3 Tbs. minced parsley
3 Tbs. butter or margarine
6 large tomatoes, peeled,
   stemmed and cut in thick
   slices
¾ cup unflavored bread crumbs
2 Tbs. butter

To Cook: In a medium skillet, over medium heat, melt 2 tablespoons butter and sauté the onion and garlic until the onion begins to brown. Add the sausage meat, salt, and sugar and sauté for 3 minutes. Add ¾ cup bread crumbs to the skillet and moisten with water mixed with soy sauce. Mix well and remove from the heat. Sprinkle with parsley. Smear the bottom and sides of the slow-cooker with 2 tablespoons butter. Place ⅓ of the tomato slices on the bottom and add a layer of the onion mixture. Repeat and end with a layer of tomatoes. Cover and cook on Low for 6 to 8 hours.

Before Serving: Heat the broiler to medium; turn the tomato mixture into an ovenproof baking dish; sprinkle thickly with ¾ cup bread crumbs, dot with butter, and broil long enough to brown the crumbs.

Makes 6 servings.

BRAISED CELERY
6 to 8 hours

I sometimes make this in the slow-cooker because it finishes slowly in the oven, where it sometimes also runs out of cooking broth.

10 *large stalks celery*   ⅛ *tsp. pepper*
1 *cup Beef Stock or Bouillon*   3 *Tbs. butter or margarine*
    (page 189)

To Cook: Cut the celery into 3-inch lengths and place with the stock and pepper in the slow-cooker. Cover and cook on Low for 6 to 8 hours.

Before Serving: In a small skillet on the stove top, simmer the cooking liquid until reduced to ½ cup. Add the butter; stir until melted. Serve over the hot celery.

Makes 4 to 6 servings.

BRAISED LEEKS
6 to 8 hours

Follow the recipe for Braised Celery, but instead of celery use 6 to 8 very large leeks, thoroughly washed and with the tops trimmed to within 2 inches of the white part. Celery is salty and so is the cooking stock, so that recipe omits salt. You may want to add salt to the leeks when the cooking is finished.

Makes 4 to 6 servings.

CELERY STUFFED WITH VEAL OR PORK
6 to 8 hours

Made from leftovers of veal or pork and the coarse outer stalks of celery and sauced with a lemony béchamel made of the cooking juices, this is a great dish for parties or for light summer meals.

2 cups cooked pork or veal, or
   1 cup pork, 1 cup veal
1 tsp. Italian herbs
1 tsp. salt
⅛ tsp. pepper
2 slices white bread
¼ cup milk
1 egg
6 to 8 large outer stalks
   celery, washed, leaves
   removed

½ cup chicken stock, or 1
   chicken bouillon cube and
   ½ cup water
2 Tbs. butter or margarine
2 Tbs. all-purpose flour
1 tsp. strained lemon or lime
   juice
1 heaping Tbs. finely chopped
   parsley

To Cook: Remove any parts of the meat that show the brown of roasting, and blend the meat in a blender until very fine. Place in a medium-large bowl and add the Italian herbs, salt, and pepper. Soak the bread in the milk until saturated; drain off all excess milk. Then beat in the egg. Beat bread-and-egg mixture into the meat mixture. Taste for seasoning and add salt, pepper, or Italian herbs if needed. Roll the mixture into a sausage about 2 or 3 inches in diameter. Cut the celery stalks to the length of the sausage. Wash them well; dry them, and with a potato peeler, lightly peel the outer side to remove strings. Tie two rows of stalks around the sausage, using white string or heavy white thread. Place the roll in the slow-cooker; add the stock. Cover and cook on Low for 6 to 8 hours, or until the celery is tender through.

Before Serving: In a small saucepan, over medium-low heat, melt the butter; stir in the flour to make a smooth paste. Beat in 1 cup of the cooking liquid, or as much as is available. Stir quickly to make a smooth sauce. Add the lemon juice and cook 1 or 2 minutes. The consistency should be that of very heavy cream. If too thick, add a little chicken stock. Just before serving, mix in the parsley. Remove the string and serve the log with the sauce poured over it. Cut it in 1-inch-thick slices (like meat loaf).

Makes 4 to 6 servings.

SAUCES AND FONDUES

VEGETABLES AND BAGNA CAUDA

The slow-cooker can do other things besides cook slowly. For instance, it keeps dips, fondues, and sauces hot without drying them out. The smaller slow-cookers are better suited to this use than larger ones. This sauce is very good with mixed fresh garden vegetables, and the recipe suggests how to use your slow-cooker to keep dips for the cocktail hour warm.

6 *medium cloves garlic,*
    peeled, minced
12 *anchovy fillets and their oil*
½ *lb. butter or margarine*
1 *cup light olive oil*
¼ *tsp. pepper*

6 *cups sticks or chunks of fresh*
    raw vegetables—zucchini,
    cucumber, asparagus,
    cauliflower, fennel, celery,
    iceberg lettuce, green
    pepper, mushrooms,
    summer squash

To Cook: In a small mortar or a wooden bowl, mash the garlic and anchovies into a paste. Turn this into the slow-cooker. Set the heat at High, cover, and let simmer for 10 minutes, or until the mixture has thickened. Stir in the butter, olive oil, and pepper; cover and cook for 3 to 5 minutes. Turn the heat to Low and keep sauce warm. Serve with the vegetables for dip sticks.

Makes 10 to 12 servings.

TOMATO SAUCE WITH EGGPLANT
6 to 8 hours

This will be enough for about 2 cups macaroni or rice (measured before cooking).

⅓ *cup olive or vegetable oil*
1 *clove garlic*
2½ *lb. very ripe Italian*
    tomatoes, chopped
1 *small eggplant, peeled,*
    diced
1 *sweet green pepper, seeded,*
    minced

1 *tsp. dried basil, or 4 leaves*
    fresh basil
4 *anchovy fillets, minced*
    (optional)
1 *tsp. salt (if no anchovy is*
    used)

To Cook: In a large skillet, over medium heat, heat the oil and sauté the garlic until golden. Discard garlic. Add the remaining ingredients and simmer briefly, scraping up pan juices. Turn into the slow-cooker. Cover and cook on Low for 6 to 8 hours. If the sauce seems a little too thin, simmer in a saucepan, over medium-high heat, to reduce it.

Makes 6 to 8 servings.

CLASSIC CHEESE FONDUE WITH VEGETABLE STICKS

Fondue is a quick-cook affair, but I find it convenient to make it in the slow-cooker for a party. Without ruining it, the cooker keeps it warm for a long time before the party and during the dipping period as well.

1 *lb. pasteurized cheese, such as Gruyère*	4 *cups sticks of fresh vegetables, such as*
1 *large clove garlic, peeled*	*zucchini, celery, cucumber,*
2 *cups dry white wine*	*or stale bread sticks,*
3 *Tbs. kirsch liqueur*	*cauliflower chunks, or sticks*
1 *tsp. cornstarch*	*of stale French bread*
⅛ *tsp. grated nutmeg*	

To Cook: Grate the cheese on the coarse side of the grater. Cut the garlic in half; rub the cut parts all over the bottom of the slow-cooker, then discard. Pour the wine into the slow-cooker, turn to High, and cover. Pour the kirsch into a small cup and stir in the cornstarch. When the wine has foamy bubbles on the surface but before it boils, begin to pour the grated cheese into it, stirring constantly. When the cheese begins to thicken and catch, stir more rapidly and add the kirsch-and-cornstarch mixture. Continue to cook, stirring, until the fondue has thickened. Sprinkle with nutmeg. Turn to Low and cover, ready to serve with crisp vegetable or bread sticks.

Makes 6 or 7 servings as an appetizer, 4 servings as a meal course.

CHEESE RAREBIT OR WELSH RAREBIT

Served on toast points, this is a Sunday-night supper, but I like it with grilled tomatoes or shredded lettuce. It isn't meant for long cooking, but it is one of the cheese dishes that benefits from the gentleness of the heat the slow-cooker supplies. A good way to use left-over yellow cheese.

1 lb. aged yellow cheese	1 tsp. salt
1 Tbs. butter or margarine	¼ tsp. dry mustard
1 cup beer	1 whole lettuce, shredded; or 4
1 medium egg, slightly beaten	ripe tomatoes, halved,
1 tsp. Worcestershire sauce	broiled

To Cook: Grate the cheese. In the slow-cooker, on High, melt the butter and stir in the beer. Cover until the beer is steaming. Turn the heat to Low, stir in the cheese, and stir until the cheese has melted. Beat in the egg and the seasonings. Cover and let cook until thickened. Stir before serving over lettuce or tomatoes.

Makes 6 to 8 servings.

TOMATO SAUCE
6 to 8 hours

This will dress 2 to 3 cups macaroni or rice (measured before cooking). A large pork chop is all the pork you need, or use a tag end cut from the large end of a pork loin roast.

⅓ cup olive or vegetable oil	3 sprigs parsley, minced; or 3
2 large cloves garlic	Tbs. minced parsley stems
¼ lb. fresh pork, chopped	¼ tsp. dried basil, or 3 leaves
4 large ripe tomatoes, peeled,	fresh basil
chopped	¼ tsp. dried oregano
2 cans (10 oz.) tomato paste	1 tsp. salt
2½ cups beef stock or water	¼ tsp. pepper

To Cook: In a large skillet, over medium-high heat, heat the oil and sauté the garlic until golden. Discard garlic. Add the pork and sauté until browned. Add the rest of the ingredients, scrape up the pan juices, and turn into the slow-cooker. Cover and cook on Low for 6 to 8 hours. If the sauce is a little thin, boil down briefly in a skillet, over medium-high heat.

Makes 4 to 6 servings.

SPANISH SAUCE
6 to 8 hours

I make this for omelettes and to serve with cold meat cuts, and sometimes serve it simply on a bed of shredded iceberg lettuce.

2 Tbs. olive or vegetable oil
1 large clove garlic, peeled, minced
2 large onions, peeled, sliced
8 very ripe Italian tomatoes, chopped

2 large sweet peppers, seeded, chopped
1 tsp. salt
⅛ tsp. pepper
1 Tbs. tomato paste
⅛ tsp. dried thyme

To Cook: Heat the oil in a large skillet, over medium heat and sauté the garlic and onion until the onion is translucent. Turn the tomatoes into the skillet and scrape up the pan juices. Turn into the slow-cooker with the remaining ingredients. Cover and cook on Low for 6 to 8 hours. If the sauce seems a little watery, simmer briefly on the stove top to thicken.

Makes enough for 6 servings.

MARENGO SAUCE
6 to 8 hours

This is a wonderful sauce for meats, grilled or baked or reheated, and nice with omelettes or on toast. Italian specialty markets usually carry dried mushrooms.

¼ cup diced salt pork
½ cup chopped onion
2 medium cloves garlic, peeled, minced
2 sprigs parsley, minced
2 Tbs. tomato paste
1 tsp. salt
⅛ tsp. pepper

½ cup dry white wine
6 very ripe Italian tomatoes, chopped
2 tsp. tomato purée
¼ tsp. dried thyme
⅛ tsp. cayenne pepper
¾ cup coarsely chopped dried mushrooms

To Cook: Place all the ingredients in the slow-cooker. Cover and cook on Low for 6 to 8 hours.

Before Serving: If the sauce seems thin, simmer briefly on the stove top. Or make a roux (page 28); stir some of the sauce into it; simmer until thickened; then combine with the rest of the sauce.

Makes enough for 4 to 6 servings.

TOMATO SAUCE FOR SPAGHETTI
6 to 8 hours

This is about as much sauce as you need for 2 cups spaghetti (measured before cooking). I like it on white beans, too. Nice with grilled hamburgers and other grilled or broiled meats.

⅓ cup olive oil
1 large clove garlic, peeled, minced
2 cans (16 oz.) tomato paste
6 large, ripe tomatoes, chopped

1 tsp. dried basil
1 tsp. dried oregano
2 cups water
1 tsp. salt
¼ tsp. pepper

To Cook: Heat the oil in a large skillet, over medium heat. Sauté the garlic until brown; sauté remaining ingredients, stirring, 5 to 10 minutes. Scrape up pan juices and turn mixture into the slow-cooker. Cover and cook on Low for 6 to 8 hours. If the sauce is a little thin, simmer for a few minutes on the stove top, to thicken.

Makes about 4 to 5 cups.

Chapter 10

Beans; Rice; Other Grains and Dried Vegetables

IN RECENT YEARS, WE'VE overlooked beans and dried grains in favor of rice and pastas, but with a slow-cooker that comes to an end. The slow-cooker makes possible and practical and economical many bean- and grain-based dishes we have been ignoring for a long time. For vegetarians, this is really good news.

Because of their high protein value, I've experimented considerably with dried beans, and I have had the advantage of advance reports on slow-pot tests run by the Dried Bean Institute of California. What we've come up with makes the bean picture very attractive for the slow-cooker owner interested in sound nutrition and a lower food budget. Dried beans are consistently listed among the best food buys. The USDA classed bean dishes among the few top alternatives to meat. A pound of dried beans measures 2 to 3 cups, depending on the variety; cooked, they make 4 to 6 or 7 cups of high-protein food. Proteins help build muscles, glands, bones, teeth, skin. Beans are a good source of thiamine and riboflavin, members of the B-vitamin complex, which remain stable under long cooking. They are also a source of iron: a ¾ cup serving provides ½ to ⅓ of a man's daily iron need and about ⅛ to ¼ of a woman's. Calcium, phosphorus, and potassium are plentiful in beans.

And beans aren't outrageous in calories. The USDA says a serving—about 4 ounces or 100 grams—contains 111 to 118 calories, depending on the variety. The USDA adds: "Beans are worth their weight in protein, and exceed peanut butter in protein content."

Beans of various kinds mix well with many other foods—fresh vegetables, meats, even rice. Corn, rice, or wheat cooked or served with beans enhance a meal's protein and balance. This gives you a strong nutritional go-ahead for making dishes the slow-cooker does particularly well—bean casserole, spicy chili beans, baked beans with molasses. Since baked beans go particularly well nutritionally with wheat and taste very good with brown bread, the old New England custom of serving them together was wiser than perhaps was realized.

COOKING DRIED BEANS
IN THE SLOW-POT

The real bonus is that beans cooked in a slow-pot do not need to be soaked or cooked in advance. If you want to use cooked leftover or frozen beans in a casserole, you can—they'll stand up very well to a second cooking period of 6 to 8 hours. This means that you can use uncooked dried, canned, and fresh cooked beans interchangeably in recipes.

More than a dozen types of dried bean are sold commercially. I've described them below and have listed how long it takes to slow-cook them on Low and High.

How do you know when they are cooked? Well, how do you know when spaghetti is cooked? Some people like spaghetti and beans "al dente," that is, a little on the chewy side. Others prefer them really soft and with lots of juice. Older, stored beans need longer cooking—perhaps an hour more—than those recently packaged, and there's no way to gauge how long the beans you buy have been on the grocer's shelf. When you plan to use beans in salads, cook them firm, not soft, so they'll keep their shape.

Here are the beans most easily found in our supermarkets:

Baby Lima: Shaped like a large lima (which is most often sold frozen). Can be used in most recipes calling for white beans, makes good main dishes and soups, and combines well with pork, beef, and lamb. Cooks in 10 to 12 hours on Low, 5 to 7 on High.

Black-Eye: In the South, these are called black-eyed peas and are part of the soul-food tradition. Very good with ham and pork derivatives or chicken. Cooks in 8 to 10 hours on Low, 4 to 5 on High.

Dark-red Kidney: Used most often in canning; very slow to cook. I cooked a batch 36 hours on Low, and they were still firm. It's better to use the light-red kidneys. Dark reds—light reds, too—are good alone or in vegetable casseroles, in hearty soups, and in combination with other beans.

Garbanzo: A cream-colored bean with a nutty flavor that appears in Spanish and Portuguese cooking; often called chick-pea. Wonderful cold in salads and in appetizers, pickled or sauced, with pork or meatballs. Mixes very well with other vegetables. These are slow to cook, and take 10 to 12 hours on Low, 5 to 6 on High.

Large Lima: Large and buttery in flavor. Very good in casseroles and soups and especially appropriate with smoked meats and cheese. Cooking time is 10 to 12 hours on Low, 5 to 6 on High.

Light-red Kidney: Like the dark red in flavor but faster to cook. The kidney bean most used in home cooking. It can be used in almost any bean recipe and is excellent with beef. Cooking time is 10 to 12 hours on Low, 5 to 6 on High.

Navy: See *Small White.*

Pink: Popular for chili con carne, barbecues, and other Mexican dishes; very good with ground beef. Cooking time is 10 to 12 hours on Low, 5 to 6 on High.

Small White: Smaller and firmer than the navy bean, which it resembles. A California bean that can be used in any recipe calling for white beans. Best with pork, beef, and lamb. Cooks in 8 to 10 hours on Low, 4 to 5 on High.

Some other beans I've seen in markets are the Great Northern, a big white bean that cooks in 10 to 12 hours on Low, 5 to 6 on High; white marrow, a buttery white bean; pinto; cranberry, which is like a pinto; and yellow-eye, a small, flat, white bean, resemble the beans listed above and are popular where they are grown in local gardens.

Dried, they cook in 8 to 12 hours on Low, 4 to 6 on High. Experiment in these time ranges and use the beans interchangeably with those called for in the recipes here. All are excellent nutritionally.

Cooking times for beans—I'll say it again—are hard to be sure of. If you find a dish cooking more slowly than expected, turn the heat to High the last few hours.

USING THE SLOW-COOKER
TO HELP THE BUDGET

Inexpensive as dried beans are, they can be even more economical for everyday use if you slow-cook large batches and freeze 1-cup lots. Canned beans are nutritionally sound but quite a bit more expensive than dried beans. Cooked beans stored in the freezer are ready to go into slow-cook recipes or to be served instead of fresh starchy vegetables.

Cook beans for freezing until they're not quite tender because freezing tends to break them down a little. After they are cooked, turn them into a big bowl set in a bed of ice so they'll chill quickly (and not go on cooking in their own heat). Then pack them into freezer cartons, seal them, label them with name and date, and place them in the quick-freeze compartment or on or under the freezing coils of your freezer. Thaw before using. If you are using them on a hot day with timed cooking, warm the container just enough to loosen the beans and turn them into the slow-cooker with the rest of the ingredients to keep them cool until the timer starts the cooking.

DRIED VEGETABLES

Besides beans, there are other dried products ideally cooked in a slow-pot. Lentils are extremely nutritious, have a delightful flavor that combines well with meat, and are included in many European recipes. Dried split peas can be slow-cooked to a purée with its own special taste. Once in a while, in a health-food store or a European specialty shop, you'll find, at very reasonable prices, packages of dried mixed vegetables. These can be slow-cooked in water to make a wonderful side dish, or they can be slow-cooked with meat and blended with the cooking juices to make a heavenly and low-calorie sauce. When you run across special buys in dried mixed vegetables, stock up on them. They are very useful in slow-cooking—just toss a handful into almost any vegetable casserole or soup to add nutrition and flavor.

The rule of thumb is to use between 2 and 3 times as much water as the measure of the dried vegetables, but this is an indication rather than a hard-and-fast rule. If in doubt, add 2½ cups. You can always add a little water after cooking or boil away any excess. You want just enough cooking liquid to provide a little sauce. If the cooked vegetables are hard and dry, this usually means there wasn't enough water. Add more and let them continue cooking on High; they will turn out just fine.

The recipes for Purée of Peas and Purée of Lentils (page 251) are basic. Experiment with these; then adapt the results to your own recipes.

Dried vegetables—like beans—vary in cooking times. If a dish is cooking more slowly than expected, turn the heat to High the last hour or two.

CEREALS AND GRAINS

A slow-cooker produces that wonder of wonders—perfectly cooked rice every time—as long as it is converted rice. Since converted rice is believed by many nutritionists to be the most nutritious, you may as well use it. Converted rice can (I've done it) cook on Low for 8 to 10 hours in the slow-cooker and stand, covered, a couple of hours without becoming too mushy. Because the slow-pot cooks rice so perfectly, vegetable-and-rice dishes—pilafs—are good candidates for slow-cooking.

There are wonderful cereals we've lost the habit of serving regularly. Wheat, rye, and barley are among them, and they make delicious replacements for rice in casseroles and richly sauced dishes. Cooked in a slow-pot, they are textured, nutty in flavor, and a delight to eat. I cook them in water, 2 times their volume plus ½ cup, and add salt and butter after cooking.

The same cereals, slow-cooked all night, are wonderful for breakfast when sweetened and served with whole milk or cream (see Chapter 13).

THE PASTAS

Spaghetti, noodles, and macaroni aren't particularly good for slow-pot cooking. Cook them in rapidly boiling salted water on the top of the stove; then combine with your slow-cooked ingredients.

BEAN RECIPES

BASIC BEAN CASSEROLE
8 to 10 hours

This is an all-purpose recipe for which you can use almost any white bean, with many kinds of meat—for instance, spareribs, ham hocks, a ham bone with meat on it, corned-beef slices, hamburger (brown it first, over medium-high heat, in a skillet), pork without too much fat. Green-chili salsa is sold in the Mexican sections of supermarkets and in specialty shops.

1 *lb. dried white beans* (2 *cups*)	1 *large onion, peeled,* *chopped*
About 2 to 3 *lb. bony meat* (*see above*); *or* 1 *lb.* *ground meat*	1 *medium clove garlic, peeled,* *minced*
6 *cups water*	1 *tsp. salt* (*omit if meat is* *corned beef*)
1 *bottle* (7 *oz.*) *green-chili* *salsa*	

To Cook: Place all the ingredients in the slow-cooker. Cover and cook on Low for 8 to 10 hours.

Makes 8 servings.

SAVORY COOKED DRIED BEANS

8 to 10 hours, or 10 to 12 hours, or 30 to 36 hours

This is a basic recipe for cooking dried beans of all sorts. If you want them plain, omit the onion, garlic, and bouillon cubes.

1 *lb. dried beans* (2 *cups*)
6 *cups water*
2 *Tbs. vegetable oil, bacon drippings, butter, or margarine*

½ *medium onion, peeled, chopped*
1 *clove garlic, peeled, halved*
1 *tsp. salt*
¼ *tsp. pepper*
4 *chicken bouillon cubes*

To Cook: Place all the ingredients in the slow-pot. Cover and cook on Low for 8 to 10 hours (black-eyed, small white), or 10 to 12 hours (all others except dark-red kidney), or 30 to 36 hours (dark-red kidney).

Makes 6 to 7 cups, depending on variety of bean.

BEANS IN CALIFORNIA SWEET-AND-SOUR DRESSING

Combine 3 cups cooked, drained garbanzos, 3 cups cooked, drained pink or light-red kidney beans, and 2 cups cooked, drained small white beans, and serve with this dressing. It is made with vinegar saved from a jar of sweet pickles.

⅔ *cup sugar*
2 *Tbs. cornstarch*
1 *tsp. onion salt*
¼ *tsp. white pepper*
⅛ *tsp. garlic powder*

½ *cup cold water*
1½ *cups boiling water*
⅔ *cup vinegar from sweet pickles*

To Cook: In a small saucepan, combine the dry ingredients. Add the cold water and stir until smooth. Slowly whip in the boiling water. Turn the heat to medium and cook, stirring constantly, until thick and clear. Blend in the vinegar.

Makes 10 servings.

BEANS VINAIGRETTE

In a ripe avocado half, serve cooked large limas, light-red kidney beans, and garbanzos, combined in equal portions and dressed with Vinaigrette Sauce (page 123).

REFRIED BEANS

Refried beans are just what the name indicates—beans that are cooked, then fried. In Mexico, they appear on most menus and are very good. Excellent with pork products and broiled or grilled meat. Pink beans, light-red kidney beans, or pinto beans are often used for this dish. Slow-cook the beans during the day and finish the dish just before dinner.

6 *cups cooked beans (see above)*	½ *iceberg lettuce, shredded*
Liquid from cooked beans	1 *medium onion, peeled, minced*
½ *cup bacon drippings or vegetable oil*	

To Cook: Drain the hot, cooked beans and reserve the liquid. In a large skillet, over medium-high heat, melt a few teaspoons of the bacon drippings. Add a few spoonfuls of beans, mashing them with the back of a wooden spoon or a potato masher. As they fry, add a little fat and mash in some more beans. As the pan dries, add a little of the cooking liquid. Continue to flatten and fry the beans, stirring often, until they are dry enough to be loosened easily from the skillet. Serve with iceberg-lettuce shreds and minced onion on the side.

Makes 6 to 8 servings.

BAKED BEANS
10 to 12 hours

Start this the day before. The beans take long cooking, but since the slow-pot cooks for just pennies a day, the beans will cost lots less than canned ones. They'll taste lots better, too. Navy beans are sometimes called pea beans.

1 *lb. dried navy beans* (2 *cups*)	¼ *cup dark-brown sugar, firmly packed*
6 *cups water*	¼ *cup dark molasses*
2 *tsp. dry mustard*	2 *Tbs. vinegar*
¼ *tsp. pepper*	⅛ *tsp. cinnamon*
1 *tsp. salt*	⅛ *tsp. ground cloves*
1 *medium onion, peeled, chopped*	¼ *lb. salt pork, cubed*

To Cook: Place all the ingredients in the slow-cooker. Cover and cook on Low for 10 to 12 hours.

Makes 4 to 6 servings.

VERMONT BAKED BEANS WITH MAPLE SYRUP
Overnight, plus 8 to 10 hours

A different way to make baked beans. Try both methods and see which you find more convenient.

1 *lb. dried pea beans*	½ *tsp. dry mustard*
3 *cups boiling water*	2 *tsp. salt*
1 *medium onion, peeled, chopped*	½ *lb. salt pork, rind on*
½ *cup maple syrup*	*Boiling water*

To Cook: Place beans and 3 cups boiling water in the slow-cooker. Cover and cook on Low overnight, or until the skins burst. Drain off the water. Put the onion in the pot. Combine the syrup, mustard, and salt and sprinkle over the beans. Press the pork down into the beans so only the rind shows. Add just enough boiling water to cover. Cover and cook on Low for 8 to 10 hours.

Makes 6 servings.

PINK-BEAN POT
10 to 12 hours

1 *lb. dried pink beans*
6 *cups water*
1 *Tbs. cumin seed*
4 *slices bacon*
1 *small onion, peeled, chopped*
½ *sweet green pepper, seeded, chopped*

1 *medium clove garlic, peeled, minced*
½ *tsp. cinnamon*
¼ *tsp. pepper*
1 *can (8 oz.) tomato sauce*
⅓ *cup catsup*

To Cook: Combine the beans, water, and cumin seed in the slow-cooker. Cover and cook on Low for 10 to 12 hours.

Before Serving: In a medium skillet, over medium heat, sauté the bacon until the fat is rendered. Add the onion, pepper, garlic, and remaining ingredients, bring to a simmer, and cook, covered, about 20 minutes. As soon as the sauce is done, combine with the beans and let them stand in the sauce until serving time.

Makes 6 to 8 servings.

LIMA-BEAN POT
10 to 12 hours

Nice with lamb, beef, and grilled meat.

2 *cups dried large limas*
6 *cups water*
1 *Tbs. vegetable oil*
½ *medium onion, peeled,*
 chopped

2 *medium cloves garlic, peeled,*
 minced
1 *tsp. salt*
¼ *tsp. pepper*
3 *beef bouillon cubes*
3 *Tbs. butter or margarine*

To Cook: Combine all the ingredients in the slow-cooker. Cover and cook on Low for 10 to 12 hours. Toss with butter before serving and add salt if needed.

Makes 8 servings.

LIMAS AND CHILIS
10 to 12 hours

This is a variation on the Lima-Bean Pot, above, and will take about 45 minutes in the oven after the beans have been cooked. Make the beans overnight, put the casserole together in the morning, and bake it just before dinner.

1 *recipe Lima-Bean Pot*
 (*above*)
¼ *tsp. dried basil*
⅛ *tsp. dried oregano*

1 *can (4 oz.) whole mild green*
 chilis
8 *oz. sharp Cheddar cheese*
¾ *cup commercial sour cream*

To Cook: Heat the oven to 325° F. Spread ⅓ of the beans (drained, reserve the liquid) in a shallow 2½-quart casserole and sprinkle ½ of the herbs over them. Tear the chilis into lengths; then cut across into ½-inch-wide pieces. Cut the cheese into strips 1 inch long and about ¼ inch wide. Sprinkle ½ of the chilis and ⅓ of the cheese over the limas. Repeat these layers; top with remaining beans and cheese. Blend the reserved bean liquid with the sour cream; taste and add salt if needed. Pour over the casserole. Bake for 30 to 45 minutes, or until it just begins to bubble.

Makes 8 to 10 servings.

RED KIDNEY BEANS AND TOMATO SAUCE
10 to 12 hours

2 cups dried light-red kidney beans	1 large onion, peeled, sliced
	2 whole cloves
1 can (8 oz.) tomato sauce	Ham bone
1 Tbs. Worcestershire sauce	1 to 2 tsp. salt
6 cups water	2 Tbs. light molasses

To Cook: Place all the ingredients in the slow-pot. Cover and cook on Low for 10 to 12 hours. Discard ham bone and cloves before serving.

Makes 4 to 6 servings.

KIDNEY-BEAN-AND-ARTICHOKE SALAD

One of the many salads you can make with cooked beans.

4 cups cooked, drained light-red kidney beans	2 jars (6 oz.) artichoke hearts, drained (marinated or plain)
1 cup French Salad Dressing (below)	3 large slices onion
1 cup minced celery	3 or 4 large radishes, sliced in rounds
½ cup chopped onion	

To Cook: Combine the beans and French Salad Dressing several hours before the salad is to be served. Just before dinner, mix the beans with the celery, onion, and artichoke hearts. Garnish with onion slices and radish rounds.

Makes 8 servings.

FRENCH SALAD DRESSING

⅓ cup olive oil	1 or 2 tsp. salt
⅓ cup vegetable oil	½ tsp. pepper
2⅔ Tbs. vinegar	1 small clove garlic, peeled, sliced (optional)
½ tsp. dry mustard	
1 tsp. sugar	

Put all the ingredients into the blender and blend at low speed for 1 or 2 minutes. Taste and add salt if you wish.

Makes about 1 cup.

TWO-BEAN CASSEROLE
10 to 12 hours

1 lb. ham	3 Tbs. light-brown sugar, firmly
1 clove garlic, peeled, minced	packed
1 large onion, peeled,	2 Tbs. prepared mustard
chopped	½ cup catsup
6 cups water	½ cup dry red wine
⅔ cup dried light-red kidney	1 tsp. salt
beans	¼ tsp. pepper
⅔ cup dried garbanzos or	
small white beans	

To Cook: Trim the fat from the ham and heat fat in a large skillet, over medium heat, until rendered. Discard the crackly bits. Cut the ham into small strips and brown lightly in the hot fat. Add the garlic and onion and sauté until the onion is transparent. Add the water, scrape up the pan juices, and turn into the slow-pot. Add the remaining ingredients. Cover and cook on Low for 10 to 12 hours.

Makes 6 to 8 servings.

BEAN CASSEROLE SABLAISE
10 to 12 hours

This is one of the best side dishes for lamb, and it is wonderful when done very slowly in an electric crockery pot. It is strongly flavored with garlic. Start the dish in the morning, and the beans will be ready when the meat is done.

2 cups dried small white	2 tsp. salt
beans	4 large cloves garlic, peeled
4 cups water	½ tsp. black pepper
⅛ lb. salt pork, cut into	
chunks	

To Cook: Place all the ingredients in the slow-cooker. Cover and cook on Low for 10 to 12 hours.

Makes 6 to 8 servings.

FOOLPROOF RICE
6 to 8 hours

What a slow-cooker can do with rice is unbelievable! The rice literally can cook for hours and hours and be perfect. Even after it's done, it stays perfect if left in the pot.

1 *cup converted rice*
2 *cups water*
2 *tsp. salt*

1 *Tbs. butter, margarine,*
 or vegetable oil

To Cook: Place all the ingredients in the slow-pot. Cover and cook on Low for 6 to 8 hours.

Makes 2 to 4 servings.

RICE-BACON-AND-CABBAGE CASSEROLE
6 to 8 hours

½ *medium white cabbage,*
 shredded
½ *cup converted rice*
2 *slices good bacon, minced*

1 *cup chicken stock, or*
 1 *chicken bouillon cube*
 and 1 *cup water*
¼ *tsp. salt*
¼ *tsp. pepper*

To Cook: In the slow-pot, layer ⅓ of the cabbage, ½ of the rice, and ½ of the bacon. Repeat, ending with a layer of cabbage. Add the stock, salt, and pepper. Cover and cook on Low for 6 to 8 hours. If there's liquid in the pot after cooking, drain it off.

Makes 4 servings.

RICE-AND-PARSLEY CASSEROLE
6 to 8 hours

This variation on plain rice will give you ideas on other ways to dress up this staple cereal. It is a very good way to fix rice to be served with plain roasted meats.

1 *cup converted rice*	2 *large cloves garlic, peeled,*
2 *cups water*	*minced*
2 *tsp. salt*	½ *cup finely minced parsley*
3 *Tbs. butter or margarine*	

To Cook: Place rice, water, salt, and 1½ tablespoons butter in the slow-pot. Cover and cook on Low for 6 to 8 hours.

Before Serving: In a large skillet, over medium heat, melt the remaining butter and sauté the garlic for 1 minute. Add the rice and mix it well with the garlic. Sprinkle the parsley over the top and stir into the rice. Serve at once.

Makes 2 to 4 servings.

RICE-AND-TOMATO CASSEROLE
6 to 8 hours

1 *Tbs. butter or margarine*	½ *tsp. chopped fresh parsley,*
½ *cup converted rice*	*or ¼ tsp. dried parsley*
1 *cup liquid from canned*	*flakes*
tomatoes	1 *tsp. salt*
1¾ *cups canned tomatoes,*	¼ *tsp. pepper*
drained	3 *Tbs. grated Parmesan cheese*

To Cook: In a medium skillet, over medium heat, melt the butter and sauté the rice, stirring constantly, until golden brown. Turn the contents into the slow-pot. Swish out the skillet with the tomato liquid and scrape into the cooker. Add remaining ingredients except cheese; stir well. Cover and cook on Low for 6 to 8 hours. Sprinkle with grated Parmesan before serving.

Makes 4 servings.

RICE-AND-TOMATO PILAF
6 to 8 hours

1 *Tbs. butter or margarine*	1 *large sweet pepper, seeded,*
½ *cup converted rice*	*diced*
1 *cup strong beef stock,*	1¾ *cups drained canned*
or 3 beef bouillon cubes	*tomatoes*
and 1 cup water	*Salt and pepper*

To Cook: In a medium skillet, over medium heat, melt the butter and sauté the rice, stirring constantly, until golden brown. Turn the contents into the slow-pot. Swish out the skillet with the stock and scrape contents into the cooker. Add remaining ingredients except salt and pepper; stir well. Cover and cook on Low for 6 to 8 hours. Before serving, taste and add salt and pepper if needed.

Makes 4 servings.

STUFFED CABBAGE ROLLS AND RICE
6 to 8 hours

Make this with leftover slices of ham, beef, or lamb. If you don't have wooden toothpicks to skewer the rolls, tie them with white thread.

1 *medium head green* *cabbage*	1 *Tbs. butter or margarine*
6 *to 8 large, thin slices* *cooked meat*	1 *medium onion, peeled,* *minced*
Salt and pepper	1 *fresh tomato, chopped*
1½ *cups converted rice*	1 *tsp. salt*
1 *cup beef stock, or 1 beef* *bouillon cube and 1 cup* *water*	⅛ *tsp. pepper*
	1 *tsp. caraway seed* *(optional)*

To Cook: Parboil the cabbage as for Stuffed Cabbage Rolls with Tomato Sauce (page 217). Remove the large outer leaves; you need 12 to 16. Arrange the leaves in pairs, one on top of the other, and cover each pair with a slice of meat. Sprinkle lightly with salt and pepper; roll up and secure with wooden toothpicks. Rub the bottom of the slow-cooker with a dab of vegetable oil. Sprinkle the rice over it; pour in the stock; add the remaining ingredients. Place the cabbage rolls on top. Cover and cook on Low for 6 to 8 hours.

Makes 6 to 8 servings.

RICE WITH MUSHROOMS AND ONIONS
6 to 8 hours

1 *cup converted rice*	1 *large onion, peeled and*
2 *cups water*	*finely minced*
2 *tsp. salt*	½ *cup coarsely chopped, wiped,*
3 *Tbs. butter or margarine*	*fresh mushrooms*

To Cook: Place rice, water, salt, and 1½ tablespoons butter in the slow-pot. Cover and cook on Low for 6 to 8 hours.

Before Serving: In a large skillet, over medium heat, melt remaining butter and sauté the onion until translucent. Add the mushrooms and sauté until all moisture is gone—3 or 4 minutes. Add the rice and mix well. Serve hot.

Makes 2 to 4 servings.

RECIPES FOR OTHER GRAINS AND DRIED VEGETABLES

CORN PUDDING
3 or 4 hours

A great corn dish you can make while you are away if you have a crockery cooker large enough to hold a 1½-quart baking dish and a trivet.

2 *cups drained whole corn*	⅛ *tsp. nutmeg*
kernels, fresh or canned	2 *Tbs. sifted all-purpose*
4 *eggs, separated*	*flour*
1 *tsp. salt*	1 *tsp. baking powder*
⅛ *tsp. pepper*	2 *Tbs. melted butter or*
1 *tsp. sugar*	*margarine*
½ *green pepper, seeded*	2 *cups scalded milk*
and minced	1 *cup hot water*

To Cook: In the blender, blend the corn at low speed; drain and turn the corn solids into a large bowl. Discard the liquid. Beat the egg yolks until thick and lemon colored. Beat in the corn, salt, pepper, sugar, green pepper, and nutmeg. Beat the flour and baking powder into the egg mixture; then beat in the melted butter. Then beat in the scalded milk. Beat the egg whites until stiff and fold into the corn mixture. Turn the pudding into a 1½-quart baking dish and cover with a lid or foil. Set a rack or trivet in the slow-cooker. Pour the hot water into the cooker and set the baking dish on the trivet. Cover the pot and cook on High about 3 or 4 hours, or until a silver knife inserted in the middle comes out clean.

Makes 6 to 8 servings.

POLENTA
8 to 10 hours

Cornmeal is a breakfast cereal in New England; elsewhere it is the basis for popular side dishes. Polenta, an Italian specialty, begins with cornmeal. Start it the night before; let it set during the day, and you are ready to fry it as a side dish for Italian foods that evening.

1½ cups cornmeal	1 tsp. salt
3 cups water	1 Tbs. butter or margarine

To Cook: Combine cornmeal, 2 cups water, and the salt in the slow-cooker. Mix well. Stir in remaining water. Cover and cook on Low for 8 to 10 hours, or until so thick a spoon will stand in it. Pour into a buttered 1½-quart ring mold and let cool.

Before Serving: Slice the polenta and fry it in butter. Or bake it briefly with a sauce of your choice. (See Chapter 9 for sauces.)

Makes 8 servings.

POLENTA WITH MEAT SAUCE
8 to 10 hours

Cornmeal cooked, cooled, and served with Meat Sauce makes a complete dinner and one children love.

1½ cups cornmeal	1 Tbs. butter or margarine
3 cups water	1 recipe Meat Sauce
1 tsp. salt	(page 72)

To Cook: Combine cornmeal, 2 cups of water, and the salt in the slow-cooker. Mix well. Stir in remaining water. Cover and cook on Low for 8 to 10 hours, or until so thick a spoon will stand in it. Pour into a buttered 1½-quart ring mold and let cool.

Before Serving: Unmold, warm, and slice the polenta and place around a large serving platter. Fill the center of the platter with meat sauce. Serve 1 or 2 slices polenta to each diner and spoon sauce over the pieces.

Makes 8 servings.

PURÉE OF LENTILS
8 to 10 hours

Dried lentils are small, meaty legumes, dark brown in color, with a nutty flavor all their own. They are good with strongly flavored meats. As they are one of the most nourishing of the legumes, nutrition buffs will love this purée.

2 cups dried lentils, well	½ tsp. dried marjoram
washed	½ tsp. sugar
2 cups water	4 Tbs. butter or margarine
2 tsp. salt	

To Cook: Place all the ingredients except the butter in the slow-cooker. Cover and cook on Low for 8 to 10 hours or until lentils are completely soft.

Before Serving: If any cooking liquid remains, turn heat to High and simmer, uncovered, until the moisture is gone. Beat the butter into the lentils and serve.

Makes 8 to 10 servings.

PURÉE OF PEAS
8 to 10 hours

This is different—a purée of dried green peas on the lines of a popular French dish, Purée St. Germain.

2 cups dried split green peas, well washed

2 cups water, or 1 cup evaporated milk and 1 cup water

2 tsp. salt

½ tsp. dill weed, optional

1 large bay leaf

½ tsp. sugar

4 Tbs. butter or margarine

To Cook: Place all the ingredients except the butter in the slow-cooker. Cover and cook on Low for 8 to 10 hours, or until peas are completely soft.

Before Serving: If any cooking liquid remains, turn heat to High and simmer, uncovered, until the moisture is gone. Discard the bay leaf. Beat the butter into the peas and serve.

Makes 8 to 10 servings.

RYE BERRIES
8 to 12 hours

This is whole-grain rye—a delicious substitute for wild rice, brown rice, or plain rice. The cooking time for cereals such as this seems to vary tremendously among slow-cookers. So the first time you cook it in your electric crock pot, plan to check on doneness every few hours. It is done when just a little chewy.

1 cup rye berries

2 cups water

1 tsp. salt

1 small onion, peeled and chopped

3 Tbs. butter or margarine

To Cook: Place all ingredients except the butter in the slow-cooker. Cover and cook on Low for 8 to 12 hours.

Before Serving: Place in a serving dish, dot with butter, and let the butter melt over the berries before serving.

Makes 4 or 5 servings.

WHEAT BERRIES
8 to 12 hours

These are a bit less nutty than the rye berries but very good.

1 cup wheat berries

2 cups water

1 tsp. salt

1 small onion, peeled and chopped

3 Tbs. butter or margarine

To Cook: Place all ingredients except the butter in the slow-cooker. Cover and cook on Low for 8 to 12 hours.

Before Serving: Place in a serving dish, dot with butter, and let the butter melt over the berries before serving.

Makes 4 or 5 servings.

BARLEY
8 to 12 hours

A change from rice—and very good with lamb and Middle European dishes.

1 *cup barley*	1 *small onion, peeled and*
2 *cups water*	*chopped*
1 *tsp. salt*	3 *Tbs. butter or margarine*

To Cook: Place all ingredients except the butter in the slow-cooker. Cover and cook on Low for 8 to 12 hours.

Before Serving: Place in a serving dish, dot with butter, and let the butter melt over the barley before serving.

Makes 4 or 5 servings.

PART SIX
COMFORT FOODS

Chapter 11

Baking in Your Slow-Cooker

You CAN IDENTIFY A comfort food right away because it always has a lot of calories and you always feel guilty as you prepare it. And the family groans with pleasure when its aroma wafts from the kitchen. Whether it's Corn Bread, Carrot Tea Bread, or Plum Pudding (pages 300, 267, 279), there's no denying the calories—especially when you load it with butter and jam or a rich sauce.

However, you do not live by your figure alone. And sometimes —after a skating party or a hard day's work in the garden—you've burned up enough calories to be able to indulge in a sweet without a tremor.

BAKING IN A SLOW-COOKER

When the slow-cooker simmers stews and casseroles and braises meats, it acts as a Dutch oven. At other times, it can be used as a small, regular oven or a steamer. Baking in an oven may heat a larger area than is needed. Slow-pot baked goods remain very moist—but flavorful. If things baked in your slow-cooker don't come out just right the first time, experiment a little, and eventually you will know how to handle them and whether you like them baked that way.

To do any true baking in a slow-cooker, you need a large unit. The low, small ones can't handle much, but it is fun to try half recipes in them. All the recipes in this section can be halved and baked in small units.

Some manufacturers—notably Rival—are selling baking units that fit inside their slow-cookers. If your cooker isn't thus equipped, you can easily improvise. Commercial baking units are tall, so that doughs can rise high. They have lids to keep the steam that forms inside the slow-cooker's cover from dripping into the batter or dough. Below the lid, side vents let steam escape into the slow-pot. A lid and venting are essential in an improvised baking container.

I have a commercial baking unit, and it does work best. However, it fits into only one of my slow-cookers—not the one made by the manufacturer of the baking unit! I also use 1½-, 2½-, and 3-quart molds as baking dishes. And a 2-pound coffee tin is wonderful for steaming puddings and baking the quick breads.

Muffin tins won't go into slow-cookers. However, Pyrex muffin cups will. I made a double-decker of 8 to 10 Pyrex cups set on a trivet and covered with a plate, topped by more cups covered with foil. Five or 6 Pyrex cups, each 2½ inches across, fit into several slow-cooker models and will hold half the average recipe. (If you have mixed muffin batter and it's too much for the baking unit or Pyrex cups, put it in a mold.)

One thing you'll find helpful is a trivet or a metal rack. If your cooker doesn't have one, measure the cooker's diameter and buy one, or try setting a Pyrex cup in the cooker. In my experience, breads and cakes are more successful when raised a little above the slow-cooker's bottom.

ABOUT BAKING RECIPES

When you are going to bake in a slow-cooker, prepare the dough or batter as you normally would. Skimp on liquids. Pour the batter or place the dough in a container that will fit inside your cooker.

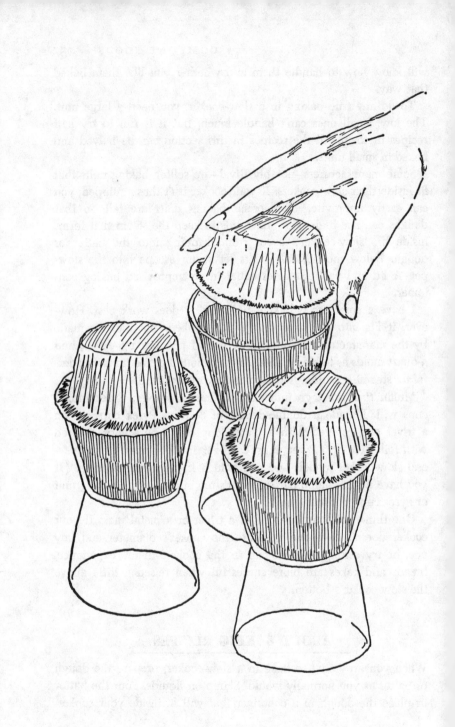

Large cookers will take 1-, 1½-, 2-, or 3-quart molds. The molds' high sides give the dough or batter space to rise under a cover.

Most of the baked dishes and many of the desserts here need a cover to keep out condensed steam. Place a piece of foil loosely enough over the baking unit or mold to let steam escape from it. I have used a small earthenware jar, rather like an old-fashioned cookie jar, for puddings. It has a rough-stoneware lid with a surface uneven enough to let inner steam out without letting condensed steam in. And I have used a Pyrex cover on a mold; I prop it slightly ajar with a twist of foil to let out steam. I like the glass cover because I can see what is happening inside the baking unit. Some of the recipes recommend propping the slow-cooker's cover a bit open.

Some doughs and batters don't need to be protected from steam —for instance, Plum Pudding is steamed rather than baked. A few batters are dense enough to absorb without harm all the condensed steam likely to fall on them. But other batters, such as that for Pound Cake, should be kept safe from steam.

USING THE TIMER FOR BAKING

While some things turn out well when baked on Low, many recipes here call for baking on High for only a few hours—not 8 to 10. If you use a timer to turn off the slow-pot, you can leave whenever you like and return to the aroma of ready-to-eat muffins or cake. If, using the timer, you delay cooking something containing baking powder and baking soda, it may be flatter than it should be. This may be because the baking powder or baking soda warmed up when the ingredients were mixed and had lost its rising power by the time baking started. Keep ingredients cool when you time baking to start several hours after you mix the batter. If the recipe calls for water in the slow-cooker, add an equivalent in ice cubes.

Slow-cooker baking doesn't produce the richly browned tops the oven does, and, as I said before, the texture of many of the baked foods is rather puddinglike. However, a topping of whipped cream, ice cream, or sweet sauce makes a slow-cooked fruit bread, for instance, a real comfort food.

DON'T LIFT THE LID DURING BAKING

During the early part of the cooking, don't lift the pot's cover. That would let out heat and slow the baking. When the baked food is almost done, lift the lid and test quickly by inserting a toothpick in the center. If it comes out clean, the food is done.

BREADS

BASIC WHITE BREAD
4 to 6 hours

Let this cool; then slice it and toast—it's rather like English muffins.

1 package dry yeast
2 cups lukewarm water
1 Tbs. sugar
4 cups unrefined or all-
   purpose flour, sifted
½ tsp. salt
2 Tbs. vegetable oil
Milk

To Cook: Preheat the slow-pot on High with the lid on. Dissolve the yeast in ½ cup of the lukewarm water with the sugar and set in a warm—not hot—place. Put the flour in a large bowl and sprinkle with salt. Make a well in the center. When the yeast is bubbly, pour the rest of the water, the yeast mixture, and the oil into the well. Stir with your fingers until all the flour has been absorbed. Grease your baking unit or a 3-quart mold and place the dough in it. Brush milk, with a pastry brush, over the top. Cover and let stand for 5 minutes in a warm place. Place on a trivet in the slow-cooker, cover the cooker, and bake on High for 4 to 6 hours.

Makes 1 loaf.

RICH WHITE BREAD
4 to 6 hours

1 package dry yeast
2 cups lukewarm whole milk
2 Tbs. sugar
4 cups unrefined or all-
    purpose flour, sifted

½ tsp. salt
2 Tbs. vegetable oil
Whole milk

To Cook: Preheat the slow-pot on High with the lid on. Dissolve the yeast in ½ cup of the lukewarm milk with the sugar and set in a warm—not hot—place. Put the flour in a large bowl and sprinkle with salt. Make a well in the center. When the yeast is bubbly, pour the rest of the lukewarm milk, the yeast mixture, and the oil into the well. Stir with your fingers until all the flour has been absorbed. Grease your baking unit or a 3-quart mold and place the dough in it. Brush milk, with a pastry brush, over the top. Cover loosely and let stand for 5 minutes in a warm place. Place on a trivet in the slow-cooker; cover the cooker and bake on High for 4 to 6 hours.

Makes 1 loaf.

SAFFRON BREAD
4 to 6 hours

This is an old New England recipe. The bread has the flavor of a sweet and spicy brioche.

1 tsp. dried saffron
2 cups lukewarm milk
½ cup butter or margarine,
    melted
½ tsp. salt
½ cup sugar
1 package dry yeast

3 eggs, slightly beaten
1½ tsp. caraway seed
¼ tsp. ground clove
¼ tsp. ground mace
½ tsp. cinnamon
4 cups all-purpose flour, sifted

To Cook: Soak the saffron in a few tablespoons of the milk. Preheat the slow-pot on High, covered. Combine remaining milk with the butter, salt, and sugar; stir until sugar dissolves. Pour in the saffron-flavored milk and discard saffron threads. Add the yeast and let rest for 5 to 10 minutes in a warm place. Add the eggs, caraway, clove, mace, and cinnamon to the milk mixture. Place the flour in a large bowl; make a well in the center and beat the milk-and-egg mixture into the flour. Turn into a slightly warmed greased 3-quart mold. Cover loosely with a plate and let stand for 5 minutes in a warm place. Set the mold with its cover in the slow-cooker; cover cooker and bake on High for 4 to 6 hours.

Makes 1 loaf.

BOSTON BROWN BREAD
6 to 8 hours

Once upon a time, little girls learned the recipe for this in rhyme:

> One cup of sweet milk,
> One cup of sour.
> One cup of cornmeal,
> One cup of flour.
> Teaspoon of soda,
> Molasses one cup.
> Steam for three hours,
> Then eat it all up.

This bread is great with baked beans and franks. It's dark and dense, and leftovers make wonderful toast.

1 cup whole-wheat flour	¾ cup dark molasses
1 cup rye flour	1½ cups buttermilk
1 cup yellow cornmeal	1 cup seedless raisins
2 tsp. baking soda	1 cup hot water
1½ tsp. salt	

To Cook: In a large bowl, combine the whole-wheat and rye flour, cornmeal, baking soda, and salt. Make a well in the center and pour in the molasses, buttermilk, and raisins. Stir until all the ingredients are combined. Grease and flour a 2-quart mold and turn batter into it. The batter should not fill more than ⅔ of the mold. Cover with foil. Set the mold on a trivet in the slow-cooker. Pour 1 cup of hot water into the pot. Cover the pot and cook on High for 6 to 8 hours. The bread is done when the top is dry and recedes from the mold. Cool on a rack for 10 minutes; then turn out and serve.

Makes 1 loaf.

RUTH MACGUIRE'S SODA BREAD
2 to 4 hours

This soda-bread recipe came to Ruth from an Irish friend via Brooklyn, but it is authentically Irish. You can glaze it with a runny mixture of sugar and milk, set to firm up and dry in a slow oven—350° F. Irish restaurants in New York always offer warm soda bread with dinner, but it isn't glazed.

1½ cups sifted all-purpose flour
1¼ tsp. baking powder
¼ tsp. baking soda
½ tsp. salt
1½ Tbs. sugar

1 tsp. caraway seed
½ cup seedless raisins
2 tsp. shortening
1 egg, slightly beaten
1 cup buttermilk

To Cook: Sift the flour, baking powder, baking soda, salt, and sugar into a large bowl. Add the caraway seed and raisins. Working with your fingers, rub the shortening into the flour mixture—or cut it in with 2 knives—until mixture is coarse and mealy. Add the egg and buttermilk and stir until you have formed a soft dough. Flour a board and turn the dough onto it. Knead dough lightly for 1 minute. Form a round loaf and make a shallow cross in the center. Place the loaf in a greased and floured 2-quart mold. Set the mold on a trivet in the slow-cooker; cover the cooker and bake on High for 2 to 4 hours, or until a toothpick inserted in the center comes out clean.

Makes 4 to 6 servings.

QUICK BREADS

APRICOT-NUT BREAD
4 to 6 hours

¾ cup dried apricots	¾ cup milk
1 cup sifted all-purpose flour	1 egg, slightly beaten
2 tsp. baking powder	1 Tbs. grated orange peel
¼ tsp. baking soda	1 Tbs. vegetable oil
½ tsp. salt	½ cup sifted whole-wheat flour
½ cup sugar	1 cup coarsely chopped walnuts

To Cook: Place the apricots on a chopping block. Sprinkle 1 tablespoon all-purpose flour over them. Dip a knife into the flour and chop the apricots finely. Flour the knife often to keep the cut-up fruit from sticking together. Sift the remaining all-purpose flour, baking powder, baking soda, salt and sugar into a large bowl. Combine the milk, egg, orange peel, and oil. Stir in the flour mixture and the whole-wheat flour. Fold in the cut-up apricots, any flour left on the cutting block, and the walnuts. Pour into a well-greased, floured baking unit or a 2-quart mold. Cover and place on a rack or trivet in the slow-cooker. Cover the cooker, but prop the lid open a fraction with a toothpick or a twist of foil to let excess steam escape. Cook on High for 4 to 6 hours. Cool on a rack for 10 minutes. Serve warm or cold.

Makes 4 to 6 servings.

BANANA BREAD
4 to 6 hours

Banana Bread leftovers keep well in the refrigerator and can be sliced and toasted. The bread also freezes well. Use overripe bananas—often they're on sale for very little.

1¾ cups all-purpose flour, sifted	⅔ cup sugar
2 tsp. baking powder	2 eggs, well beaten
¼ tsp. baking soda	1½ cups well-mashed, overripe banana (2 or 3 bananas)
½ tsp. salt	½ cup coarsely chopped walnuts (optional)
⅓ cup shortening	

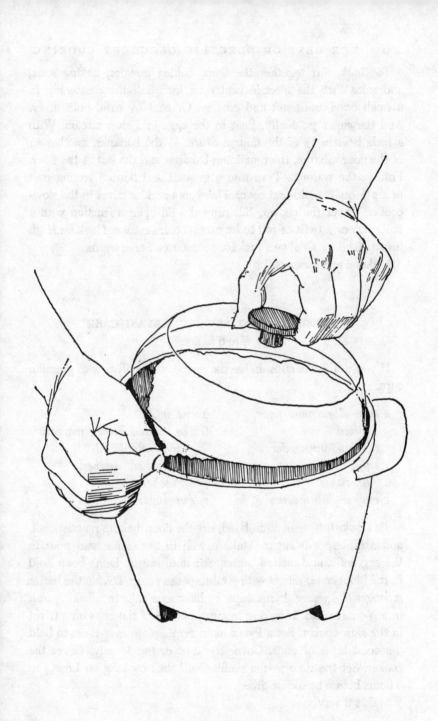

To Cook: Sift together the flour, baking powder, baking soda, and salt. With the electric beater on low, fluff the shortening in a small bowl, until soft and creamy. Or beat by hand until fluffy. Add the sugar gradually. Beat in the eggs in a slow stream. With a fork, beat in ⅓ of the flour mixture, ½ the bananas, another ⅓ of the flour mixture, the remaining bananas and the last of the flour. Fold in the walnuts. Turn into a greased and floured baking unit or a 2½-quart mold and cover. Place on a rack or trivet in the slow-cooker. Cover the cooker, but prop the lid open a fraction with a toothpick or a twist of foil to let excess steam escape. Cook on High for 4 to 6 hours. Cool on a rack for 10 minutes. Serve warm.

Makes 6 to 8 servings.

BLUEBERRY MUFFINS OR BREAKFAST CAKE
4 to 6 hours

If you use Pyrex cups, halve the recipe: that will fit 4 to 5 muffin cups.

2 *cups all-purpose flour,*	1 *cup milk*
sifted	6 *Tbs. melted butter, margarine*
3 *tsp. baking powder*	*or vegetable oil*
1 *tsp. salt*	1 *cup washed, drained*
2 *Tbs. sugar*	*blueberries*
1 *egg, slightly beaten*	3 *Tbs. sugar*

To Cook: Into a medium bowl, sift the flour, baking powder, salt, and 2 tablespoons sugar. Make a well in the center and pour in the egg, milk, and melted butter. Stir until mixed. Don't beat. Fold in the blueberries mixed with 3 tablespoons sugar. Divide the batter among well-greased Pyrex cups, or bake as a cake in a baking unit or a 3-quart mold. If baking in cups, place half the cups on a trivet in the slow-cooker. Set a Pyrex mold or pie plate over them to hold a second layer of cups. Cover the tops or top loosely. Cover the cooker. Set the time so the muffins will start cooking on Low 4 to 6 hours before breakfast time.

Makes 8 servings.

CARROT TEA BREAD
4 to 6 hours

This is a New England favorite. You can top it with a sugar-and-milk glaze or frost it with vanilla-frosting mix.

1 *cup all-purpose flour*	2 *eggs*
1 *cup sugar*	½ *cup vegetable oil*
1 *tsp. baking powder*	4 *cups grated raw carrots*
½ *tsp. salt*	(*about 4 medium carrots*)
1 *tsp. cinnamon*	½ *cup chopped pecans*

To Cook: Measure the flour, sugar, baking powder, salt, and cinnamon into a sifter. Sift 3 times into a medium bowl. With an electric beater on high, beat the eggs until frothy and lemon colored. Toward the end, dribble in the oil. With the beater on low, add the flour mixture a little at a time. Fold in the carrots and pecans. Pour into a well-greased and floured baking unit or a 3-quart mold and cover. Place in the slow-cooker. Cover the cooker, but prop the lid open a fraction with a toothpick or a twist of foil to let excess steam escape. Bake on High for 4 to 6 hours, or until a toothpick inserted in the center comes out clean.

Makes 6 servings.

CRANBERRY BREAD
4 to 6 hours

This is a Cape Cod specialty. In the restaurants there, a basket of sliced cranberry bread is served with each meal. It's best buttered and eaten fresh, but leftovers—toasted and buttered—make a wonderful breakfast food. Cranberry Bread freezes well and keeps fresh for many days in the refrigerator if it is well wrapped in plastic.

2 *cups fresh cranberries*	½ *tsp. salt*
(½ *lb.*)	6 *Tbs. butter or margarine at*
2 *cups all-purpose flour,*	*room temperature*
sifted	1 *egg*
1 *cup sugar*	1 *Tbs. grated orange peel*
½ *tsp. baking powder*	½ *cup orange juice*
½ *tsp. baking soda*	½ *cup walnuts, chopped*

To Cook: A quarter cup at a time, chop the cranberries in the blender on low. Don't purée them, which will happen if you blend them too long. Into a large bowl, sift the flour, sugar, baking powder, baking soda, and salt. With 2 knives, cut the butter into the flour mixture until it looks like coarse meal. Combine the egg, orange peel, and orange juice and stir into the flour mixture until well blended. Fold in the cranberries and the walnuts. Turn into a greased and floured baking unit or a 3-quart mold; cover. Place the mold on a rack or trivet in the slow-cooker. Cover the cooker, but prop the lid open a fraction with a toothpick or a twist of foil to let excess steam escape. Cook on High for 4 to 6 hours. Bread is done when a toothpick inserted in the center comes out clean. Cool on a rack for 10 minutes. Serve warm or cold.

Makes 8 servings.

DATE-NUT BREAD
4 to 6 hours

This is on the sweet side but awfully good. Children love it for breakfast or for afternoon snacks. Wrapped and refrigerated, it will keep fresh for several days, or you can freeze leftovers.

¾ *cup walnuts*	1 *tsp. vanilla extract*
1 *cup pitted dates*	1 *cup sugar*
½ *cup all-purpose flour, sifted*	1 *cup all-purpose flour, sifted*
3 *Tbs. shortening*	1½ *tsp. baking soda*
¾ *cup boiling water*	½ *tsp. salt*
2 *eggs*	

To Cook: Chop the walnuts coarsely with a knife (the blender tends to make them into mush). Place the dates on a chopping board, sprinkle ½ cup of flour over them, and chop them. If you keep the dates well mixed with the flour, they won't stick to the knife as you work. Place the dates in a colander and shake over the chopping board to remove as much flour as possible. Place the dates in a bowl, add the shortening and boiling water, and let stand as you prepare the batter. Beat the eggs well with a fork, add the vanilla, and then add the sugar. Scrape all the flour from the chopping board and combine it with 1 cup of flour, the baking soda, and the salt. Beat the flour mixture into the egg mixture. Add the date mixture and beat just enough to blend all the ingredients. Fold in the nuts. Pour into a greased, floured baking unit or a 2-quart mold; cover. Set on a trivet or rack in the slow-cooker. Cover the cooker, but prop the lid open a fraction with a toothpick or a twist of foil to let excess steam escape. Cook on High for 4 to 6 hours. Cool on a rack for 10 minutes. Serve warm.

Makes 4 to 6 servings.

PUMPKIN-BUTTER BREAD
4 to 6 hours

This is really best made with butter. Serve it warm, with more butter. Toast, refrigerate, or freeze leftovers.

1½ cups all-purpose flour, sifted	¼ tsp. grated nutmeg
½ tsp. salt	2 eggs
½ tsp. baking soda	1 cup sugar
½ tsp. baking powder	1 cup drained canned pumpkin
¼ tsp. cinnamon	¾ cup melted butter
¼ tsp. ground ginger	½ cup chopped nuts

To Cook: Sift the flour, salt, baking soda, baking powder, cinnamon, ginger, and nutmeg into a large bowl. With an electric beater on high, whip the eggs until frothy; add the sugar gradually as you beat. With the beater on low, beat in the well-drained pumpkin (make sure there's as little moisture as possible left in the pumpkin) and the butter. Whip in the flour mixture; then fold in the chopped nuts. Pour into a baking unit or a greased and floured 2-quart mold and cover. Set on a trivet or rack in the slow-cooker. Cover the cooker, but prop the lid open a fraction with a toothpick or a twist of foil to let excess steam escape. Cook on High for 4 to 6 hours. When a toothpick inserted in the center comes out clean, it is done.

Makes 4 to 6 servings.

CAKES

POUND CAKE FROM A MIX
4 to 6 hours

Real pound cake from scratch takes a pound of eggs, a pound of flour, and a pound of butter—which makes it really expensive. The mix is good, though dense.

1 *package* (16 oz.) *pound-*   ⅔ *cup water*
    cake mix   2 *eggs*

To Cook: Turn the cake mix, water, and eggs into a large mixing bowl and beat by hand 300 times. Do it by hand—this gives it a more from-scratch texture. Pour the batter into a greased and floured baking unit or a 3-quart mold. Set it on a trivet in the slow-cooker, and cover the top. Cover the cooker; prop the lid open a fraction with a toothpick or a twist of foil to let excess steam escape. Cook on High for 4 to 6 hours. When a toothpick inserted in the center comes out clean, the cake is done. Cool on a rack for 10 minutes before you turn it out.

Makes 8 servings.

CHERRY POUND CAKE
4½ to 6½ hours

My mother used to make this from scratch, but it's much easier to use a mix. Refrigerate leftovers, wrapped in plastic film.

1 *package* (16 oz.) *pound-*   20 to 30 *maraschino cherries,*
    cake mix   *drained*
⅔ *cup water*   3 *Tbs. all-purpose flour*
2 *eggs*

To Cook: Turn the cake mix, water, and eggs into a large mixing bowl and beat with an electric beater on low until well blended. In a small bowl, combine the cherries with the flour. Toss them well in the flour so that all their moisture is absorbed. Pour the batter into a greased and floured baking unit or a 3-quart mold. Drop the cherries into the batter from high enough up so they sink into it. (This maneuver keeps all the cherries, which are heavier than the batter, from sinking to the bottom of the cake.) Place the baking unit or mold on a trivet in the slow-cooker and cover. Cover the slow-cooker; prop the lid open a fraction with a toothpick or a twist of foil to let excess steam escape. Cook on High for 4½ to 6½ hours. When a toothpick inserted in the center comes out clean, the cake is done. Cool on a rack for 10 to 15 minutes before you turn it out. Let it cool thoroughly before serving.

Makes 10 to 12 servings.

PINEAPPLE POUND CAKE
4½ to 6½ hours

1 package (16 oz.) pound-
    cake mix
⅔ cup pineapple juice,
    drained from a 16-oz. can
    of pineapple tidbits

2 eggs
1½ cups drained pineapple
    tidbits
3 Tbs. all-purpose flour

To Cook: Turn the cake mix, pineapple juice, and eggs into a large mixing bowl and beat with an electric beater on low, until well blended. In a small bowl, combine the pineapple tidbits with the flour. Toss them well in the flour so that any moisture is absorbed. Fold the tidbits into the batter. Pour the batter into a greased and floured baking unit or a 3-quart mold. Place in the slow-cooker and cover. Cover the cooker, but prop the lid open a fraction with a toothpick or a twist of foil to let excess steam escape. Cook on High for 4½ to 6½ hours. When a toothpick inserted in the center comes out clean, the cake is done. Cool on a rack for 10 to 15 minutes before you turn it out. Let cool thoroughly before serving.

Makes 10 to 12 servings.

EASY ORANGE CAKE
4½ to 6½ hours

This is very nice with an orange-butter icing—sweet butter whipped with confectioners' sugar and orange-juice concentrate to which has been added 1 tablespoon grated orange peel.

1 *package* (16 oz.) *pound-cake mix*	2 *eggs*
⅔ *cup orange juice*	3 *Tbs. grated orange peel*

To Cook: Place the cake mix, orange juice, and eggs in a large bowl and beat by hand 300 times. Add the grated peel for the last round of beating. Pour the batter into a well-greased and floured baking unit or a 3-quart mold. Place in the slow-cooker and cover. Cover the cooker, but prop the lid open a fraction with a toothpick or a twist of foil to let excess steam escape. Cook on High for 4½ to 6½ hours. When a toothpick inserted in the center comes out clean, the cake is done. Cool on a rack for 10 minutes before turning out.

Makes 10 to 12 servings.

APPLE CAKE
6 to 8 hours

1 *cup all-purpose flour, sifted*	4 *cups sliced, pared, cored tart apples*
1½ *tsp. baking powder*	
½ *tsp. salt*	½ *tsp. cinnamon*
1 *Tbs. sugar*	¼ *tsp. nutmeg*
¼ *cup shortening*	2 *Tbs. sugar*
1 *egg, slightly beaten*	½ *cup apricot jam*
¼ *cup milk*	2 *Tbs. melted butter*

To Cook: Into a medium-large bowl, sift together the flour, baking powder, salt, and 1 tablespoon sugar. With 2 knives cut in the shortening until mixture is mealy. Make a well in the center and drop in the egg and milk. Stir to form a smooth batter. Turn into a greased, floured baking unit or a 3-quart mold. Arrange the apple slices in rows on top, pushing them halfway into the batter. In a small bowl, mix the cinnamon, nutmeg, and 2 tablespoons sugar. Sprinkle over the apple slices and dot with apricot jam. Drizzle butter over all. Place on a trivet in the slow-cooker and cover. Cover the cooker, but prop the lid open a fraction with a toothpick or a twist of foil to let excess steam escape. Cook on High for 6 to 8 hours. Serve lukewarm.

Makes 6 servings.

Chapter *12*

Slow-Cook Desserts

CUSTARDS AND COMPOTES and puddings, these are the sweets the crockery cooker does very well. They all taste terrific after a few hours in the slow-pot's gentle heat. The slow-cooker can do other desserts, too—you'll find cakes and fruit breads, for instance, in the preceding chapter, and some of the recipes in Chapter 13 make very good desserts.

CUSTARDS IN SLOW-COOKER

Eggs are not only more nutritious but more delicious when cooked very slowly. Since eggs are the setting ingredient in custards like those grandmother made with fresh dairy products, custards do well in slow-pots. There are some variations on the custard theme in this chapter, but many more custard-based desserts are suited to slow-cooking. You can adapt your recipes to the cooking times here.

Because slow-pots cook at varying speeds, you must test my timing. Insert a silver knife in the custard after the shorter cooking time suggested: If it comes out with grains of half-cooked custard and a yellow sheen of uncooked custard, cook for another hour or so. If a slow-to-cook custard may wreck a dinner party, finish it in a 350° F. oven. Set the baking mold in a pan half filled with boiling water.

You can make custard sauce in the slow-cooker, of course. Cook it on High and keep stirring as it thickens. I make mine in a double-boiler because the double-boiler top is easier to wash than the slow-pot and cooking time is similar.

COMPOTES AND COOKED FRUITS

Fresh fruits single or mixed, cook beautifully in the slow-pot. We're out of the habit of cooking fruit—apples, peaches, pears, apricots, and all—perhaps because we tend to rely on canned fruit in the winter. Use the recipe for Fresh-Fruit Compote (page 285) as a basic approach to cooking any fruit. The fruit can be served on ice cream or with a custard sauce, a popular and nutritious old-fashioned dessert. Or make more elegant concoctions, such as Poires Hélène and Peach Melba (pages 289, 290).

PUDDINGS

Puddings, though usually inexpensive, can be glamorous. We're accustomed to making them quickly from packaged preparations, but the flavor is just not as good as that of homemade puddings. When you have a slow-cooker, making them isn't a big job, and it's worthwhile nutritionally.

The best system is to start a pudding cooking late at night. The next morning, put it in the refrigerator to chill all day. Then your slow-pot is free to cook other good things for dinner—and the dessert is finished.

Cook puddings in a mold or soufflé dish, rather than right in the cooker. It is easier to wash than the cooker and can be used as a serving dish.

BLUEBERRY GRUNT

3 to 5 hours

Traditionally, this is served with Colonial pudding sauce, a combination of 3 cups of heavy cream and ⅔ cup of soft maple sugar. Blueberry Grunt used to be cooked in muslin or yarn pudding bags that looked rather like a man's sock. The bags were dipped into boiling water, floured, and filled while still hot. Blueberry Grunt is nice with chilled maple syrup.

2 cups cake flour, sifted
4 tsp. baking powder
½ tsp. salt
2 Tbs. sugar
2 Tbs. butter or margarine

2 Tbs. light molasses
⅞ cup milk
1 cup blueberries
All-purpose flour

To Cook: Sift together the first 4 ingredients. Cut the butter into

the dry mixture and stir in the molasses and milk. In a small bowl, combine the blueberries and enough flour to coat them. Then gently fold the blueberries into the batter. Turn into a greased 3-quart soufflé dish or mold, set on a trivet or Pyrex cup in the slow-cooker, and cover loosely with foil. Prop the slow-cooker cover open a fraction with a twist of foil. Cook on Low for 3 to 5 hours, or until a straw inserted in the center comes out fairly dry.

Makes 8 servings.

BLACKBERRY PUDDING

Follow the recipe for Blueberry Grunt (above), but substitute ripe blackberries for blueberries.

CAPE COD CRANBERRY PUDDING
3 to 5 hours

Another old-fashioned dessert which, like mincemeat, relies on chopped suet for body and flavor.

1 cup cake flour, sifted	½ cup unflavored bread crumbs
1 tsp. baking powder	⅔ cup finely chopped suet
½ tsp. salt	1 cup cranberries
⅓ cup light-brown sugar, firmly packed	1 egg, well beaten
	⅓ cup milk

To Cook: Sift the flour, baking powder, and salt together 3 times. Mix in thoroughly the sugar and bread crumbs. Add the suet and cranberries; then fold in the egg and milk. Turn into a buttered 3-quart mold or soufflé dish, cover loosely with foil, and set on a trivet or Pyrex cup in the slow-cooker. Cover the cooker and cook on Low for 3 to 5 hours.

Makes 6 servings.

APPLE PANDOWDY
3 to 4 hours

A cookbook published in 1880 gives a pandowdy recipe in **para-graph form**: "Fill a heavy pot heaping with pleasant apples, sliced. Add 1 cup molasses, 1 cup sugar, 1 cup water, 1 teaspoon cloves, 1 teaspoon cinnamon. Cover with baking powder biscuit crust, sloping over the apples. Bake overnight. In the morning, cut the hard crust into the apple. Eat with yellow cream or plain." Here's a similar recipe to try in your slow-cooker.

4 *cups sliced apples*	¼ *cup butter or margarine*
2 *Tbs. strained lemon juice*	⅓ *cup all-purpose flour*
½ *cup light-brown sugar,*	¼ *tsp. cinnamon*
firmly packed	¼ *tsp. nutmeg*

To Cook: The apples should be peeled, quartered, cored, and cut in ½-inch-thick slices. Toss the slices thoroughly in the lemon juice. Then arrange in a buttered 3-quart soufflé dish. In a large bowl, working with 2 knives, blend the sugar, butter, flour, cinnamon, and nutmeg until the butter is cut into pea-size chunks. Sprinkle the flour mixture over the apples; keep mixture away from the edge of the dish. Set the dish on a Pyrex cup or a trivet in the slow-cooker; cover loosely with foil. Cover the cooker and cook on High for 3 to 4 hours.

Makes 4 to 6 servings.

HONEYCOMB PUDDING
2 to 4 hours

An old-fashioned puddingy-custard. The first time you make it, check the timing carefully. It may be ready sooner than you expected. It is done when a silver knife inserted in the center comes out clean.

3 *Tbs. butter or margarine*	1 *cup all-purpose flour*
2 *Tbs. cream or whole milk*	¼ *tsp. salt*
3 *medium eggs, separated*	½ *tsp. cinnamon*
1 *cup light molasses*	¼ *tsp. nutmeg*
1 *Tbs. strained lemon juice*	

To Cook: Melt the butter in a small saucepan and transfer to a large bowl. Stir in the milk, well-beaten egg yolks, molasses, and lemon juice. Into a medium bowl, sift together the flour, salt, cinnamon, and nutmeg. Combine with the butter-and-milk mixture. Beat the egg whites until they form glossy—not dry—peaks, and fold gently into the flour mixture. Turn into a buttered 2- or 3-quart mold; set it on a trivet or a Pyrex cup in the slow-cooker, and cover loosely with foil. Cover the cooker and cook on Low for 2 to 4 hours.

Makes 4 to 6 servings.

BREAD PUDDING, DOMINIQUE'S WAY
2 to 3 hours

Dominique Baur, a lovely French girl who helped me test the recipes in this book, made pudding with saved-up chunks of sliced French bread.

4 egg yolks	Pinch salt
2 cups light cream	5 cups cubed, stale French
¼ cup sugar	bread
½ tsp. vanilla extract	¼ cup dry sherry
	1 jar (10 oz.) raspberry jam

To Cook: Beat the yolks until frothy and lemon colored. Mix in all remaining ingredients except the jam. Toss until the bread is soft and has absorbed a lot of the liquid. Spoon in layers into a buttered 2-quart baking dish and dribble raspberry jam between layers. Cover loosely with foil and set on a trivet in the slow-cooker. Pour ½ cup of hot water into the cooker, cover it, and cook on High for 2 to 3 hours.

Makes 6 servings.

SUET PUDDING
5 to 7 hours

Suet is the fine fat from beef used in mincemeat (page 284). This antique recipe relies on it for the richness of its texture. The pudding doesn't exactly fit today's concept of light, bright eating, but it was popular long ago and is fun to serve at a traditional meal, such as Christmas or Thanksgiving dinner.

1 cup sugar
2 tsp. baking powder
1 tsp. ground allspice
1 tsp. cinnamon
1 tsp. salt
1 cup chopped suet, beaten
  soft
3 egg yolks, well beaten

½ cup light molasses
1 cup whole milk
½ cup shredded citron peel
2 medium apples, peeled, cored,
  diced
½ cup seedless raisins
1½ cups dried bread crumbs
3 egg whites, whipped stiff
Foamy Sauce (below)

To Cook: Sift together 3 times the sugar, baking powder, allspice, cinnamon, and salt. Stir into the suet. Stir in the eggs, molasses, and milk. Add the citron, apples, raisins, bread crumbs. Fold in the egg whites. Turn into a greased 3-quart mold or soufflé dish; tie a linen cloth over the top. Set the dish on a trivet or Pyrex cup in the slow-cooker. Cover the cooker and cook on Low for 5 to 7 hours, or until firm. Serve warm with Foamy Sauce.

Makes 8 servings.

FOAMY SAUCE

½ cup sugar
½ cup butter or margarine
2 tsp. water

1 medium egg, well beaten
½ tsp. vanilla extract

To Cook: In a small saucepan, over medium-low heat, stir together the sugar, butter, and water until mixture boils. Remove from heat and keep warm. Just before serving, stir in the egg and vanilla.

PLUM PUDDING
5 to 6 hours

This recipe is a descendant of Ruth Macguire's great-grandmother's plum pudding—a traditional Christmas-dinner dessert. It is flambéed with rum and served with a hard sauce on the side. Ruth makes it several weeks before Christmas and lets it ripen in a cool, dark closet, well wrapped in several thicknesses of rum-soaked cheesecloth and overwrapped with foil.

1 cup all-purpose flour	½ lb. unflavored dried bread
¾ tsp. salt	crumbs
½ tsp. baking powder	½ lb. beef suet, beaten soft
½ tsp. ground allspice	½ lb. light-brown sugar
2 tsp. ground ginger	3 medium apples, peeled, cored,
¼ tsp. nutmeg	and chopped fine
½ lb. seedless dark raisins	Grated peel of ½ lemon
2 oz. candied citron peel	¼ cup dark rum
½ lb. dried currants	¼ cup apple cider
½ lb. golden seedless raisins	4 eggs, well beaten
3 oz. slivered almonds	

To Cook: Sift the flour, salt, baking powder, allspice, ginger, and nutmeg into a very large bowl. Stir in the remaining ingredients one at a time until all are added. Grease a 3-quart pudding mold or a regular mold. Turn pudding mixture into the mold. Cover with a square of clean linen and tie linen with string. Place on a trivet in the slow-cooker and add 2 cups of water to cooker. Cover and cook on High for 5 to 6 hours.

Makes 10 to 12 servings.

INDIAN PUDDING
2 to 3 hours

The most popular pudding in the past century was Indian pudding, which was baked for hours in the brick ovens of the day or, if the great oven was not heated, boiled for hours in a linen bag. The slow-cooker does this spicy cornmeal dessert beautifully. You can make it with half-and-half instead of milk if you want a richer pudding.

3½ cups cold milk	½ tsp. salt
⅓ cup yellow cornmeal	½ tsp. ground ginger
2 eggs	1 tsp. cinnamon
¼ cup dark molasses	4 Tbs. butter or margarine
½ cup light-brown sugar,	¾ cup golden seedless raisins
firmly packed	½ pint light or heavy cream

To Cook: Over medium heat, in a large saucepan, heat 3 cups of the milk. Combine ½ cup milk with the cornmeal and turn into the saucepan. Stir continually until the mixture begins to thicken. Lower the heat and stir 20 minutes more. Beat the eggs in a small bowl and stir in the molasses, sugar, salt, ginger, and cinnamon. Cut the butter into the cornmeal mixture and stir in the raisins. Add the egg mixture; whip briskly; then pour into a buttered 3-quart mold. Cover the mold. Pour 1 cup water into the slow-cooker. Place the mold on a rack or trivet in the cooker. Cover the cooker and cook on High for 2 to 3 hours. Serve warm, with cream.

Makes 8 servings.

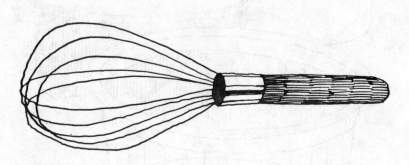

RICE PUDDING WITH BOURBON
4 to 6 hours

I make this with leftover rice, but you can start from scratch by cooking ½ cup raw rice as directed on the package.

3½ cups milk
1 cup cooked white rice
3 eggs, slightly beaten
⅓ cup sugar
1 Tbs. vanilla extract
½ cup golden seedless raisins

1½ tsp. grated lemon peel
1 tsp. nutmeg
2 Tbs. butter or margarine
3 Tbs. bourbon or dark rum
½ cup sweetened whipped cream

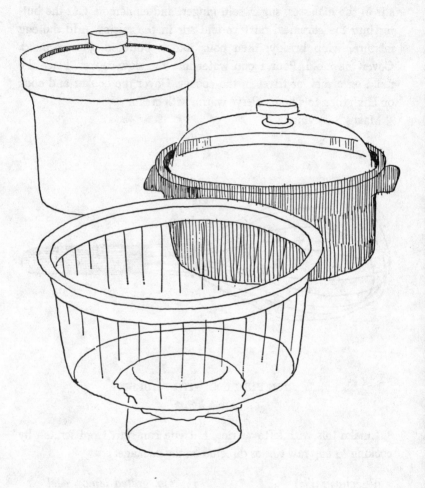

To Cook: Warm the milk, and pour it over the rice. Into the eggs, beat the sugar, vanilla, raisins, and lemon peel. Stir the milk and rice into the egg mixture. Scrape into a buttered 3-quart soufflé dish and set on a Pyrex cup or a trivet in the slow-cooker. Cover the dish with a square of foil. Sprinkle with nutmeg and dot with butter. Cover the cooker and cook on Low for 4 to 6 hours. Turn into a serving bowl and stir in the bourbon. Serve the pudding lukewarm, with a dollop of sweetened whipped cream on top.

Makes 6 to 8 servings.

ALL-DAY RICE PUDDING
8 to 12 hours

This used to be made in a very slow oven and cooked for hours, until most of the milk had evaporated. It must be stirred several times during the cooking, so it's not an absentee-cook dish.

1 *tsp. butter or margarine*	½ *tsp. salt*
1 *cup converted rice*	1 *cup seedless raisins*
4 *cups whole milk*	1 *tsp. vanilla extract*
1 *cup sugar*	

To Cook: Butter the bottom of the slow-cooker. Combine the rice, milk, sugar, and salt in the cooker. Cover, prop the lid partially open with a foil twist, and cook on Low for 3 to 4 hours. After the first hour (it could be the second) stir the mixture thoroughly and cover again. Repeat the procedure twice during this part of the cooking. After the 3 or 4 hours, add the raisins and the vanilla, and continue cooking. Stir whenever a brown film forms on the pudding. Cook 5 to 8 hours longer. It is ready when very thick. Let cool slightly before serving.

Makes 6 to 8 servings.

MAPLE-SYRUP RICE PUDDING
4 to 6 hours

1 *cup converted rice*	½ *cup sugar*
2 *cups milk*	½ *cup heavy cream, whipped*
¼ *tsp. salt*	*Maple syrup*

To Cook: Combine rice, salt, milk, and sugar in a 2-quart mold; stir once. Cover loosely with foil; place on a trivet in the slow-cooker. Cover the cooker, set a twist of foil under the cover to let a little steam escape, and cook on Low for 4 to 6 hours, or until the rice has absorbed all the milk. Let cool.

Before Serving: Fold the whipped cream into the rice; mound on a serving dish and dribble maple syrup over the top. Serve a small pitcher of maple syrup on the side.

Makes 4 to 6 servings.

NO-EGG RICE PUDDING
4 to 6 hours

Madame Bertrand, my landlady in Southern France, made this rice pudding in an old ceramic saucepan on the top of her wood-burning stove.

1 *cup converted rice*	½ *tsp. nutmeg*
2½ *cups milk*	*Peel of ½ lemon, slivered*
⅔ *cup sugar*	½ *tsp. vanilla extract*
½ *cup golden seedless raisins*	½ *cup heavy cream or half-*
½ *tsp. salt*	*and-half, chilled*

To Cook: Place all the ingredients except the cream in the slow-cooker and stir once. Cover and cook on Low for 4 to 6 hours. Serve lukewarm, with chilled heavy cream.

Makes 8 to 10 servings.

HOMEMADE MINCEMEAT
16 to 20 hours

This takes 16 to 20 hours of cooking time, and without a slow-cooker it's a chore. First the meat is cooked for 8 to 10 hours; then the mincemeat is put together and cooked an additional 8 to 10 hours. If you don't have a food chopper, you can try to blend the ingredients in your blender, but it's tiresome. However, it's fun to try once, and homemade mincemeat is both economical and very good in pies and tarts. Put it up in jars and save it for Christmas gifts.

1 lb. lean chuck beef, cut into
    1-inch cubes
2 or 3 cups water
2 lb. tart apples, peeled and
    cored
2⅔ cups seedless raisins
2½ cups currants
¼ lb. candied citron peel

2 tsp. salt
1 Tbs. nutmeg
2 cups sugar
1 cup apple cider
1 Tbs. ground cloves
1 Tbs. cinnamon
¼ lb. ground beef suet, minced

To Cook: Place the beef in the slow-cook pot with enough water to cover. Cover and cook on Low for 8 to 10 hours, or until very tender. Turn off the heat. Remove the meat, but leave 1 cup of the broth in the pot. Put the meat through a food chopper, with the apples, raisins, currants, and citron. Add this and all the other ingredients to the broth in the slow-cooker; stir well. Cover and cook on Low for 8 to 10 hours more. Spoon into clean, dry, canning jars; seal, and store in the refrigerator. Or process for 10 minutes in a boiling-water bath.

Makes enough for four 8-inch pies.

FRUIT DESSERTS, CUSTARD, FONDUE

FRESH-FRUIT COMPOTE
5 to 7 hours

This is a basic recipe for cooking fresh fruits in the slow-cooker. Use it to make compote of pears, apples, cherries, peaches, plums, nectarines, or apricots. You can use mixed fruits or a single fruit. Use compote of pears and peaches to make classic desserts such as Poires Hélène and Peach Melba (pages 289 and 290).

2 cups water
1 cup sugar
¼ tsp. salt

5 cups halved or quartered,
    peeled fresh fruit
Peel of ¼ lemon, slivered
½ tsp. vanilla extract

To Cook: Place all the ingredients except the vanilla in the slow-cooker. Cover and cook on Low for 5 to 7 hours. Remove the cover, turn off the heat, and stir in the vanilla. Chill before serving.

Makes 6 to 8 servings.

COMPOTE OF DRIED FRUIT
10 to 12 hours

For special occasions, serve this with bourbon-flavored whipped cream.

1 *cup dried prunes*	1 *cup dried apricots*
1 *cup dried golden seedless*	2½ *cups water*
raisins	*Peel of ¼ lemon, slivered*

To Cook: Place all the ingredients in the slow-cooker. Cover and cook on Low for 10 to 12 hours, or overnight. Chill before serving.

Makes 8 to 10 servings.

SWEET-CIDER APPLESAUCE
3 to 4 hours

This once was called bean-pot applesauce and was made in a real bean pot.

8 *large apples, peeled, cored,*	½ *tsp. cinnamon*
quartered	⅛ *tsp. salt*
3 *Tbs. strained lemon juice*	*Cider to cover (about 4 cups)*
½ *cup sugar*	

To Cook: Toss the apples with the lemon juice and layer in the slow-cooker with the sugar and cinnamon mixed with salt. Pour in enough cider to barely cover the apples. Cover, but prop the lid open with a small twist of foil to let some steam escape. Cook on Low for 3 to 4 hours, or until the fruit is just tender.

Before Serving: In a small saucepan, boil down the cooking liquid just enough to strengthen its flavor; then pour over the fruit. Chill before serving.

Makes 4 to 6 servings.

BAKED STUFFED APPLES
3 to 5 hours

Following the method described below, you can bake apples plain. Stuffed as in this recipe, they make a real party dessert. If you bake them plain, put a little sugar on the apple top and ¼ cup of water in the slow-cooker.

6 *medium, tart, red apples*	¼ *cup soft butter or margarine*
1 *cup light-brown sugar*	2 *cups very hot water*
¼ *cup golden seedless raisins*	3 *Tbs. orange-juice concentrate*
1 *Tbs. grated orange peel*	

To Cook: Wash, core, and stem the apples, but don't peel them. Stand them in a buttered mold and stuff them with ⅔ cup of the brown sugar, the raisins, and the orange peel. Fill the tops of the core cavities with butter and sprinkle the remaining sugar over the tops. Place the mold in the slow-cooker and pour the hot water into the cooker. Sprinkle the orange-juice concentrate over the apples. Cover the cooker and cook on Low for 3 to 5 hours, or until the apples are tender.

Makes 6 servings.

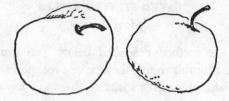

MOTHER'S APPLESAUCE
6 to 8 hours

8 *to* 10 *medium, tart, apples,*   ½ *tsp. salt*
    peeled, cored, and sliced   ½ *tsp. cinnamon*
½ *cup water*   1 *tsp. vanilla extract*
½ *cup sugar*   2 *Tbs. butter or margarine*

To Cook: Place the apples in the slow-cooker along with the water, sugar, salt, and cinnamon. Cover and cook on Low for 6 to 8 hours. Remove the cover, turn the heat off, and stir in the vanilla and the butter. Serve warm or chill before serving.

Makes 6 to 8 servings.

PAPA'S APPLESAUCE
6 to 8 hours

8 *to* 10 *medium, tart, apples,*   ½ *cup sugar*
    peeled, cored, and sliced   1 *Tbs. grated orange peel*
½ *cup orange juice*

To Cook: Place all the ingredients in the slow-cooker. Cover and cook on Low for 6 to 8 hours. Serve warm or chilled.

Makes 6 to 8 servings.

STEWED RHUBARB
6 to 8 hours

4 *cups 2-inch pieces rhubarb*   2 *Tbs. butter or margarine*
½ *to* ¾ *cup sugar*   ½ *tsp. vanilla extract*
½ *cup water*

To Cook: Place the rhubarb in the slow-cooker along with the sugar and water. Cover and cook on Low for 6 to 8 hours. Remove the cover, turn off the heat, and stir in the butter and the vanilla. Chill before serving.

Makes 6 to 8 servings.

QUICK RHUBARB MOUSSE
6 to 8 hours

4 cups 2-inch pieces rhubarb
½ to ¾ cup sugar
½ cup water
2 Tbs. butter or margarine

½ tsp. vanilla extract
1 pint heavy cream, whipped,
    unsweetened

To Cook: Place the rhubarb in the slow-cooker along with the sugar and water. Cover and cook on Low for 6 to 8 hours. Remove the cover, turn off the heat, and stir in the butter and the vanilla. Drain away most of the juice. Fold the rhubarb into the whipped cream. Turn into a serving bowl, cover, and chill for a few minutes in the freezer before serving.

Makes 8 to 10 servings.

STEWED APRICOTS
10 to 12 hours

Do these overnight, like Stewed Prunes (page 301).

1 lb. dried apricots
3 cups water

1 Tbs. grated orange peel
1 tsp. Cointreau (optional)

To Cook: Place the apricots, water, and orange peel in the slow-cooker. Cover and cook on Low overnight, or 10 to 12 hours. Serve chilled, with a dash of Cointreau.

Makes 6 to 8 servings.

POIRES HÉLÈNE

This is a classic dessert from the turn of the century. To make it, you need prepared chocolate sauce and Fresh-Fruit Compote made with halved pears.

8 scoops vanilla ice cream
8 pears, cooked as for Fresh-
    Fruit Compote (page
    285)

¾ cup chocolate sauce

Before Serving: In each serving dish, put 1 scoop of ice cream and place 2 pear halves on top. Drizzle on chocolate sauce.

Makes 8 servings.

PEACH MELBA

For this classic dessert, you need fresh raspberries and Fresh-Fruit Compote made with halved peaches.

2 cups fresh raspberries	4 peaches, cooked as for Fresh-
Sugar to taste	Fruit Compote (page 285)
1 Tbs. kirsch	1 quart vanilla ice cream

Before Serving: Wash and stem the raspberries and purée in a blender on low speed, adding sugar a little at a time. Do not make the berries overly sweet. Stir in the kirsch and chill for several hours. Place the ice cream in a serving bowl in scoops and set the peach halves on top. Cover with raspberry purée.

Makes 8 servings.

QUICK APRICOT WHIP

Combine 1 recipe for Stewed Apricots (page 289), drained and mashed, with 1½ cups sweetened whipped cream. Pour a little of the cooking juice over each serving. Add a dash of Cointreau or a pinch of slivered almonds, if you wish. Also good with a little grated chocolate.

Makes 6 to 8 servings.

QUICK PRUNE WHIP

Combine 1 recipe for Stewed Prunes (page 301), drained, pitted, and mashed, with 1½ cups sweetened whipped cream. Pour a little of the cooking juice over each serving. For parties, dress up with slivered almonds.

Makes 6 to 8 servings.

CARAMEL CUSTARD
2 to 4 hours

A custard dessert to serve with caramel sauce. Make it a day ahead so it can be chilled; or bake it overnight using the timer to start it, and chill it until dinner time.

4 medium eggs	4½ cups sugar
1 tsp. vanilla extract	½ cup boiling water
3½ cups milk	2 cups hot water

To Cook: Beat the eggs with an electric beater until thick. Add the vanilla and beat until lemon colored. Add the milk and 2½ cups of the sugar; with the beater on low, combine well. Butter a 2-quart mold. In a heavy, medium-size skillet, over very low heat, melt the remaining 2 cups of sugar. When it begins to bubble and turn brown, stir to combine it all. When the caramelizing sugar is a medium brown, pour ½ into the mold. Pour the boiling water into the caramel in the skillet. Stir, over low heat, until the mixture bubbles. Turn off heat; let cool on top of the stove; then chill.

Pour the egg-and-milk mixture into the mold. Pour the hot water into the slow-cooker and place the mold on a trivet or rack in the cooker. Cover mold loosely with foil. Cover the pot, but prop the lid open a fraction with a toothpick or a twist of foil to let excess steam escape. Cook on High for 2 to 4 hours, or until a silver knife inserted in the center comes out clean. Chill, covered, in the refrigerator; then unmold and serve with caramel sauce over the top.

Makes 6 to 8 servings.

CHOCOLATE FONDUE
2 to 4 hours

One of the wonderful things a slow-cooker can do is melt chocolate without burning it. That's a trick restricted in the past to the top of a double boiler. It's a bore, of course, to have to wash the slow-cooker after melting just a couple of squares of chocolate.

6 *squares unsweetened chocolate*	3 *Tbs. brandy*
1 *cup sugar*	½ *cup heavy cream*
½ *cup butter or margarine*	*Stale pound or angel cake, cut*
¼ *tsp. salt*	*into "fingers"*

To Cook: Combine all the ingredients, except cake, in the slow-cooker. Cover and cook on High for 15 to 20 minutes; then turn to Low and cook, covered, for 2 to 4 hours. Serve with fingers of sliced, stale cake for dipping.

Makes 6 to 8 servings.

Chapter 13

Breakfast Foods to Cook Overnight

COMPOTES OF DRIED FRUITS, whole grains and cereals, and some old-fashioned dishes, such as scrapple, are among the foods the slow-cooker can prepare overnight. Set them in the slow-pot before you go to bed, and when you wake up, you'll wonder who is cooking something that smells so good. In many areas, as I have mentioned, electrical rates are lower at night than during the day. So overnight cooking has a double appeal: you get up to a ready-to-serve breakfast at half the price.

BREAKFAST FRUITS

Prunes, raisins, and apricots are among the dried fruits that make delicious morning eating. You could serve canned fruit, of course, but the cost would be considerably more. Another advantage of preparing fruit yourself is that you can flavor it as you wish. A little vanilla does wonders for prunes and raisins. Grated orange peel in apricots and peaches adds a whole new dimension to their flavor.

The breakfast fruits are very nice served with buttered toast or buttered English muffins.

In Chapter 12, you'll find other slow-cook fruit recipes—Baked Stuffed Apples (page 287), for instance—fine to cook overnight for breakfast.

WHOLE-GRAIN CEREALS AND RICE

Whole-grain cereals make wonderful breakfast foods, and nearly all of them benefit from overnight cooking in the slow-pot. Try them on family members who hate to eat in the morning. The texture of Cornmeal Mush (page 301), swimming in butter and the nutty flavor of Wheat or Rye Berries (page 252) in milk or light cream appeal to palates jaded by cornflakes. After such hearty fare, no one will be dying for a candy bar or coffeecake halfway through the morning.

Rye berries and wheat berries are available at most health-food stores, which, by the way, are a good source for old-fashioned foods to slow-cook, such as dried fruits and vegetables. Yellow and white cornmeal, whole wheat, and Irish oats are sold by most markets.

The recipe for Rice-and-Raisin Breakfast (page 300) can be adapted to any other fruit. Rice and apricots would be nice. Plain rice with brown sugar, cream, and a bit of cinnamon is good, too. Rice is very nutritious. Adele Davis, late grande dame of the health-food world, recommended in particular converted rice (if white rice is called for), and that is the type the slow-cooker does best. Brown rice cooks just as well, but takes a little longer. It, too, is good with brown sugar and raisins. It's chewier, but some people prefer that texture.

In my experience, nothing goes wrong with the cooking of grains, but I imagine that liquid might be left in some slow-pots when the cooking is finished. If so, turn the heat to High; when the liquid is boiling, uncover and simmer a few minutes until the liquid has evaporated.

BREAKFAST BREADS

Chapter 11 has several very good recipes for breads made with bananas, cranberries, pumpkin, and other fruits. These are splendid breakfast foods.

BREAKFAST RECIPES

SCRAPPLE
8 to 10 hours

The fried scrapple served in Pennsylvania restaurants today reminds me of sausage. It's a combination of cornmeal and variety meats from a pig—once again, everything but the squeal. With a slow-cooker, you can get the long cooking out of the way overnight. Add the cereal in the morning, chill, and serve the following day. Making scrapple is not one of the most profitable ways to spend your cooking time, but it is fun to try. Keep the finished loaves in the refrigerator. Slice, fry, and serve with scrambled eggs, sautéed apple slices, and maple syrup.

2 *lb. pork neck bones or any other bony pieces*	½ *lb. pork liver (optional)*
4 *cups boiling water*	1 *cup cornmeal*
1 *tsp. salt*	1 *cup cold water*
1 *medium onion, peeled, chopped*	2 *tsp. salt*
	½ *tsp. dried sage*
6 *peppercorns*	⅛ *tsp. nutmeg*
1 *bay leaf*	*Dash cayenne pepper*

To Cook: Place the pork pieces, boiling water, salt, onion, peppercorns, and bay leaf in the slow-cooker. Cover and cook on Low overnight, or about 8 to 10 hours. If you are using pork liver, add it for the last hour of cooking.

Remove the meats from the cooker and let cool. Remove meat from the bones and put all meat through food grinder. Strain the cooking liquid (there should be 4 cups) and discard peppercorns and bay leaf. Place the liquid in the top of a double boiler and bring to a boil. Combine the cornmeal, cold water, 2 teaspoons salt, and other seasonings. Half fill the double-boiler bottom with boiling water and bring to a rapid boil. Place the top over it and when the cooking liquid is simmering, stir in the ground meat and dribble in the cornmeal mixture, stirring constantly. When the mixture has thickened, stir 2 minutes. Cover, reduce heat, and cook 10 minutes. Scrape into 2 bread-loaf tins rinsed in cold water; let cool. Then cover and refrigerate until firm, or overnight. To serve, cut into slices a little over ½ inch thick and sauté in butter or bacon drippings, as you would sausage.

Makes 2 loaves; 6 to 8 servings.

SAUSAGE-STUFFED APPLES
6 to 8 hours

These apples are an old-fashioned New England lunch food that my family occasionally enjoys for winter breakfast. I prepare them the night before and set them on a trivet over ice cubes in the slow-pot. The timer starts them cooking about 5 hours before breakfast time. Traditionally, they are served with corn muffins.

6 to 8 large, firm, tart apples   About ½ cup fresh bread crumbs
1 lb. sausage meat

To Cook: Wash the apples; remove the cores and a little of the apple around them. Set each on a small loose cup made of a square of foil and then on a trivet. In a medium skillet, over medium heat, sauté the sausage meat, stirring constantly, until the fat is flowing. Mix in enough bread crumbs to absorb the fat and toss crumbs and meat well. Stuff the apples with this mixture. Don't pack it too hard, or it will be gluey when cooked; pack it lightly. Place the trivet in the slow-cooker with about 12 ice cubes all around. Cover, set the timer to start cooking on Low, 5 or 6 hours before breakfast.

Makes 6 to 8 servings.

BUBBLE AND SQUEAK
4 to 6 hours

In England, this is customarily served for breakfast, but it is, to my taste, a little too heavy that early in the day. It is essentially a vegetarian dish, although mixed scraps of meat are sometimes added.

2 *cups shredded cabbage, cooked, drained*	1 *tsp. salt*
1 *cup mixed vegetables (leftovers, or canned and drained)*	2 *Tbs. cream or half-and-half*
	2 *Tbs. vegetable oil*
	2 *eggs, slightly beaten*
1 *cup spinach, cooked, drained*	1 *cup grated cheese*
	2 *Tbs. finely chopped parsley*
¼ *tsp. nutmeg*	2 *Tbs. finely chopped onion*
	Grated cheese

To Cook: Mix all the ingredients except the last in a soufflé dish. Cover loosely with foil; set in the slow-cooker on a trivet or Pyrex cup. Cover and cook on Low for 4 to 6 hours.

Before Serving: Top with grated cheese and bake in an oven heated to 375° F. for 30 minutes, or until brown.

Makes 4 to 6 servings.

STEAMED FIG PUDDING
6 to 8 hours

A modern version of an old New England dessert, this makes a wonderfully different breakfast. Traditionally it is served with a sweet sauce; instead, sprinkle with brown sugar and add a little whole milk.

1 *lb. dried figs*	½ *cup sugar*
2 *Tbs. all-purpose flour*	2 *eggs*
1 *cup suet or butter*	1 *tsp. soda*
1 *cup light molasses*	3 *cups cake flour, sifted*
¾ *cup very cold milk*	½ *tsp. salt*
1 *tsp. grated lemon peel*	

To Cook: In a bowl, combine the figs and 2 tablespoons flour and chop the figs finely. Keep the knife floured and fig bits tossed in the flour, so they won't stick together. Cut in suet, and then mix in the

remaining ingredients. Turn into a greased 3-quart mold or soufflé dish; cover loosely with foil; set in the slow-cooker on a trivet or Pyrex cup. Cover the cooker and cook on Low overnight, or 6 to 8 hours.

Makes 6 to 8 servings.

OATMEAL PUDDING FOR BREAKFAST
4 to 6 hours

This is from *In the Kitchen,* written in 1875 and dedicated to the cooking class of the Young Ladies' Saturday Morning Club of Boston. We find it heavy as a dessert, but wonderful for breakfast on cold, glum mornings. It is customarily served with chilled Maple-Sugar Sauce (below) or maple syrup.

4 cups milk
2 cups oatmeal
3 eggs
½ lb. suet or butter
¼ lb. seedless raisins
¼ lb. currants

1 tsp. salt
½ cup sugar
¼ tsp. cinnamon
½ tsp. nutmeg
Maple-Sugar Sauce

To Cook: In the morning, scald the milk and mix the oatmeal into it. Let stand all day. Before bedtime, beat the eggs until light and frothy. Stir the other ingredients into the eggs. Combine with the oatmeal and turn into the well-greased slow-cooker. Cover and cook on Low for 4 to 6 hours, or longer. Serve with Maple-Sugar Sauce. Makes 8 servings.

MAPLE-SUGAR SAUCE

½ lb. maple sugar
4 Tbs. hot water

¼ lb. butter or margarine

To Cook: Put the sugar between 2 layers of waxed paper and roll with a rolling pin until it is in crumbs. Turn into a small saucepan and simmer with the hot water until clear, 5 to 10 minutes. Add the butter and simmer, stirring, until butter has melted.

CORNMEAL APPLESAUCE
4 to 6 hours

A thick, apple-flavored sauce made with potatoes once was popular with roast pork. This is a modern version. We like it for breakfast. Cook overnight, using the timer to start it.

2 cups water
1 tsp. salt
1 cup yellow cornmeal

4 tart apples, peeled, cored, sliced
3 Tbs. butter or margarine

To Cook: Pour the water into the slow-cooker, add the salt, and stir in the cornmeal and apple slices. Cover and cook on Low for 4 to 6 hours.
Makes 5 servings.

GINGERBREAD
4 to 6 hours

I make gingerbread from a packaged mix because it's as good as any recipes I've ever tried and inexpensive as well as easy. Serve it warm with butter and marmalade or jam. Or serve it for dessert with whipped cream or ice cream.

1 package gingerbread mix
1 Tbs. melted butter, margarine, or vegetable oil

2 Tbs. grated candied citron rind

To Cook: Combine the gingerbread mix with the ingredients as instructed on the package. Then add the melted butter and citron. Pour into a greased 2-quart mold; cover loosely with foil; place on a trivet or Pyrex cup in the slow-cooker. Prop the cooker's cover very slightly open with a twist of foil to let excess steam escape. Cook on High for 4 to 6 hours. When the top is firm to the touch, the gingerbread is done.

Makes 6 to 8 servings.

RICE-AND-RAISIN BREAKFAST
8 to 10 hours

You can make this with leftover rice, but it's better made overnight this way in a slow-cooker.

1 *cup converted rice*	¼ *cup sugar*
2¼ *cups water*	1 *Tbs. grated orange peel*
1 *Tbs. butter or margarine*	1 *cup seedless raisins*
¼ *tsp. salt*	*Half-and-half or light cream*

To Cook: Combine everything but the half-and-half in the slow-cooker. Cover and cook on Low overnight or 8 to 10 hours. Serve warm in the morning with chilled half-and-half or light cream.

Makes 4 servings.

CORN BREAD FROM SCRATCH
2 to 3 hours

Packaged mix is so successful you really don't need to make corn bread from scratch, but the mix costs more. I grease the mold with bacon drippings.

1¼ *cups all-purpose flour*	1 *egg, slightly beaten*
¾ *cup yellow cornmeal*	1 *cup milk*
¼ *cup sugar*	⅓ *cup melted butter or*
4½ *tsp. baking powder*	*vegetable oil*
1 *tsp. salt*	

To Cook: In a medium bowl, sift together the flour, cornmeal, sugar, baking powder, and salt. Make a well in the center. Turn the egg, milk, and melted butter into the well and beat until dry mixture is just moistened. Turn into a greased 2-quart mold, cover with a plate, and place on a trivet or rack in the slow-cooker. Cover the cooker and cook on High for 2 to 3 hours.

Makes 6 servings.

STEWED PRUNES
10 to 12 hours

Do these overnight. They make a great breakfast served warm with cream and toasted, buttered whole-wheat bread.

1 *lb. dried unpitted prunes*	*Peel of ¼ lemon, in strips*
3 *cups water*	*½ tsp. vanilla extract*

To Cook: Place everything but the vanilla in the slow-cooker. Cover and cook on Low for 10 to 12 hours, or overnight. Remove the cover, turn off the heat, and add the vanilla. Turn into a serving bowl and let cool to lukewarm; before serving, remove peel.

Makes 6 to 8 servings.

STEWED GOLDEN RAISINS
10 to 12 hours

1 *lb. dried golden seedless*	3 *cups water*
raisins	*½ tsp. vanilla extract*

To Cook: Place the raisins and water in the slow-cooker. Cover and cook on Low for 10 to 12 hours, or overnight. Remove the cover, turn off the heat, and add the vanilla. Turn into a serving bowl and let cool to lukewarm before serving.

Makes 6 to 8 servings.

CORNMEAL MUSH
6 to 8 hours

You can have cornmeal mush perfectly cooked and waiting when you get up.

½ *cup cornmeal*	*Butter or margarine*
½ *tsp. salt*	*Salt*
3 *cups water*	

To Cook: Place cornmeal, ½ tsp. salt, and the water in the slow-cooker. Cover and cook on Low for 6 to 8 hours.

Before Serving: Spoon into big cereal or soup plates and top each with 1 or 2 tablespoons of butter. Offer salt with it rather than sugar.

Makes 4 to 6 servings.

WHEAT-BERRY BREAKFAST

Follow the recipe for cooking Wheat Berries (page 252). Let the berries cook overnight and in the morning serve them with half-and-half (or milk), sugar, and chopped fruit or blueberries.

Makes 4 or 5 servings.

RYE-BERRY BREAKFAST

Follow the recipe for cooking Rye Berries (page 252). Let the berries cook overnight and in the morning serve with half-and-half (or milk) and brown sugar, honey, or corn syrup.

Makes 4 or 5 servings.

Chapter 14

Jams, Relishes, and Preserves to Slow-Cook

THERE ARE SOME drawbacks and some advantages to making jams, relishes, and preserves in a slow-cooker.

One of the advantages is that the flavor is wonderful. The Old-Fashioned Marmalade on page 309 is the most orange-tasting marmalade I have ever made. The very long cooking extracts all the flavor from the peels, and you really can tell the difference. However, the marmalade is darker than that quick-cooked on the stove. If you are making preserves for gifts, you may consider that a drawback.

Another advantage is that you can put everything into the slow-cooker and go away for several hours—or overnight—until the next step in the process is due. I like starting slow-pot preserves at night after the children have gone to bed. Cutting all those bits and pieces is relaxing as long as I'm not trying to do six other things at the same time.

CHOOSING PRESERVING RECIPES
FOR THE SLOW-COOKER

Not all preserving recipes are suitable for a slow-cooker—rather, not all make sense. In conventional jam and relish making, ingredients are cooked in their own juices and with water and sugar in an open kettle, usually while the cook stirs. The kettle is uncovered so the liquid will boil away in steam, leaving a thickened mass of solids. You can, of course, cook any jam or relish the slow way. However, if the ingredients really should be cooked quickly in just a little liquid, slow-cooking isn't as good as stove-top cooking.

The slow-cooker does do well with ingredients whose flavors are extracted slowly. Also, it can cook sugar without burning it, so you don't have to stand over the pot, stirring.

The recipes here are variations on stove-top recipes I've used for years and are representative of those I believe work well in a slow-cooker. Use them to adapt your own favorites.

COOKING TIME

I haven't discovered any real difference in flavor between jams and preserves cooked 10 hours and those cooked 14. The latter may have a somewhat stronger flavor. This may not be true of all recipes, but seems to be true of most. This means that once you have started the cooking in your slow-pot, there isn't a really critical moment when you should stop it.

PROCESSING SLOW-COOKED PRODUCTS

If you are accustomed to making preserves in an open kettle and don't as a rule process, you may want to omit that step in the slow-cooker recipes here. (Processing means placing the filled, sealed containers in a boiling-water bath to sterilize the contents.) However, I must recommend processing, particularly when preserves are to be stored at warm house temperatures. If you don't want to process and are making only a few jars, store them in the refrigerator.

If you've never made preserves, here are some things you should know:

Containers: If you are going to process the preserves, it is best to use the glass canning jars with tight-fitting lids sold in hardware stores and many markets. These will stand up to the boiling temperatures. For nonprocessed preserves you can use found glass jars —peanut-butter jars, or what have you. Before filling containers, run them through the dishwasher; the high heat will come close to sterilizing them. Let them dry before you fill them. Leave ½-inch headroom between the preserves and the jar rim. Seal found containers with melted paraffin about ¼ to ½ inch thick. When the paraffin is cool, cap the jars or cover them with Saran Wrap or foil, tied in place.

Filling the jars: Pour the preserves through a wide-mouth funnel to avoid dripping on the jar rim. Drippings are difficult to wipe really clean, and they could attract insects or spoil during storage. Leave ½-inch headroom in jars to be sealed with paraffin (see above). Leave ¼-inch headroom in jars to be capped and processed. Don't fill them right to the top; that would make them hard to handle, and the caps would be covered with the jars' sticky contents.

Processing: Processing, as I said, is a matter of boiling the filled, sealed jars. The kettle for the boiling-water bath should be deep enough to allow for 1 or 2 inches of bubbling water above the jars' tops. Processing time for a great many products is 10 minutes at altitudes 1,000 feet or less above sea level. For every 1,000 feet above this altitude, add 1 minute to the time. Thus, up to 1,000 feet above sea level, you process 10 minutes. Up to 2,000 feet, you process 11 minutes. Up to 3,000 feet, you process 12 minutes. And so on.

Jars must stand on a trivet or a rack in the kettle, which could be a very large pressure cooker or any large kettle that has a lid. Set the trivet in the kettle and half fill it with boiling water. As the jars are ready, place them on the trivet. When all are in, pour very hot water down the side of the kettle (not over the jars) and keep adding more until the jar tops are 1 or 2 inches under water. Put on the cover; bring the water to a boil; then start timing the processing. When the time is up, remove the jars. Let them cool about 12 hours before storing. If you are using a pressure cooker as a boiling water bath, omit the gasket and set the lid loosely on the kettle, so steam can escape.

JAMS, RELISHES, AND PRESERVE RECIPES

PEACH-ORANGE BUTTER
11 to 13 hours

4 *lb. ripe peaches*	2 *tsp. cinnamon*
2 *cups orange juice*	½ *tsp. ground cloves*
About 2 *or* 3 *cups sugar*	1 *tsp. ground allspice*

To Cook: Pit the peaches, but don't peel them. Cut into small pieces and place in the slow-cooker with the orange juice. Cover and cook on Low for 10 to 12 hours. Do not stir. Rub the peaches through a sieve. Measure pulp and juice together and add ⅔ cup sugar for each cup. Add the spices. Cover and cook on High 1 hour. Pour into clean, dry ½-pint canning jars. Seal and process for 10 minutes in a boiling-water bath. Or bottle and store in the refrigerator.

Makes 3 to 4 pints.

APPLE BUTTER
11 to 13 hours

The big advantage in making preserve butters in a slow-cooker is that you don't have to stir or stand over the pot waiting to stir. Adapt your favorite fruit-butter recipes to fit the instructions and cooking time here.

2 *quarts sweet cider*	¼ *tsp. cinnamon*
4 *lb. sweet but tart apples,*	¼ *tsp. ground allspice*
peeled, cored, and sliced	⅛ *tsp. ground cloves*
About 3 *cups sugar*	1 *tsp. salt*

To Cook: Place the cider and the apples in the slow-cooker. Cover and cook on Low for 10 to 12 hours. Do not stir. Rub the apples through a sieve; measure the apples and add as much sugar as there is apple. Add the spices and salt and return to the cooker. Cover and cook on High for 1 hour. Pour into clean, dry, ½-pint canning jars. Seal and process for 10 minutes in a boiling-water bath. Or bottle and store in the refrigerator.

Makes 4 to 5 pints.

GINGERY APPLE BUTTER
8 to 10 hours

You can buy fresh ginger root at specialty grocers and Oriental food shops. It keeps well frozen.

5 *cups chopped, cored and*   Peel of 1 lemon, cut into
    peeled sour apples   *thin shavings*
    (*4 to 6 apples*)   2-*inch piece of fresh ginger*
5 *cups sugar*   *root, minced*
½ *cup water*

To Cook: Combine all ingredients in the slow-cooker. Cover and cook on Low for 8 to 10 hours or until the apple pieces are transparent and the juice very thick. Pour into clean, dry 8-ounce canning jars. Seal and process for 10 minutes in a boiling-water bath.

Makes about 3½ pints.

CARROT JAM
8 to 10 hours

Nice served as a jam, but best as a sweet relish with poultry.

2 *cups grated raw carrots*   *Juice and grated peel of*
    (*3 or 4 medium carrots*)   1 *lemon*
1½ *cups sugar*   ¼ *tsp. ground cloves*
½ *tsp. salt*   ¼ *tsp. ground allspice*
1 *cup water*   ¼ *tsp. cinnamon*

To Cook: Combine all ingredients in the slow-cooker. Cover and cook on Low for 8 to 10 hours or until thickened. Pour into clean, dry, 8-ounce canning jars. Seal and process for 10 minutes in a boiling-water bath.

Fills 5 or 6 (8 oz.) jars.

PINK PINEAPPLE JAM
6 to 8 hours

1 *large pineapple*	½ *lemon, sliced very thin*
½ *cup water*	½ *cup maraschino cherries*
2½ *cups sugar*	*and juice*

To Cook: Slice the top from the pineapple about 1 inch from the base of the leaves. Slice off the bottom about ¼ inch up. Peel the pineapple and remove any eyes that remain. Slice the pineapple meat from the core—the hard, pale inner section. Then chop the meat. Combine the pineapple and its juice, the water, sugar, and lemon in the slow-cooker. Cover and cook on Low for 6 to 8 hours. If the juice is thin when the cooking is over, boil on High, stirring, until thickened—10 or 15 minutes. Stir in the cherries and their juice for the last 3 minutes of cooking. Pour into clean, dry, 6-ounce jelly glasses or 8-ounce canning jars. Seal and process for 10 minutes in a boiling-water bath.

Fills about 3 (8 oz.) jars.

RHUBARB-STRAWBERRY CONSERVE
5 to 7 hours

This will be darker than if you made it on the stove top, but it's good—and easy.

1 *lb. rhubarb (about 3 cups,*	1 *cup water*
cut up)	4 *cups sugar*
1 *pint strawberries*	
(about 2 cups)	

To Cook: Remove the rhubarb leaves and coarse tips. Cut the stalks into 2-inch lengths and measure 3 cups. Rinse the berries quickly under cold water; drain well; then hull and slice them. Place the fruits in the slow-cooker; add the sugar and water; stir well. Cover and cook on Low until the conserve has thickened—about 5 to 7 hours. If the conserve still is watery turn the heat to High, uncover, and stir while it simmers and reduces—about 10 to 20 minutes. Skim off the foam and pour into clean, dry, 6- or 8-ounce canning jars. Seal and process 10 minutes in a boiling-water bath.

Fills 4 or 5 (8 oz.) jars.

OLD-FASHIONED MARMALADE
11 to 13 hours

A basic recipe for orange marmalade. Adapting the principles here, you can slow-cook your own marmalade combinations. Do the first cooking overnight; complete the marmalade in the morning.

6 *medium navel oranges*	*Water*
1 *medium lemon*	*Sugar (about 4 cups)*

To Cook: With a sharp knife, cut the peel from the oranges and lemon in large sections. Remove the orange sections from the white membrane holding them. Seed the fruit. Cut oranges and lemon into small pieces. Cut the peel on a slant into slivers. Mix peel and fruit in a large bowl; then measure, packing very firmly. Add an equal quantity of water; turn into the slow-cooker. Cover and cook on Low for 10 to 12 hours. Measure the mixture; add an equal quantity of sugar; return to the slow-cooker. Cover and cook on High for 1 hour. Turn into clean, dry, 8-ounce canning jars. Seal and process 10 minutes in a boiling-water bath.

Fills 5 or 6 (8 oz.) jars.

APPLE-AND-TOMATO BUTTER
6 to 8 hours

2½ *lb. ripe tomatoes, washed,*	2 *cups sugar*
peeled (8 to 10 medium)	*1-inch stick cinnamon*
2 *medium sour apples,*	1 *blade dried mace*
peeled, cored	6 *whole cloves*
½ *cup water*	*1-inch piece fresh ginger root*
1 *cup cider vinegar*	

To Cook: Slice the tomatoes and apples into thick chunks. Combine them in the slow-cooker and stir in the water, vinegar and sugar. Tie the spices and ginger root in a cheesecloth square and add to the cooker. Cover and cook on Low for 6 to 8 hours, or until thickened. If it hasn't thickened enough during the cooking period, turn the heat to High; uncover and simmer, stirring, for 10 to 20 minutes. When it is really thick, remove the spice bag and pour into clean, dry, 8-ounce canning jars. Seal and process for 10 minutes in a boiling-water bath.

Fills 4 or 5 (8 oz.) jars.

GREEN TOMATO CATSUP
8 to 10 hours

4 lb. green tomatoes, peeled, sliced (16 to 18 small)

2 medium onions, peeled, sliced

½ cup cider vinegar

1 cup light-brown sugar, firmly packed

2 tsp. salt

½ tsp. black peppercorns

½ tsp. ground allspice

½ tsp. ground ginger

½ tsp. cinnamon

1½ tsp. prepared mustard

1 Tbs. pickling spices

To Cook: Combine all the ingredients in the slow-cooker. Cover and cook on Low for 8 to 10 hours. Rub through a sieve. If the catsup is thin, return to the cooker and simmer, stirring, on High for 10 to 20 minutes, or until thickened. Pour into clean, dry 8-ounce or 1-pint canning jars. Seal and process for 10 minutes in a boiling-water bath.

Fills 4 or 5 (8 oz.) jars.

CATSUP WITH CELERY
8 to 10 hours

This is easy to make if you have a food chopper.

12 large ripe tomatoes, peeled, chopped fine

2 large stalks celery, chopped fine

4 large onions, peeled, chopped fine

1 sweet red pepper, seeded, chopped fine

1 Tbs. salt

1 cup cider vinegar

½ lb. light-brown sugar

To Cook: Place the chopped vegetables in the slow-cooker. Add the remaining ingredients and stir well. Then cover and cook on Low for 8 to 10 hours, or until thickened. If it is still a little thin after the cooking period, turn the heat to High; uncover and simmer, stirring, 10 to 20 minutes. Pour into clean, dry, 8-ounce canning jars. Seal and process for 10 minutes in a boiling-water bath.

Fills 5 or 6 (8 oz.) jars.

APRICOT CHUTNEY
6 to 8 hours

5 cups chopped fresh, pitted apricots

2 medium white onions, peeled, sliced

1 cup white raisins

1½ cups light-brown sugar, firmly packed

1¾ cups cider vinegar

2 Tbs. mustard seed

2 Tbs. celery seed

½ tsp. nutmeg

¼ cup finely cut crystallized ginger

1 tsp. salt

Juice and chopped pulp of ½ seeded lemon

Chopped peel and pulp of ½ seeded orange

½ sweet green pepper, seeded, chopped fine

To Cook: Combine all the ingredients in the slow-cooker. Cover and cook on Low for 6 to 8 hours, or until thick. Pour into hot, clean, dry 8-ounce or 1-pint canning jars. Seal and process for 10 minutes in a boiling-water bath.

Fills 5 or 6 (8 oz.) jars.

INDEX